TWENTIETH CENTURY VIEWS

The aim of this series is to present the best in contemporary critical opinion on major authors, providing a twentieth century perspective on their changing status in an era of profound revaluation.

Maynard Mack, *Series Editor*
Yale University

G. B. SHAW

G. B. SHAW

A COLLECTION OF CRITICAL ESSAYS

Edited by

R. J. Kaufmann

Prentice-Hall, Inc.   *Englewood Cliffs, N. J.*

A SPECTRUM BOOK

19593

Contents

Contents

G. B. SHAW

Introduction

by R. J. Kaufmann

Fifteen years after his death at the patriarchal age of ninety-four, George Bernard Shaw is still very much alive. There have been professional Shavians almost from the beginning, for his brighter contemporaries, standing close to the quick machinery of his remarkable mind, knew that if Shaw was not quite the definitive cultural miracle he designedly proclaimed himself to be, he was close enough to it to be very special indeed. But a great writer's reputation is insecure with only partisan enthusiasms to sustain it. What is needed is not fanatic approval but an active body of skeptical opinion, curious and intelligent, about the strategic virtues of the work of any candidate for greatness. If an artist continues to compel the interest of such a jury of readers and critics, his greatness is assured. The work of George Bernard Shaw has been undergoing this trial by scrutiny in the last two decades; his reputation has been rendered firmer by this ordeal. A critical picture of Shaw is emerging, unequivocal enough to project a strong image, but not so simple as to balk continuing curiosity. In educated opinion, Shaw now stands as the greatest all-round English dramatist since Shakespeare. His long acknowledged prowess as a prose writer of classic lucidity and enviable readableness has been extended to include less obvious qualities—historical prescience, keen social responsibility, and (what was most often denied) a fine sense of artistic form.

George Bernard Shaw is a regiment in himself. He lived so long, wrote so much, talked so endlessly and so dismayingly well, embraced so many careers, and invented so many gospels, it is no wonder lesser men have sometimes tired of his relentless brilliance. Offended, they have sniped at his self-advertised eminence and hoped for his death long before it occurred in 1950 to end nearly a century of ebullient disturbing of the peace. Shaw touched public life and sacrosanct prejudices at many points. He isolated key issues decade after decade. Being completely committed to public argument, he left countless openings for those intent on the fault-finding pleasures. There will be occasion to recall his faults, for few of Shaw's better critics now see the need to conceal them. In fact, it is quite against the quirky, impudent, and passionately hopeful manner we designate "Shavian" to refuse intelligent resistance to his pressing artistic attacks. Like his more memorable characters, Shaw searched for opposition and, like them, he was most vital when he found it. The reader of his plays, his criticism, his political polemics, and the whole shelf of stimulants to social sanity which he provided during seventy active years on the cultural stage is on trial constantly.

To meet the demands of the modern megalopolitan forms of existence, forms now general but which were only maturing during his lifetime, Shaw invented an art. To play Socrates to the modern metropolis required new techniques of argument, a vast fund of highly liquid knowledge, a fast and gay mind, a personality visible from a great distance, and a strong imperviousness to the perils of the public acceptance which brilliant charm and comic gifts must earn for their possessor. These requirements specify the formula for Shaw's primal invention: the Shavian *persona*, GBS. Shaw invented himself in much the same way that he invented his long procession of vital, talky characters: Mrs. Warren, Dick Dudgeon, Candida, *his* Julius Caesar, Lady Cicely, John Tanner, Broadbent, Undershaft, Liza Doolittle, Mrs. Hushabye, and Saint Joan. Like these characters, Shaw's invented public self is neither a simple magnification of his inner self nor an arbitrary contradiction of it. It could not have been habitable for so long, nor so emotionally durable, had it been only arbitrarily related to the predilections and facts of Shaw's nature. His best characters are likewise durable and difficult to subvert.

One of the fruitful mysteries of Shaw's art is why his special distortions in character-drawing should provoke such different reactions among his readers. Honest men divide on the question of his grasp of human motive. His contemporaries were similarly divided about Shaw's own nature: cold, interstellar, intellectualized beyond humanity he seemed to some; others were equally convinced of his earnest care for them and for mankind and remarked his naked kindliness, his full attention to their mutual work, his ability to listen and to respond and thereby to help them realize their latent powers as actors, writers, or social beings. Routinely accused of extreme self-conceit, to his most perceptive friends Shaw was peculiar in his extreme selflessness. This selflessness showed in his remarkable immunity to insult. He could not be provoked to lose his temper or to take offense, despite the saturated state of keen excitement in which he moved. His stronger characters display a similar immunity to distraction, and are strong insofar as they take their emotional (as well as their social) cues from themselves rather than from others. This almost eerie degree of independence, while in no sense devoid of passion—his characters are more energetic than the run of mankind and are eager to laugh, to find the good and, finding it, to pursue it with ardour—is the Shavian hallmark. What Shaw did with himself he does with his best characters.

On the Keatsian assumption that the world is "a vale of soul making," and with a strong, though abnormally high-spirited, puritanical infusion of desire to serve the godly will of Life, Shaw progressively stripped his life of idle excrescences, thus leaving himself free to meet the manifold necessities of reality as lightly burdened as possible. It is no accident that an almost obsessive metaphor of Shaw's depicts life as a tossing ship, sailing free but storm-threatened and destined for the rocks. Shavian man needs to keep control of this exciting movement on cleared decks. A sense of imperturbable purpose in an epoch of hesitation, divided loyalties, and corrupting doubt made Shaw seem a monster of cold-blooded efficiency to some, a "smiling sewing machine" to Yeats, an intellectual eunuch to H. G. Wells, and to others a revoltingly frivolous social engineer. What is most interesting about these responses is not their fractional truth content, nor their contentious falsity, but that so many highly intelligent observers should have been distracted by Shaw's invented personality into such crass variants of biographical fallacy. Shaw *wanted* strong reactions to himself and to his art. As an artist, he knew that he himself must be a place where strong opinions met. He knew that in a world of repressed and conventionalized responses, of deadened moral reflexes, a measure of solvent anger (the harsher complement to the solvent of laughter) was crucial to raise the temperature of perception. His art is one of productive strife between official sentiments and actual feelings even more than it is a comedy of ideas.

If we compare Socrates and Shaw, we can find more than a superficial likeness. Just as we reach beyond the caricatured Socrates condemned by the Athenian jury in the *Apology*, or the silly Socrates of the fatuous "think-shop" in Aristophanes' *The Clouds*, it is easy enough to separate Shaw, the artist-thinker, from all the instruments of moral vexation he devised to force the pace of thought in a time that (subsequent history argues) needed even stronger measures than Shaw employed to shake it into awareness. The fact is that Shaw was historically awake earlier, more persistently, and with less compromise than any of his contemporaries. He was more rather than less serious than other men, as comic geniuses often are. That poised generation of late Victorians and Edwardians which he tried to sting, ridicule, argufy, or charm into awareness *was* asleep to imperative historical realities. He used every artistic device available and even invented new ones to relieve their bewitchment. When Shaw said that the only imagination worth having is "the power to imagine things as they really are," he was echoing Shelley, another passionately earnest man, and he was never more serious. But neither his artist's ingenuity nor his resilient seriousness could prevail. The comforts of convention triumphed over all invitations to self-scrutiny and the social order Shaw criticized with fond contempt committed suicide in the First World War. There has been no organic resurrection.

The War cut through the heart of Shaw's mature career. As an artist, despite the appearance of *Saint Joan* in 1923, he was never quite the same thereafter. The total defeat of reason in the mindless horror of that futile war impaired Shaw's motive confidence, although, in the thirty years still remaining to him, his fanatic gaiety and his fertility in comic situation and dialogue manufactured a secondary *oeuvre* important enough to establish a lesser artist. His typical industry and vigor should not be allowed to conceal a diminishing faith in social man. Shaw worked on in bright despair.

To sense something tragic in Shaw's well-managed life as a committed artist may seem on the face of it ridiculous. He was immensely successful in all measurable ways. He began poor, without the initial social leverage so indispensable in nineteenth-century England; he died wealthy by his own efforts. He was an Irish intruder, under-educated and socially gauche when he arrived in England at the age of twenty in 1876. When he died in 1950, he was a national institution in his own frail person, privileged and quoted everywhere, while his plays were being acted all over the world—even in London. At the end, a Labour government, which his brilliant early efforts in the Fabian Society had helped to inaugurate and bring to a position of strength and influence, had been strongly entrenched in power for five effective years. What is tragic goes beyond even the bleak isolation of Shaw's last years, when he lived on after his friends were dead, entombed within the consecration of his great age and his final assignment to the cultural niche he had sought—that of accredited sage. In a sense all his marvelous activity had been a failure. In the plays of George Bernard Shaw, failure is generally exposed to ridicule, but the failure of a great man through misunderstanding and consequent trivialization of his proffered gifts is tragic. The potentiality of tragedy is to be found in Shaw's early and immutable consecration of himself to purging Civilization's folly.

He knew early what he must do. Before he embarked on his long, fertile career as a playwright, Shaw had been a ranking music critic, an industrious though unsuccessful novelist, and a great drama critic. In this last capacity, as a phase of his life-long campaign against spiritual sleep, he strove to rouse the British theater from its torpid and mechanical habits of "Sardoodling" domestic comedies and romanticizing Shakespeare and history. He wrote then: "melodramatic stage illusion is not an illusion of real life, but an illusion of the embodiment of our romantic imaginings." To counteract these practices he provided highly-colored and amusing plays which used the systematic illusions of art to confront men with their unromanticized compulsions and conditioned preferences. The central strategies of his dramatic art repeatedly introduce characters free from illusions and burdensome affectations into the charade-like pageantry of what is taken for actuality but is more truly the faded apparatus of a social existence as fatally divorced from its own motives as conventional stage acting from current behavior. His Candida is candid; his Bluntschli is blunt; though like Shaw himself there is an engaging courtesy accompanying their hardness and their immunity to obligatory sentiment. His Caesar—dry, casual, and persistently didactic—is, therefore, fascinating in an historic environment where such qualities (theoretically considered) should have been deadly to artistic success. All his great characters are great teachers or good learners—or both.

Shaw tried to entice a generation, even two generations, to shed their "artificial mentalities," to step through the looking-glass into mature responsibilities. He did this with unfailing courtesy, beguiling wit, and a diminishing reputation for the very seriousness which drove him on. Apropos of Tolstoy's adverse critics, Shaw said, "Alas, nothing is plainer to a dupe of all the illusions of civilization than the folly of the seer who penetrates them." In the process of achieving public acceptance, Shaw was trapped in an anteroom to this house of illusions and became "the embodiment" of the public's "romantic imaginings" about him as an effervescent, golden-witted clown, bereft of true social responsibility. Unlike Socrates, he was not accorded the dignity of physical martyrdom for his beliefs. To be thus sealed off could not be recompensed by any amount of uncomprehending adulation and attention. Adulation was not important to him, and attention, which was, could not be a satisfactory substitute for effective social use of what he had labored for with his own peculiar version of religious dedication. The critics whose essays are gathered into a patterned sequence in this anthology endeavor to set Shaw free from the bonds of misunderstanding.

II

This volume opens with an ovation from Shaw's younger contemporary, the German playwright Bertolt Brecht. Brecht shared Shaw's conviction that the theater can be a palace of truth if the playwright knows enough about the two essentials which make drama vital: actual human circumstances and the craft of the theater. They shared as well a healthy courage by which their drama is committed to a higher didacticism. Each devised a dramatic art that utilized parable to please and to teach simultaneously. Brecht's ovation is a form of testimony to his affinity to Shaw, the social-artist, and his sensitivity to Shaw's originality. This originality was partly a function of Shaw's extraordinary balance of self-detachment and social passion. The perceptive essay which follows Brecht's, written by the psychiatrist, Erik H. Erikson, deals with Shaw's manufacture of his own nature out of a blend of keen realism and self-fantastication. Erikson's larger concern is with the process by which we adjust public ideologies to our own convictions in our metaphysically disoriented time. Since Shaw's exceptional steadfastness of conviction was the ballast for his artistic impudence, Erikson's wise discussion of how Shaw derived a secure identity from the crisis of an inadequate familial and cultural environment provides a useful point of entry into subsequent investigations of Shaw's artistic habits.

"Style," Whitehead said, "is the ultimate morality of mind." This epigrammatic insight is particularly relevant to George Bernard Shaw, for his morality is welded to his idiosyncratic style—a style so distinct that we now have the word "Shavian" to designate it. Richard M. Ohmann is interested in this congruence of Shaw, the man, and "Shaw," the style. Like Erikson, he searches into Shaw's repudiations of an inadequate way of life to find the roots of Shaw's literary style. Mr. Ohmann is trained in the methods of sophisticated modern linguistics. The results of his enquiry help further to distinguish what is special in Shaw's rendering of experience and what will be consistently apparent in subsequent essays: Shaw's use of language rests on keen artistic scruples and is the consistent, qualifying lens through which we learn the exact prescription of Shaw's reforming vision.

Because Shaw's style is so personal and because the sharp flavor of his dialogue is the first thing apparent on encountering his art, it is often overlooked that Shaw's power as an artist finally rests on his ability to create interesting characters—men and women excited by life and possessing the power to infect others with their convictions—and to place them within an effective comic design. Shaw was possessed himself by a commodious monomania for a life of high quality for all men, but he was primarily a maker of comedies. In one of the most thoughtful essays in the group, Bruce R. Park seeks to make Shaw's aesthetic assumptions visible to unsympathetic critics. Shaw's comic art needs to be judged in harmony with its own very ambitious assumptions. Unlike most playwrights, Shaw did a great deal of thinking outside as well as inside the theater. He knew more, rather than less, than most of his critics about the crises of the social order he embodied in his art. This advantage in general knowledge reverses the normal relationship between critic and artist. Mr. Park conducts the kind of quiet and informed case which makes it impossible to credit a good many hardy clichés about Shaw's intentions. There is rich irony in the intellectual strategy of critics who, in tediously re-exposing Shaw's puritanism and defects of passion, fail to perceive their own solemn suspicions of the happy excesses of comedy and the extent to which Shaw, like T. S. Eliot, invented a new "music of ideas"—one thematically wider than conventional opinion can hear. Mr. Park's argument concludes the first phase of the volume and opens the way to a roughly chronological sequence of essays on the plays themselves.

This central portion of the volume is opened, appropriately, by the most articulate of contemporary Shavians: Eric Bentley. In his discussion of "The Making of a Dramatist," Mr. Bentley uses the dozen plays of the miraculous decade from the beginning of Shaw's playmaking career to the completion of *Man and Superman* in 1903, with the appearance of which

Shaw's "major phase" may be said to begin. What he might be said to do is to substantiate, in rich detail, Mr. Park's more theoretically presented claim for the high coherency of Shaw's comic art. From the beginning, Shaw's plays have a strong personal flavor and betray a deep interest in what Mr. Bentley calls "the emotional substance" of his characters. The truth steadily emerges that George Bernard Shaw was *more* stirred by basic passions than most dramatists. One way of tracing the fascinating curve of his development is to watch how his knowledgeable fear of passion's turbulent effects gradually overmasters his connoisseur's delight in the ways passion can work. What also emerges from Mr. Bentley's exploration of this formative decade is an appreciation of Shaw's instinct for seminal dramatic situations. This sense was, of course, not infallible—and the essay is intelligently critical of Shaw's variable success—but it was strong from the beginning.

Comic drama, as much as tragic, depends on the dramatist's capacity to embody adequately comprehensive conflicts of will and principle in sufficiently definite, imaginatively localized situations. Norbert F. O'Donnell addresses himself to Shaw's typical handlings of human conflict. Shaw was a Socialist, and the more immediately accessible terms of his dramatic arguments are strongly social, often polemically so. Mr. O'Donnell, while not denying the relevance of this Shavian bias, rightly concentrates on Shaw's still more basic preoccupation with the world as a competition of individual wills. Shaw, as a good dramatist must be, was of two minds about the virtues of individualism. As a reasonable Socialist, he saw the necessity of subordinating private libido to public order; but he had a taste, too, for the glamour of the masterly will, and as he grew older there was an increasing disgruntlement with the sloshing inefficiencies of mass democracy. This self-division results in a productive ambivalence of tone in his plays. Mr. O'Donnell calls the result "Shavian tragicomedy." The term is dubious, but the justifying analysis of Shaw's concentration on the conflict of wills in such plays as *Captain Brassbound's Conversion, Caesar and Cleopatra,* and *Pygmalion* is cogent and illuminating. GBS, man and artist, was fascinated by self-confidence and by its negation, "intimidation."

Nowhere are these Shavian concerns more difficult to sort out with critical precision than in *Major Barbara*; ascertaining its exact tone is perhaps the premier problem in Shavian criticism. Louis Crompton's "Shaw's Challenge to Liberalism" is concerned solely with this important play (1905), which marks an important turning point in Shaw's inner development. By a judicious blending of structural analysis with biographical and historical evidence, Mr. Crompton provides an intelligible reading of this difficult drama of ideas. His essay shows that Shaw used his plays as a means of public thinking on the ideological conflicts of his time. His ambivalence was a function of his incisive political realism: he saw early the devastating role demagoguery and manipulation of new forms of destructive power were going to play in the determination of political affairs in the twentieth century. Because of the egoistic flippancy of the Shavian verbal attack, it is often hard for critics to realize that he sometimes dramatized what he saw happening below the surface of historical change, not what he advocated or longed for. To understand *Major Barbara*, such discriminations must be made.

In the essay "Bernard Shaw: The Face Behind the Mask," drawn from his outstanding book, *The Theatre of Revolt*, Robert Brustein develops the theme of self-division into a cogent general analysis of Shaw's latent nihilism in the face of the metaphysical inconsequence of routine existence. Mr. Brustein then applies these insights in close readings of two of the finest plays: *Man and Superman* and *Heartbreak House*. He has some stern reservations about Shaw's artistic self-control, but his formidable interpretations proceed from a conviction of Shaw's secure place as a major artist. V. S. Prichett, in his *Times* obituary for GBS, stated a charge against which Shaw cannot be wholly defended: "Shaw was no more free than Voltaire from the irresponsibilities of a chaotically lucid mind which changed focus too fast for his own eye." But Shaw's dextrous opportunisms were indispensable to the comic dramatist. The cross which he has had to bear is simply the inability of his readers to remember that he is the ventriloquist behind *all* voices in his dramatic debates. Reading the entire canon, the critic might more fairly convict Shaw of fanatic obsession than of irresponsible instability. Shaw himself said, "The man of letters who is more than a confectioner is a prophet or nothing." Prophets are uncomfortable social bedfellows, but it is as a prophet—a seer of the still hidden course our temporal follies lay down for us—that Shaw is best understood. His later work is a series of reactions to the pressures of that desperation which Mr. Brustein discloses as working within Shaw.

The remaining five essays in the volume work from widely different critical assumptions to support this notion of the centrality of the prophetic in Shaw's artistic behavior. The sequence starts with G. Wilson Knight's synoptic interpretation of "Shaw's Integral Theatre." With his usual percipience, Mr. Knight shows the almost rampant vitality of a theme of bisexualism in Shaw's plays and how this, in turn, advertises Shaw's comprehensive concern for the wholeness of being. He also shows how integral Shaw's settings are to his dramatic plan. Shaw was a visionary of a peculiarly well-informed, socially-engaged type. He was consequently a composer of integrated imaginative environments, as his visually precise stage directions testify. The mystic strain Mr. Knight stresses receives its most candid (and prolonged) airing in *Back to Methuselah*. This work of Egyptian magnitude—five plays in one—is the least negotiable of all Shaw's works. Margery M. Morgan, in a sympathetic essay, discovers a self-consistency and care in its design which extends without breach from the most generalized quasi-metaphysical assumptions to the tiniest details. Alone among Shaw's most serious work, this play requires a competent apologia. Miss Morgan's learned and spirited interpretation provides just that.

Saint Joan, considered by many to be Shaw's finest play, followed hard on *Back to Methuselah*. No one has found a critically more fruitful approach to *Saint Joan* than Louis L. Martz, who, in "The Saint as Hero," discusses it together with T. S. Eliot's *Murder in the Cathedral* as a distinguished modern attempt to renovate dramatic tragedy. T. R. Henn, in his terse essay "The Shavian Machine," also has his say on *Saint Joan*, but only after he has found fresh things to say about the "problem of tragedy" and about two prior Shavian approaches to the tragic: *Mrs. Warren's Profession* and *The Doctor's Dilemma* (from Shaw's early and middle phases, respectively). For all the virtuosity of its opening dialogue, the latter, which Shaw designated "A Tragedy," is a failure in those terms. Shaw could not convincingly animate an antisocial artist. In seeking to understand a talent as extensive as Shaw's, it is advantageous to establish the margins at which his mastery evaporates. This is one of the numerous virtues of Mr. Henn's contribution.

The final selection is a short, little-known essay by Irving Fiske which establishes, by modest collocation, an interesting affinity between George Bernard Shaw and William Blake. Shaw said of it, "Hundreds of articles have been written about me and forgotten. This is the one I would have published and circulated as widely as if I had written it myself." Who could resist such an invitation? Mr. Fiske's little essay makes its effect quietly and cumulatively. It requires no additional endorsement from me.

What grows on one in studying Shaw is how much his work is designed as a drama of spiritual *recreation* in all the senses of that word. He is cheering, for he had the rare gift of superabundant gaiety—more gaiety than he needed to sustain himself. He is witty and he provokes wit. His comic world is comic without being trivial or portentous. His drama is also studiously re-creative. He worked in a society which he could see was exhausted by false burdens of gentility and depressed by inadequate goals: "This soul's prison we call England." For him the role of the artist was not merely to exhort but to induce imaginatively the healing "appetite for fruitful activity and a high quality of life." As an artist, he conjured up a long sequence of controlled visions of what can be as well as what is. In his late play, *Too True to Be Good* (1932), one of his characters seems to be impersonating Shaw when he says:

> My gift is divine: it is not limited by my petty personal convictions. It is a gift of lucidity as well as of eloquence. Lucidity is one of the most precious of gifts: the gift of the teacher: the gift of explanation. I can explain anything to anybody; and I love doing it.

Just claims to greatness can be made for Shaw. His work does have contemporary relevance. A final estimation of his weaknesses will sharpen our sense of this relevance without subverting his greatness, for cogency in art is achieved by bold subordination and Shaw was both bold and cogent. Part of his greatness lies in his extravagant emphasis. Naturally, there was a cost. We can start from his passion for explanation.

Shaw was more aggressively intelligent than most artists. He pretended and perhaps came to believe that he always knew what he was talking about. His calculated omniscience extended beyond immediate dramatical business to his audience's proper obligations and, most damagingly, to the quality and color of his characters' souls. There is something disagreeably Pauline about Shaw as he shepherds and instructs the congregations on stage and in the stalls in their whole duty as men. Despite all his wit, there is a taint of humorlessness in this drive to pin us to honesty's wall, perpetually to set us straight or to trick us into shamed acquiescence. Many of the best artists often do not "know" what they are talking about. Their vision grows from within, not, of course, without control but in humble compliance with what they see; they learn and we learn with them. But Shaw nearly always has a brief. He has prepared his case. He is determined to expose the fatuity of our position and to articulate his own. Being phenomenally adept verbally and possessing all the debater's skills, he prevails in argument but at some expense to our sense of the roundness of experience. We obscurely feel vital reserves in his richest characters have been suppressed, that they cannot be so neatly labelled nor so artfully propelled towards prescribed goals. Shaw the artist, like Shaw the man, periodically talks too much and is too knowing. By the relentless chaperonage of our responses, our pleasure in the spirited world of his plays is curtailed. He begs us to think, but refuses to let us do so. We suspect, thus, there is more of John Tanner in Shaw than of Saint Joan. His pedantic vocation lessens the "negative capability" Keats so loved in Shakespeare. Often Shaw does lack this nurturing restraint in judgment and consequent feminine receptivity to the exact texture of others. Hence Shaw often creates characters who do not engage our whole spirit—only our admiration, our intellect, or our snobbery.

Snobbery, being a jealous claim to special access joined to a compulsion to umpire the claims of others, fascinated Shaw. He was not wholly free of its backwash, a partial servitude which limits his genius at the same time it sharpened his eye as a comic writer. His plays are unduly preoccupied with the abrasions of snobbery and class-warfare as it is practiced in drawing rooms, commercial offices, restaurants, and on country terraces. Overpleased by his own perky and hypothetical superiority to meaner, middle-class social tactics, too eager to display his virtuosity in "putting people down" or in pulling rugs from beneath pomposity, Shaw reveals something of the vengeful provincial in his subversion of all dignity. His generalized kindliness cannot wholly conceal the gleeful Irish sniggerings of one who is never taken in. Perhaps still greater writers than Shaw have a margin of self-confident serenity which enables them to be "taken in" enough to grasp just how the world is when we participate in its illusions. They know such momentary surrenders to the conventional vision will not permanently harm their reputation for acuteness and will surely enlarge their understanding. In short, Shaw remained for too long a defiant *enfant terrible* at the price of a residuum of permanent adolescence and a partially blinding spiritual pride which reduced him to the silly conviction that he *must* be able to understand Hitler, Stalin, and Mussolini, when in sad truth he lacked experience to comprehend them. This weakening strain in his artistic equipment is in question when Shaw's technically admirable characterization, a process of musical subtlety, is caricatured by critics as heartless puppetry.

Shaw thoroughly understood *certain types* of highly conventionalized beings and, what is very rare, *certain types* of exceptionally gifted people, as Broadbent in *John Bull's Other Island* and Henry Higgins in *Pygmalion* illustrate. He found means to establish these types memorably within his comic world. He understood the inner terms of moral determination and spiritual obstinacy as well as any dramatist. Although different in every other respect, Mrs. Warren and Saint Joan are alike in genuinely possessing these qualities. Surely, too, only Shakespeare, Molière, and Dickens have a comparable ability to make trivial people and boring ones into such fascinating characters. *Fanny's First Play* is a minor triumph in provoking interest in paltriness. Yes, Shaw depicted well those parts of human behavior to which he had sympathetic access; but his sovereignty was narrower than he admitted, and much that is humanly crucial is sheared off in plays where he tries to reach past the closely related, twin realms of the absurdly farcical and the dedicatedly fanatical. When he takes the measure of the medical profession in *The Doctor's Dilemma* or of practical politics in *The Apple Cart*, we are oppressed by cleverness bereft of sympathetic insight. His drama, at its best, thrives on the "extreme situations" beloved of modern existentialists. Like existentialist heroes, his best characters strive to save their private vision in a compromised, though well-upholstered, world.

One of the still-to-be-digested facts about Shaw is this: he is godfather, if not actually finicky paterfamilias, to the theater of the absurd, enthusiasts of which scornfully disown him. It is not just that his mad playlet, *Passion, Poison and Petrifaction; or The Fatal Gazogene*, could be played in a double bill with Pinter, Ionesco, Frisch, or Kopit (with Shaw's name suppressed and a few trivialities of period terminology expunged) and pass for the latest concoction of comic anarchy—with characters eating statues, drenching each other with siphons, and dying in farcical epiphany in the most modish postexistential style—but also that Shaw's sense of art as medley, art as teetering on the brink of formal dissolution, is often like theirs in baroquely disposing mortified sexuality and melodramatic religiosity, effete hysteria and social catastrophe all within one canvas of statement. Shaw's determined rationality, his relentless programs for spiritual self-help, and his vision of social patterns survived the waves of anarchy and hilarious nihilism only by a monstrous infusion of *will*, both in his private recipes for existence and in his gradual capitulation to that *Will* driving through the center of our crazy existence, which he finally came to worship in the form of the Life-Force— a needed token of redeeming possibility.

As acute a critic as Brigid Brophy, in her very "far-out" book, *Black Ship to Hell*, and (less reputably) Colin Wilson, have responded to this element in Shaw; but quite perceptive enthusiasts for absurd theater have mistaken Edwardian trappings for the essential Shaw and the façade of school-masterly assurance for the nervous substance of his art. This familiar pattern of critical superficiality hopefully will not endure when Shaw's work has been safely distanced by time and ceases to blight competitive aspirations to originality. It should be remembered that Shaw financed, with his Nobel Prize funds, English translations of Strindberg, whose genius is detectable everywhere in the new efforts at irreverence and destructive absurdity. For example, Edward Albee's internationally acclaimed *Who's Afraid of Virginia Woolf?* is transposed and uneconomical Strindberg with an admixture of Shavian drawing-room dialectic only slightly disguised by un-Shavian reliance on obscenities.

Knowing the theater for the complex instrument it is, Shaw held professional casts spellbound (and a more vain, less compliant audience is hard to assemble) while he spontaneously acted and blocked out his latest play, reading the entire text with full accompaniment of gesture and grimace. Of all these actors and managers, only the dogmatic Beerbohm Tree is known to have resented this drilling or to have questioned Shaw's mastery of the practical art of making a play live in three dimensions. This technical mastery can be felt in the rhythms, the quick and often faultless accretion of detail after fusing detail, as a Shavian scene unfolds. It is part of the pleasure of reading the best available criticism of Shaw to realize that so far we have only cleared his name of slanders on his deliberate artistry. Competent demonstrations of the minute exactitude with which Shaw built his scenes is still before us. Like Ibsen, who has now been freed from similar misunderstanding, Shaw's poetic power is not to be judged by his spasmodic, self-conscious, now faded attempts at "fine writing," but by the nervous vitality with which his lines follow the contours of practical emotions and create an original syntax to express the precise qualities of his characters' wills.

Shaw came to drama through music and he felt Mozart to be his master as much as Molière and Shakespeare. Shaw is great because all his vast social involvement, all his hectoring gospel urge, all his fanatic curiosity was most alive for him, as for us, in the plastic terms of dramatic art. As in a fugue, social themes are observed, blurred, lost and then recovered in the progression of a single, artfully crafted scene. His mastery of experience is most complete in the great *ensemble* numbers in his plays, as in the opening scene of *Man and Superman*, the final sequence of *Major Barbara* or the Inquisition in *Saint Joan*, when lyric opinions he advocated or cherished are made to hold their own in the strenuous polyphony of alien views.

Ovation for Shaw

by Bertolt Brecht

I. *Shaw's Terror*

Shaw himself has experienced and subsequently suggested that any person, in order to express frankly an opinion on anything, has to overcome a certain congenital fear—that of being presumptuous. He has taken care early in his career to prevent people from molesting him with insincere incense burning. (But he has done it without shrinking from being considered famous. He knows that the tools of an honest man must always include boisterous self-advertising. He proudly declines to hide his light under a bushel.)

Shaw has used a large part of his ingenuity to inhibit people to such a degree that they would need to have extreme insensitivity to prostrate themselves in admiration before him.

It should be clear by now that Shaw is a terrorist. The Shavian terror is an unusual one, and he employs an unusual weapon—that of humor. This unusual man seems to be of the opinion that there is nothing fearful in the world except the calm and incorruptible eye of the common man. But this eye must be feared, always and unconditionally. This theory endows him with a remarkable natural superiority; and by his unfaltering practice in accordance with it, he has made it impossible for anyone who ever comes into contact with him—be it in person, through his books, or through his theater—to assume that he ever committed a deed or uttered a sentence without fearful respect for this incorruptible eye. In fact, young people, whose main qualification is often their love of mettle, are often held to a minimum of aggressiveness by their premonition that any attack on Shaw's habits, even if it were his insistence on wearing peculiar underwear, would inevitably result in a terrible defeat of their own thoughtlessly selected apparel. If one adds to this his exploding of the thoughtless, habitual assumption that any-

"Ovation for Shaw" by Bertolt Brecht. From *Modern Drama*, II (September 1959), 184–187. Translated by Gerhard H. W. Zuther. Copyright © 1959 by A. C. Edwards. Reprinted by permission of A. C. Edwards and *Modern Drama*. Originally published in *Berliner Börsen-Courier*, July 25, 1926.

thing that might possibly be considered venerable should be treated in a subdued manner instead of energetically and joyously; if one adds to this his successful proof that in the face of truly significant ideas a relaxed (even snotty) attitude is the only proper one, since it alone facilitates true concentration, it becomes evident what measure of personal freedom he has achieved.

The Shavian terror consists of Shaw's insistence on the prerogative of every man to act decently, logically, and with a sense of humor, and on the obligation to act in this manner even in the face of opposition. He knows very well how much courage it takes to laugh about the ridiculous and how much seriousness it takes to discover the amusing. And, like all purposeful people, he knows, on the other hand, that the most time-consuming and distracting pursuit is a certain kind of seriousness which pervades literature but does not exist anywhere else. (Like us, the young generation, he considers it naïve to write for the theater, and he does not show the slightest inclination to pretend that he is not aware of this: he makes far-reaching use of his naïveté. He furnishes the theater with as much fun as it can take. And it can take a lot. What draws people to the theater is, strictly speaking, so much nonsense, which constitutes a tremendous buoyancy for those problems which really interest the progressive dramatic writer and which are the real value of his pieces. It follows that his problems must be so pertinent that he can be as buoyant about them as he wishes to be, for the buoyancy is what people want.)

II. *Shaw Vindicated in the Face of His Own Dark Premonitions*

I seem to remember that Shaw recently expressed his opinion about the future of the drama. He says that in the future people will no longer go to the theater in order to understand. He probably means that mere reproduction of reality curiously fails to give the impression of verisimilitude. The younger generation will not contradict Shaw on this point. But I feel that Shaw's own dramatic works were able to overshadow those of his contemporaries exactly because they unflinchingly appealed to the intellect. His world is composed of opinions. The fate of his characters is identical with their opinions. Shaw, in order to have a play, invents some complications which provide his characters with opportunities to vent their opinions extensively and to have them clash with ours. (These complications can never be old and familiar enough to suit Shaw; here he really has no ambition whatever: a thoroughly ordinary usurer is worth his weight in gold; he stumbles on a patriotic girl in history, and the only important thing is that his audience be equally familiar with the story of this girl, that the sad end of the usurer be well known and gleefully anticipated, so that he can upset all the more completely our old-fashioned concepts of these types and—above all—our notions of the way these types think.)

Probably all of his characters, in all their traits, are the result of Shaw's delight in upsetting our habitual prejudices. He knows that we have the terrible habit of forcing all the attributes of a certain kind of people into one preconceived, stereotyped concept. In our imagination the usurer is cowardly, sneaky, and brutal. We would not think of permitting him to be even a little courageous, sentimental, or soft hearted. Shaw does.

Concerning heroes, Shaw's degenerate successors have awkwardly amplified his refreshing conviction—that heroes are not exemplary scholars and that heroism is a very inscrutable, but very real conglomeration of contradictory traits—to mean that neither heroism nor heroes exist. But even this does not bother Shaw. It seems he considers it healthier to live among common people than among heroes.

In the composition of his works Shaw proceeds with utmost frankness. He does not mind writing under the continuous scrutiny of the public. In order to make his judgments more emphatic, he facilitates this scrutiny: he unremittingly stresses his own peculiarities, his very individualistic taste, even his own (little) weaknesses. Thus he cannot fail to reap gratitude. Even where his opinions clash with those of the younger generation, he is listened to with glee: he is—and what more can be said about a man—a good fellow. Besides, his time preserves opinions better than emotions and moods. It seems that of all the things produced in this epoch opinions are the most durable.

III. *Essential Contagiousness: Humor*

It is characteristically difficult to find out the opinions of other European authors. But I assume that concerning literature they hold approximately the same view, to wit, that writing is a melancholy business. Shaw, whose opinions about everything are widely known throughout the world, clearly sets himself deliberately apart from this view of his colleagues. (It is not his fault—rather a thorn in his side—that his all-pervasive difference of opinion from the general views of the other European writers does not appear clearly enough, since the others do not even publicize those few convictions which they actually have.) But Shaw will at least agree with me when I say that Shaw likes to write. On his head there is no room for the crown of a martyr. His literary preoccupation does not separate him from life. On the contrary. I do not know whether it is an indication of talent, but the effect of his unmistakeable serenity and his contagious good humor is extraordinary. Shaw actually succeeds in giving the impression that his mental and bodily health increases with every sentence he writes. Reading him is perhaps not exhilarating in a Dionysian manner, but it is undeniable that it is amazingly conducive to good health. And his only enemies—if we must mention them at all—are obviously exclusively people to whom health is much less of a concern.

I cannot remember a single one of Shaw's "characteristic" ideas, although I know, of course, that he has many; but I remember many things which he discovers to be characteristic of other people. In his own estimate, at any rate, his temper is more important than his individual opinions. And that speaks well for a man like him.

I feel that a theory of evolution is central for him, one which, in his opinion, differs considerably and significantly from another theory of evolution of definitely lower calibre. At any rate, his faith that man is capable of infinite improvement plays an important role in his works. It will be clearly recognized as a sincere ovation for Shaw when I admit without blushing that I unconditionally subscribe to Shaw's view although I am not thoroughly acquainted with either of the two theories mentioned above. The reason? A man with such keen intellect and courageous eloquence simply deserves my complete confidence. This is all the more true as I have considered—always and in any situation—the forcefulness of an expression more important than its immediate applicability and a man of stature more important than the sphere of his activity.

Biographic: G.B.S. (70)
on George Bernard Shaw (20)

by Erik H. Erikson

When George Bernard Shaw was a famous man of seventy, he was called upon to review and to preface the unsuccessful work of his early twenties, namely, the two volumes of fiction which had never been published. As one would expect, Shaw proceeded to make light of the production of his young adulthood, but not without imposing on the reader a detailed analysis of young Shaw. Were Shaw not so deceptively witty in what he says about his younger years, his observations probably would have been recognized as a major psychological achievement. Yet, it is Shaw's mark of identity that he eases and teases his reader along a path of apparent superficialities and sudden depths. I dare to excerpt him here for my purposes only in the hope that I will make the reader curious enough to follow him at every step of his exposition.[1]

G.B.S. (for this is the public identity which was one of his masterpieces) describes young Shaw as an "extremely disagreeable and undesirable" young man, "not at all reticent of diabolical opinion," while inwardly "suffering ... from simple cowardice ... and horribly ashamed of it." "The truth is," he concludes, "that all men are in a false position in society until they have realized their possibilities and imposed them on their neighbors. They are tormented by a continual shortcoming in themselves; yet they irritate others by a continual overweening. This discord can be resolved by acknowledged success or failure only: everyone is ill at ease until he has found his natural place, whether it be above or below his birthplace." But Shaw must always exempt himself from any universal law which he inadvertently pronounces;

"Biographic: G.B.S. (70) on George Bernard Shaw (20)" by Erik H. Erikson. From *Identity and the Life Cycle* by Erik H. Erikson (New York: International Universities Press, Inc., 1959), pp. 102–110. Copyright © 1959 by International Universities Press, Inc. Reprinted by permission of the publishers and the author. The pages reprinted are only part of a paper entitled "The Problem of Ego Identity."

[1] Excerpts quoted here are from G. B. Shaw, *Selected Prose* (New York: Dodd, Mead & Company, 1952).

so he adds: "This finding of one's place may be made very puzzling by the fact that there is no place in ordinary society for extraordinary individuals."

Shaw proceeds to describe a crisis (of the kind which we will refer to as an *identity crisis*) at the age of twenty. It is to be noted that this crisis was not caused by lack of success or the absence of a defined role but by too much of both: "I made good in spite of myself, and found, to my dismay, that Business, instead of expelling me as the worthless impostor I was, was fastening upon me with no intention of letting me go. Behold me, therefore, in my twentieth year, with a business training, in an occupation which I detested as cordially as any sane person lets himself detest anything he cannot escape from. In March 1876 I broke loose." Breaking loose meant to leave family and friends, business and Ireland, and to avoid the danger of success without identity, of a success unequal to "the enormity of my unconscious ambition." He granted himself a prolongation of the interval between youth and adulthood, which we will call a *psychosocial moratorium.* He writes: ". . . when I left my native city I left this phase behind me, and associated no more with men of my age until, after about eight years of solitude in this respect, I was drawn into the Socialist revival of the early eighties, among Englishmen intensely serious and burning with indignation at very real and very fundamental evils that affected all the world." In the meantime, he seemed to avoid opportunities, sensing that "Behind the conviction that they could lead to nothing that I wanted, lay the unspoken fear that they might lead to something I did not want." This *occupational* part of the moratorium was reinforced by an *intellectual* one: "I cannot learn anything that does not interest me. My memory is not indiscriminate; it rejects and selects; and its selections are not academic. . . . I congratulate myself on this; for I am firmly persuaded that every unnatural activity of the brain is as mischievous as any unnatural activity of the body . . . Civilization is always wrecked by giving the governing classes what is called secondary education . . ."

Shaw settled down to study and to write as he pleased, and it was then that the extraordinary workings of an extraordinary personality came to the fore. He managed to abandon the *kind* of work he had been doing without relinquishing the work *habit*: "My office training had left me with a habit of doing something regularly every day as a fundamental condition of industry as distinguished from idleness. I knew I was making no headway unless I was doing this, and that I should never produce a book in any other fashion. I bought supplies of white paper, demy size, by sixpence-worths at a time; folded it in quarto; and condemned myself to fill five pages of it a day, rain or shine, dull or inspired. I had so much of the schoolboy and the clerk still in me that if my five pages ended in the middle of a sentence I did not finish it until the next day. On the other hand, if I missed a day, I made up for it by doing a double task on the morrow. On this plan I produced five novels in five years. It was my professional apprenticeship. . . ." We may add that these first five novels were not published for over fifty years; but Shaw had learned to write as he worked, and to wait as he wrote. How important such initial *ritualization of his worklife* was for the young man's inner defenses may be seen from one of those casual (in fact, parenthetical) remarks with which the great wit almost coyly admits his psychological insight: "I have risen by sheer gravitation, too industrious by acquired habit to stop working (*I work as my father drank*)." He thus points to that combination of *addictiveness* and *compulsivity* which we see as the basis of much pathology in late adolescence and of some accomplishment in young adulthood.

His father's "drink neurosis" Shaw describes in detail, finding in it one of the sources of his biting humor: "It had to be either a family tragedy or family joke." For his father was not "convivial, nor quarrelsome, nor boastful, but miserable, racked with shame and remorse." However, the father had a "humorous sense of anticlimax which I inherited from him and used with much effect when I became a writer of comedy. His anticlimaxes depended for their effect on our sense of the sacredness (of the subject matter) . . . It seems providential that I was driven to the essentials of religion by the reduction of every factitious or fictitious element in it to the most irreverent absurdity."

A more unconscious level of Shaw's oedipal tragedy is represented—with dreamlike symbolism—in what looks like a screen memory conveying his father's impotence: "A boy who has seen 'the governor' with an *imperfectly wrapped-up goose under one arm* and *a ham in the same condition under the other* (both purchased under heaven knows what delusion of festivity) *butting* at the garden wall in the belief that he was *pushing open the gate*, and *transforming his tall hat to a concertina* in the process, and who, instead of being overwhelmed with shame and anxiety at the spectacle, has been so *disabled by merriment* (uproariously shared by the maternal uncle) that he has hardly been able to rush to the rescue of the hat and pilot its wearer to safety, is clearly not a boy who will make tragedies of trifles instead of *making trifles of tragedies*. If you cannot get rid of the family skeleton, you may as well make it dance." It is obvious that the analysis of the psychosexual elements in Shaw's identity could find a solid anchor point in this memory.

Shaw explains his father's downfall with a brilliant analysis of the socioeconomic circumstances of his day. For the father was "second cousin to a baronet, and my mother the daughter of a country gentleman whose rule was, when in difficulties, mortgage. That was my sort of poverty." His father was "the younger son of a younger son of a younger son" and he was "a downstart and the son of a downstart." Yet, he concludes: "To say that my father could not afford to give me a university education is like saying that he could not afford to drink, or that I could not afford to become an author. Both statements are true; but he drank and I became an author all the same."

His mother he remembers for the "one or two rare and delightful occasions when she buttered my bread for me. She buttered it thickly instead of merely wiping a knife on it." Most of the time, however, he says significantly, she merely "accepted me as a natural and customary phenomenon and took it for granted that I should go on occurring in that way." There must have been something reassuring in this kind of impersonality, for "technically speaking, I should say she was the worst mother conceivable, always, however, within the limits of the fact that she was incapable of unkindness to any child, animal, or flower, or indeed to any person or thing whatsoever. . . ." If this could not be considered either a mother's love or an education, Shaw explains: "I was badly brought up because my mother was so well brought up. . . . In her righteous reaction against . . . the constraints and tyrannies, the scoldings and browbeatings and punishments she had suffered in her childhood . . . she reached a negative attitude in which having no substitute to propose, she carried domestic anarchy as far as in the nature of things it can be carried." All in all, Shaw's mother was "a thoroughly disgusted and disillusioned woman . . . suffering from a hopelessly disappointing husband and three uninteresting children grown too old to be petted like the animals and the birds she was so fond of, to say nothing of the humiliating inadequacy of my father's income."

Shaw had really three parents, the third being a man named Lee ("meteoric," "impetuous," "magnetic"), who gave Shaw's mother lessons in singing, not without revamping the whole Shaw household as well as Bernard's ideals: "Although he supplanted my father as the dominant factor in the household, and appropriated all the activity and interest of my mother, he was so completely absorbed in his musical affairs that there was no friction and hardly any intimate personal contacts between the two men: certainly no unpleasantness. At first his ideas astonished us. He said that people should sleep with their windows open. The daring of this appealed to me; and I have done so ever since. He ate brown bread instead of white: a startling eccentricity."

Of the many elements of identity formations which ensued from such a perplexing picture, let me single out only three, selected, simplified, and named for this occasion by me.

The Snob

"As compared with similar English families, we had a power of derisive dramatization that made the bones of the Shavian skeletons rattle more loudly." Shaw recognizes this as "family snobbery mitigated by the family sense of humor." On the other hand, "though my mother was not consciously a snob, the divinity which hedged an Irish lady of her period was not acceptable to the British suburban parents, all snobs, who were within her reach (as customers for private music lessons)." Shaw had "an enormous contempt for family snobbery," until he found that one of his ancestors was an Earl of Fife: "It was as good as being descended from Shakespeare, whom I had been unconsciously resolved to reincarnate from my cradle."

The Noisemaker

All through his childhood, Shaw seems to have been exposed to an oceanic assault of music making: the family played trombones and ophicleides, violoncellos, harps, and tambourines—and, most of all (or is it worst of all) they sang. Finally, however, he taught himself the piano, and this with dramatic noisiness. "When I look back on all the banging, whistling, roaring, and growling inflicted on nervous neighbors during this process of education, I am consumed with useless remorse. . . . I used to drive [my mother] nearly crazy by my favorite selections from Wagner's Ring, which to her was 'all recitative,' and horribly discordant at that. She never complained at the time, but confessed it after we separated, and said that she had sometimes gone away to cry. If I had committed a murder I do not think it would trouble my conscience very much; but this I cannot bear to think of." That, in fact, he may have learned the piano in order to get even with his musical tormentors, he does not profess to realize. Instead, he compromised by becoming—a music *critic*, i.e., one who *writes* about the noise made by others. As a critic, he chose the *nom de plume* Corno di Bassetto—actually the name of an instrument which nobody knew and which is so meek in tone that "not even the devil could make it sparkle." Yet Bassetto became a sparkling critic, and more: "I cannot deny that Bassetto was occasionally vulgar; but that does not matter if he makes you laugh. Vulgarity is a necessary part of a complete author's equipment; and the clown is sometimes the best part of the circus."

The Diabolical One

How the undoubtedly lonely little boy (whose mother listened only to the musical noisemakers) came to use his imagination to converse with a great imaginary companion is described thus: "In my childhood I exercised my literary genius by composing my own prayers . . . they were a literary performance for the entertainment and propitiation of the Almighty." In line with his family's irreverence in matters of religion, Shaw's piety had to find and rely on the rockbottom of religiosity which, in him, early became a mixture of "intellectual integrity . . . synchronized with the dawning of moral passion." At the same time it seems that Shaw was (in some unspecified way) a little devil of a child. At any rate, he did not feel identical with himself when he was good: "Even when I was a good boy, I was so only theatrically, because, as actors say, I saw myself in the character." And indeed, at the completion of his identity struggle, i.e., "when Nature completed my countenance in 1880 or thereabouts (I had only the tenderest sprouting of hair on my face until I was 24), I found myself equipped with the upgrowing moustaches and eyebrows, and the sarcastic nostrils of the operatic fiend whose airs (by Gounod) I had sung as a child, and whose attitudes I had affected in my boyhood. Later on, as the generations moved past me, I . . . began to perceive that imaginative fiction is to life what the sketch is to the picture or the conception to the statue."

Thus G.B.S., more or less explicitly, traces his own roots. Yet, it is well worth noting that what he finally *became* seems to him to have been as *innate* as the intended reincarnation of Shakespeare referred to above. His teacher, he says, "puzzled me with her attempts to teach me to read; for I can remember no time at which a page of print was not intelligible to me, and can only suppose that I was born literate." However, he thought of a number of professional choices: "As an alternative to being a Michelangelo I had dreams of being a Badeali (note, by the way, that of literature I had no dreams at all any more than a duck has of swimming)."

He also calls himself "a born Communist" (which, we hasten to say, means a Fabian Socialist), and he explains the peace that comes with the *acceptance of what one seems to be made to be*; the "born Communist . . . knows where he is, and where this society which has so intimidated him is. He is cured of his MAUVAISE HONTE. . . ." Thus "the complete outsider" gradually became his kind of complete insider: "I was," he said, "outside society, outside politics, outside sport, outside the Church"—but this "only within the limits of British barbarism . . . The moment music, painting, literature, or science came into question the positions were reversed: it was I who was the Insider."

As he traces all of these traits back into childhood, Shaw becomes aware of the fact that only a *tour de force* could have integrated them all: ". . . if I am to be entirely communicative on this subject, I must add that the mere rawness which so soon rubs off was complicated by a deeper strangeness which has made me all my life a sojourner on this planet rather than a native of it. Whether it be that I was born mad or a little too sane, my kingdom was not of this world: I was at home only in the realm of my imagination, and at my ease only with the mighty dead. Therefore, I had to become an actor, and create for myself a fantastic personality fit and apt for dealing with men, and adaptable to the various parts I had to play as author, journalist, orator, politician, committee man, man of the world, and so forth. In this," so Shaw concludes significantly, "I succeeded later on only too well." This statement is singularly illustrative of that faint disgust with which older men at times review the inextricable identity which they had come by in their youth—a disgust which in the lives of some can become mortal despair and inexplicable psychosomatic involvement.

The end of his crisis of younger years Shaw sums up in these words: "I had the intellectual habit; and by natural combination of critical faculty with literary resource needed only a clear comprehension of life in the light of an intelligible theory: in short, a religion, to set it in triumphant operation." Here the old Cynic has circumscribed in one sentence what the identity formation of any human being must add up to. To translate this into terms more conducive to discussion in ego-psychological and psychosocial terms: Man, to take his place in society, must acquire a "conflict-free," habitual use of a dominant *faculty*, to be elaborated in an *occupation*; a limitless *resource*, a feedback, as it were, from the immediate *exercise* of this occupation, from the *companionship* it provides, and from its *tradition*; and finally, an intelligible *theory* of the processes of life which the old atheist, eager to shock to the last, calls a religion.

Born to Set It Right:
The Roots of Shaw's Style

by Richard M. Ohmann

Born to Set It Right

In making himself the critic of things as they are, Shaw places himself in the position of outsider. Everyone, to be sure, can imagine a better world than the present one; everyone has some grievances. But Shaw does not want the *status quo* merely doctored up a bit, and few can face such a wholesale scrapping of traditions as he does propose. The poor, who might profit by revolution, have no voice, and even if they had they would balk at many of Shaw's iconoclasms—his attacks on marriage and conventional religion, for example. The middle class, the very group that leans most heavily on established institutions, is the class with a voice to use in defending them. Thus Shaw finds that "civilized society is one huge bourgeoisie" (M&S, xv),[1]

"Born to Set It Right: The Roots of Shaw's Style" by Richard M. Ohmann. From *Shaw: The Style and the Man* by Richard M. Ohmann (Middletown, Conn.: Wesleyan University Press, 1962), pp. 74–90 and 101–08. Copyright © 1962 by Wesleyan University. Reprinted by permission of the author and the Wesleyan University Press. The pages printed here are only part of the chapter entitled "The Posture of Opposition."

The quotations from Shaw included here are reprinted by permission of The Public Trustee and The Society of Authors.

[1] My references to Shaw's works are, wherever possible, to *The Ayot St. Lawrence Edition of The Collected Works of Bernard Shaw* (New York, 1930–32). Page references apply also to *The Works of Bernard Shaw* (London, 1930–32), for which the same type was used. In the following key to my in-text references the volumes belong to The Ayot St. Lawrence edition unless otherwise specified.

And	*Androcles and the Lion, Overruled, Pygmalion*
Back	*Back to Methuselah*
Delusions	*Doctors' Delusions, Crude Criminology, Sham Education*
Dilemma	*The Doctor's Dilemma, Getting Married, The ShewingUp of Blanco Posnet*
EPWW	*Everybody's Political What's What?* (London, 1944)
Essays	*Essays in Fabian Socialism*
IK	*The Irrational Knot*
Imm	*Immaturity*

and that to be against the middle class is to be against almost everybody. Enemy of the people (for their own good) is therefore a role that meshes naturally with Shaw's ideas. It is also intensely congenial to him just as a stance.

Shaw was born into a family that asked (and deserved) little tribute of reverence. He did look up to his father at first, until he discovered that the senior Shaw, who liked to give thunderous lectures on the evils of drink, was himself a tippler. This revelation of hypocrisy and weakness left a scar on Shaw's attitude toward parental authority. His mother, long-suffering and admirably talented, was nonetheless too remote and cold a figure to be idealized. He was surrounded, too, by various eccentric uncles—one whose "profanity and obscenity in conversation were of Rabelaisian exuberance" (SSS, 15), and one who went harmlessly insane—and watched over by a kind of surrogate father, the musician Lee, who ate unfashionable brown bread and criticized doctors, and whose influence on Shaw's home "accustomed me to the scepticism as to academic authority which still persists in me" (SSS, 14). Hardly a conventional group of sacrosanct elders.

But more important still was the atmosphere of laxity that surrounded the young George Bernard. The children were treated as adults, left to their own devices unencumbered by demands for obedience, by guidance, or by love; their upbringing lacked both Victorian austerity and Victorian sentimentality. No one attempted to nurture in Shaw a sense of sin. Quite the contrary, in fact. His father would occasionally rebuke him for scoffing at the Bible, but would conclude the defense by stating, "with an air of perfect fairness, that even the worst enemy of religion could say no worse of the Bible than that it was the damndest parcel of lies ever written" (Imm, xxiii). Deaths were common in Shaw's big family, and to save time at funerals the family coaches would maintain a lugubrious pace only until reaching the city limits, then tear at a gallop to the burial ground, which lay some distance away, while the family often passed the time by speaking ill of the deceased. Mockery of death and mockery of religion were appropriately set against a background of Mrs. Shaw's music, and punctuated by Mr. Shaw's drunken sprees. And yet at the same time the family maintained the most absurd

IWG	*The Intelligent Woman's Guide to Socialism and Capitalism*
JBOI	*John Bull's Other Island, How He Lied to Her Husband, Major Barbara*
M&S	*Man and Superman*
Mis	*Misalliance, The Dark Lady of the Sonnets, Fanny's First Play*
PPU	*Plays Pleasant and Unpleasant* (2 vols.)
QI	*The Quintessence of Ibsenism, The Perfect Wagnerite, The Sanity of Art*
SSS	*Sixteen Self Sketches, Standard Edition* (London, 1949)
StJ	*Saint Joan, The Apple Cart*
Too True	*Too True to Be Good, Village Wooing & On the Rocks. Three Plays by Bernard Shaw* (London, 1934)
War	*What I Really Wrote About the War*

pretensions of superiority: they were after all Protestants; they were descended from gentry, albeit unimpressively; they were in wholesale, not retail, trade, and Shaw's father could criticize him for playing with the son of an ironmonger. Of this class snobbery Shaw remarks, "I remember Stopford Brooke one day telling me that he discerned in my books an intense and contemptuous hatred for society. No wonder!" [2] Sensitive to this hypocrisy, and receptive to the permissiveness and skepticism, Shaw seems never to have felt awe toward authority, seems almost to have been "born free from many of the venerations and inhibitions which restrain the tongues of most small boys," as he said to Hesketh Pearson.[3] In any case he is always ready to ridicule his elders, from his own father to cultural father-figures like Darwin.

If his family origins disinclined him to accept the world as he found it, education stamped his skepticism in still more deeply. His schooling "operated by a succession of eye-openers each involving the repudiation of some previously held belief, and consequently of my conviction of my father's infallibility," so that he thinks the learning process a "ceremony of disillusion" (EPWW, 155) at each step of advance. Nor did his informal education—Marx, Henry George, Bellamy—do anything to dilute his conviction that whatever is is misunderstood, and that most of what is is wrong. His first novel, *Immaturity*, ends symbolically with a negative shake of the hero's head.

Throughout his life Shaw wrote as an *opponent;* and this stance had its origins in his reaction against the entrenched Victorian smugness which prevailed during his boyhood and through his first quarter-century in London. It has become fashionable lately to deny that the Victorians were smug, and to see them instead as deeply troubled by the crumbling of old creeds and the mushrooming of new problems. This is true, certainly, of the great writers, but their voices gain in heroic timbre precisely because of the emptiness into which they cry. In the face of their jeremiads the great bourgeoisie remains complacent and conservative, as perhaps it always has been. It is against that conservatism—against a collective mind that is shocked by the New Woman, thinks socialists cads, subscribes to a comfortably tailored blend of middle-class Christianity and scientific materialism, and holds all kinds of selfish cant as gospel—that Shaw writes.

During the Spanish-American War he read an account of an American commander who, upon seeing the Spanish fleet burned, gathered his men

---

[2] "In the Days of My Youth," from *Mainly About People*, Sept. 17, 1898. Quoted by Archibald Henderson in *George Bernard Shaw: Man of the Century* (New York: Appleton-Century-Crofts, 1956), p. 16.
[3] Quoted in Hesketh Pearson's *G. B. S.; A Full Length Portrait* (New York and London: Harper and Row, Publishers, Inc., 1942), p. 21.

together and declared his belief in God Almighty. On reading this, Shaw concluded that "if I am sane, the rest of the world ought not to be at large. We cannot both see things as they really are." [4] Not infrequently his critiques of society do give the impression that Shaw is the only sane man in a world of the feebleminded and the deluded, but at least this egotism stems more from a conviction of the world's folly than from a sense of his own infallibility. Though he sometimes says, "How right I am!" he more often says, "How misguided the others are!" And against their madness he sets himself to write.

At the end of his life he describes the Shavian crusade against error:

> My Everybody's What's What is only an attempt by a very ignorant old man to communicate to people still more ignorant than himself such elementary social statics as he has managed to pick up . . . in the course of a life . . . spent largely in discovering and correcting the mistakes into which his social antecedents and surroundings led him. (EPWW, 366)

The cardinal truth about society is that it lacks knowledge and self-awareness: "What is wrong with the prosaic Englishman is what is wrong with the prosaic men of all countries: stupidity" (M&S, xix). For their stupidity his home remedy is a heavy dose of truth, administered by himself, but he sees their ignorance as so deep and so soothing that they desperately resist enlightenment. Thus he has it that audiences and critics rejected "Too True to Be Good" because its honesty had been too much for them, "as if I had hit them in some new and unbearably sore spot" (Too True, 3).

Throughout *What I Really Wrote About the War* he adopts the role of Cassandra, or the voice in the wilderness: in wartime people hunger for palliation with special acuteness. To Shaw, "Common Sense About the War," in spite of its relative sanity, seems "the cruelest use I have ever had to make of my pen." He would like to have spared amiable people the "unbearable" truth about power diplomacy, but "could not indulge these innocents" because his business "was to clear our case of false claims" (War, 116–17). Elsewhere he speaks of "Common Sense" as "that intolerable document which afterwards turned out to be so exasperatingly right in every detail" (388), and of the people's "prayers to be shielded from that terrible thing, the truth" (48). One article ends: "I can promise nothing beyond another unheeded cry in the wilderness" (394); and another begins: "I told you so" (395). At the same period he was writing the Webbs that after thirty years of telling Englishmen "the truth as far as human judgment is capable of the truth, I find that they remain invincibly persuaded that I am a mischief maker, a liar, and a wrecker." [5] In all this he is un-

---

[4] "In the Days of My Youth," quoted by Henderson, p. 48.
[5] Quoted by Henderson, p. 377.

questionably sincere, yet he brings extra gusto to the part because it so admirably suits his self-image of Shaw the facer of unpopular truths and shatterer of illusions, Shaw the opposer, Shaw the wise fool. Unsurprisingly, it is a part that he assigns to some of the most memorable figures in his work: Owen Jack and Sidney Trefusis in the novels, Captain Shotover, Jack Tanner, Saint Joan, and many others in the plays.

Shaw's choice of allies throws into relief his choice of role. Against Victorian well-being he champions the cosmic uneasiness of Schopenhauer, Nietzsche, Butler, Marx, Ruskin, Morris, and Carlyle, and the artistic rebelliousness of Wagner, Ibsen, Chekhov, Gorky, and the French Impressionists. For reinforcement he throws Jesus at the establishment. In this company alone Shaw feels at ease.

With this posture of revolt, his preference for change (as outlined in Chapter II [in Richard M. Ohmann's book *Shaw: The Style and the Man*— EDITOR'S NOTE]) jibes nicely. A civilization cannot progress, cannot remake itself, except through the destruction of old institutions: "Every step of progress means a duty repudiated, and a scripture torn up" (QI, 20). To change is to deny the claims of what is. To conventional people, therefore, progress seems regress, for it always entails the relinquishing of previous advances and once-revolutionary ideals. Such people denounce as an enemy of society the free spirit who mocks ideals, though he is actually performing a service by "sweeping the world clear of lies" (QI, 45). Shaw does accept the necessity of social rules—thus his rejection of anarchism for its "terrifying danger and obvious inconvenience" (QI, 320)—but no law is so absolute that it can stand up forever, and all laws, creeds, and systems of ethics, "instead of making society better than its best unit, make it worse than its average unit, because they are never up to date" (QI, 317). Thus the duty of the man of genius with a conscience is almost invariably to attack, since many can be found to defend. The worst philistines of all are journalists and artists who take it as their duty merely to *reflect* the "ignorance and prejudice of their readers" (QI, 330), rather than trying to reform them.

It is worth noting, apropos of Shaw's contrariness, that he does not rest content with assaults on the enemy's weak points. Rightly he contrasts himself with Molière, who makes his doctors mercenary hembugs, and with Dickens, who attacks revivalist preachers by having Stiggins first get drunk on pineapple rum and finally be kicked into a horse trough. Shaw "strikes at Hector or Achilles, not at Thersites." [6] It has often been remarked that most of his dramatic villains make a strong case for themselves. Such devil's disciples as Mrs. Warren, Morell, the Inquisitor, and the Devil himself in "Man and Superman" are far from being straw men or buffoons. Similarly, he directs his satire and invective at such able opponents as the medical profession, experimental science, Darwinism, conventional theism, and the

[6] Henderson, p. 740.

free enterprise system. He generally strikes at the pillars of society, not at the aberrations.

As I have pointed out, Shaw considers wholesale rebellion such as this essential to progress, and his argument for tolerance turns on the necessity for granting as much leeway as society can bear to the discontented servants of the Life Force. Yet on the subject of tolerance Shaw has conflicting feelings. There is much of the authoritarian in his intellectual make-up: his intolerance of mediocrity, his passion for social order, his hatred for random drifting, all put him out of patience with the painfully lethargic movements of a free society. Some of this impatience spills over into tempered admiration of Mussolini, Stalin, even Hitler, and into such rigid systems as state-controlled genetics. But the pressure of his relentless individualism is too powerful for this other complex of motives. A fully disciplined society might take it upon itself to hamstring its Wagners, Ibsens, and Shaws, and the moral claustrophobia in England is quite severe enough without contemplating such anti-utopian extensions of authority. So Shaw consistently supports freedom. He reluctantly accepts democracy as the means of transition to communism; compulsion will not work because "we *hate* masters" (Essays, 89). He stoutly opposes censorship because "an attack on morals may turn out to be the salvation of the race" (Dilemma, 385). And he writes tracts proposing a bill of rights for children and "controversial education" to "tear away the camouflage from commercial civilization" (Delusions, 332). The act of opposition is as necessary to the human race as the sexual act, and must be jealously protected from the anxious reprisals of the ins. Shaw has ambiguous feelings about authority, but finally he is neither contradictory nor vague in his advocacy of tolerance.

In her study of perception in prejudiced and unprejudiced children Else Frenkel-Brunswik finds a correlation too great to be fortuitous between intolerance of perceptual and conceptual ambiguity and "strength of hostility, of power-orientation, of externalization, and of rigid stereotyping." [7] This conjunction has more than passing interest; I suggested in Chapter I [in Richard M. Ohmann's *Shaw: The Style and the Man*—EDITOR'S NOTE] that Shaw is inhospitable toward conceptual ambiguity, and in this chapter that his characteristic authorial stance is in part hostile. There is no need to seek a too rigorous application of Frenkel-Brunswik's terms. Shaw is power-oriented only in being immensely *interested* in power, not in wanting to prostrate himself before it. He stereotypes his opponents only to the extent of finding them all lacking in wit. As for "externalization" of aggressions and weaknesses, that is the mark of a paranoid, and to call Shaw a paranoid would be to substitute diagnosis for literary criticism. Shaw has good reason for thinking himself besieged by enemies, since he goes so far out of his way

[7] Jerome S. Bruner and David Krech, *Perception and Personality* (Durham, N.C.: Duke University Press, 1950), p. 141.

to create them.[8] "Hostility," finally, has some connotations quite inappropriate to Shaw's outlook on life; he is too warm-blooded and too flamboyant to decapitate his enemies with any emotion but the warrior's joy of battle. But if Frenkel-Brunswik's terms do not pin Shaw down like a botanical specimen, they do at least come close. Hand in hand with Shaw the man of genius goes Shaw the antagonist, the gadfly, the outrager of stodgy people, the opponent of majorities. I have laid some of his lapses in common sense (antivivisection, etc.) at the door of rigid categorizing; they also reflect, obviously, his unwillingness to be on the side of the majority or to find repose in yea-saying. In the light of such alternate explanations it is especially convenient to find psychologists linking the epistemic stance of the leveler with the rhetorical stance of the nay-sayer.

no, No, NO

The passage that follows is an example of Shaw playing the patient man of reason, beleaguered by the intolerable pigheadedness of the vivisectors. Anyone who knows the ABC of Science, he says, knows that men must not seek knowledge by criminal methods:

> He knows that there are fifty ways of ascertaining any fact; that only the two or three worst of them are dirty ways; that those who deliberately choose the dirty ways are not only morally but intellectually imbecile; that the "clean-handed man with the scalpel" is a humbug who has to buy his brains from the instrument maker; that it is ridiculous to expect that an experimenter who commits acts of diabolical cruelty for the sake of what he calls Science can be trusted to tell the truth about the results; that no vivisector ever accepts another vivisector's conclusions nor refrains from undertaking a fresh set of vivisections to upset them; that as any fool can vivisect and gain kudos by writing a paper describing what happened, the laboratories are infested with kudos hunters who have nothing to tell that they could not have ascertained by asking a policeman except when it is something that they should not know (like the sensations of a murderer); and that as these vivisectors crowd humane research workers out of the schools and discredit them, they use up all the endowments and bequests available for their purposes, leaving nothing for serious physiological research. (Delusions, 142–43)

Anybody may know this, but Shaw tells him all the same. Each of his "that" clauses denies one proposition in the vivisectionists' creed, and the sentence

[8] Though I do not wish to press the point, there is more than a little paranoia in the running battles Shaw carries on in letters to the daily papers, where apparently he was subject to considerable abuse. And he does seem to take a special delight in relating the trials to which his superiority makes him subject. Of Mussolini's regime he says, "I, being a bit of a psychologist myself, also understood the situation, and was immediately denounced by the refugees and their champions as an anti-democrat, a hero-worshipper of tyrants, and all the rest of it." (*The Simpleton*, 117)

amounts to a demolition job on the whole structure of their argument. Often when Shaw gets up steam for one of these colossal series, his fires are those of anger. The syntactical heaping-up that betokens a similarity relationship also serves him rhetorically, to smother his audience, as it were: he confronts the opposition, not with one argument, but with ten. Such superabundance has special propriety in the crusade against entrenched opinion, which needs to be jostled rudely before it can be dislodged. Note, too, the language of exaggeration in this passage—"fifty ways of ascertaining any fact," "it is ridiculous," "diabolical cruelty," "no vivisector ever," "any fool," "have nothing to tell," "all the endowments," "leaving nothing." Hyperbole, like the Shavian catalogue, can be understood in terms both of the epistemology of equivalence and of the rhetoric of opposition.

The same holds true for the devices of comparison. One of Shaw's favorites contains an explicit form of negation, "no more———than———." But he uses the others to deny or contradict almost as regularly. His analogies seek measuring sticks for the villainy or illogicality of his opponents, and his comparisons of degree often work by *reductio ad absurdum* ("could not manage a baked potato stand honestly and capably, much less a coal mine"— IWG, 122). When he highlights the similarities between one period and another he often does so pejoratively in order to emphasize the moral corruption of both; here, for example, he presses both the series and the "as" of equality into such a comparison:

> Already in the twentieth century there has been as much brute coercion and savage intolerance, as much flogging and hanging, as much impudent injustice on the bench and lustful rancor in the pulpit, as much naive resort to torture, persecution, and suppression of free speech and freedom of the press, as much war, as much of the vilest excess of mutilation, rapine, and delirious indiscriminate slaughter of helpless non-combatants, old and young . . . as we can find any record of from the days when the advocacy of liberty was a capital offence and Democracy was hardly thinkable. (Mis, 103–4)

The catalogue bulges with invective and exaggeration, as Shaw annihilates the ascription of tolerance and humanity to his contemporaries. One could follow the thread of opposition through other equivalence forms, and through the forms of discontinuity as well—particularly semantic shock, redefinition, word-coining, and paradox. But it will be more profitable at this point to scan new and more concentrated evidence of denial and opposition.

To begin with macrostylistics, Shaw frequently compounds the structure of a whole piece from a set of negations. Take that quintessence of Shavianism, "The Revolutionist's Handbook." After a preface concluding that "Revolutions have *never* lightened the burden of tyranny" (italics mine), John Tanner's first chapter outlines the need for controlled breeding, but in doing so it begins with a denial that transfiguration of institutions is ever more than change from Tweedledum to Tweedledee, and ends with a warning that the goal of breeding must be neither a race of mindless athletes nor a race of Sunday School prigs. Chapter Two also carries a burden of negation: it brushes aside the twin obstacles of property and marriage; rejecting first the revolutionist's contention that they are important; second, the idea that society will much feel their departure; and third, the conventional notion that cohabitation and procreation are necessarily connected. Then, via a discussion of the Oneida community, Tanner disposes of the hope that great leaders and great creeds can raise a people above its natural level. The fourth chapter makes short work of the supposed objections of human instinct to regimented genetics. With the fifth we are back to the need for a race of supermen, the argument being that democracy cannot thrive when the electorate has feet of clay. Then another quick vault, this time to a denial that prudery represents instinctive resistance to the Life Force. Chapter Seven returns to political realities, and disposes of the ideas (1) that social reform is a solution, (2) that violence is any help, (3) that man has progressed during recorded history, and (4) that he is even capable of progress without a mutation in character. The next chapter takes up the third of these denials, and debunks a whole series of alleged modern achievements. With Chapter Nine, Tanner returns to the denial that social progress *can* occur, barring evolutionary progress. He concludes by rejecting the idea that breeding can be controlled in a *laissez-faire* society—a devious way to arrive at the necessity of socialism!

On this gathering of positions Shaw imposes very little logical coherence; transitions are, as usual, his weak point. What does hold his arguments together is the posture of denial, for the little book stands united with itself against both the conventional dogmas of capitalism and those of socialism as well. Many of Shaw's arguments could as easily have been cast as affirmations rather than denials, but whenever possible he elects the negative mode, as if his positions will gain sharpness from being honed against those of imagined antagonists.[9]

The patterns of negation that give structure to Shaw's arguments are naturally reticulate in miniature on the level of sentence and phrase: one cannot constantly refute without ever saying "not," and negative forms abound in his prose. A single page from an open letter to Frank Harris contains thirteen of them:

> you can learn nothing about your biographees from their sex histories
> The sex relation is not a personal relation
> could not endure one another for a day
> you would be none the wiser

---

[9] It bears repeating that "The Revolutionist's Handbook" is written by Jack Tanner, who perhaps exceeds even Shaw in obstreperousness. But his rhetoric, like his revolutionism, differs from that of his creator in degree, not in kind.

I was not impotent
I was not sterile
I was not homosexual
not promiscuously
I never associated
nor had any scruples
I was not attracted
my first adventure did not occur until
Do not misunderstand this   (SSS, 113)

Admittedly, Shaw is up on his hind legs here, and to a certain extent he is
contradicting actual statements made by the improbable Harris. But the
high incidence of negatives obtains elsewhere, though less spectacularly. To
take a longer and more typical sample, six pages of *The Intelligent Woman's
Guide* (360–65) contain, respectively, seven, nine, nine, eight, six, and twelve
of these forms (thirty-five "nots," six "nos," five "nors," three "nevers,"
and two "nothings"), an incidence considerably higher than the norm for
other writers.

But such a rigidly limited measure of negation is far from telling the whole
story. These same six pages, for instance, display a number of other forms
of denial and opposition: "the *wrong* way to put it," "the very *last thing*
the . . . worker wants," "the common trick of . . . is a foolish one," and
so forth. To get at the full sweep of negation in Shaw's prose it is necessary
to make a fuller and less formal analysis. Consider another page, this time
from the Preface to "John Bull's Other Island" (JBOI, xvi). To begin with
there are nine negative forms. In addition, there are several words that
imply opposition or denial somewhat less directly: "without," "only" (implying a completeness not attained), and the prefixes "un-" and "out-" ("out-
wit," etc.). Then there are the signs of syntactical opposition, "although"
and "instead." But the largest group of negative words are those that have
a looser association with invective, those with negative connotations. In
such words and phrases the passage abounds:

violently shoved	conspire	blockhead
stumbling blindly	assassinate	blockheads
backward	deeper and deeper	compelled
crush	shame	supercilious
weaknesses	lack	tongue-tied
terrors	enemy	exposing
misery	shams	denouncing
bayonets	hypocrisies	lose
embarrass	servitude	discount
bully	illusions	miss

Such words sustain the rhetoric of opposition not because of any formal
characteristics but because of their meanings, and because of the freight of

emotion associated with them, emotion whose burden is condemnatory. The total number of words I have enumerated so far is forty-eight, on a page that contains only some three-hundred-odd words all told: more than one word out of seven signals opposition.

This is about as far as measurement can go, but it still is not the limit of the passage's negativism. For one thing, syntactical juxtaposition sometimes works to bring out a conflict. For example, a sentence with an explicit negative—"We [Ireland] cannot crush England as a Pickford's van might crush a perambulator"—precedes one with no negative forms: "We are the perambulator and England the Pickford." The force of the earlier negative carries over into this sentence, so that its effect is to *deny* the suggestion that Ireland is stronger than England. In addition, the second sentence contains an internal opposition, the contrast between a Pickford and a perambulator, which is indicated only by the grammatical pairing of two words with disparate referents. As syntax works to diffuse an atmosphere of opposition, so does the tone of the whole section. "England" becomes a term of invective in itself, since in the context of Shaw's anti-imperialist argument England is the main villain. And in a series such as this: "a supercilious, unpopular, tongue-tied, aristocratic Protestant Parnell," the distaste attaching to the first three terms carries over to give "aristocratic" and "Protestant" unfavorable connotations that they would not necessarily possess otherwise, and establishes "Parnell" as something to be against. To the effects of syntax and connotation must be added, finally, the effects of irony, which often serves to invert what would ordinarily be terms of approbation. Thus when Shaw speaks of "any mysterious Irish pluck, Irish honesty, Irish bias on the part of Providence, or sterling Irish solidity of character," he is deploring, not pluck and honesty themselves, but the Celtic sentimentality that insists on taking such virtues as the special property of the Irish. Irony, as a means of speaking to the happy few over the heads of the ignorant many, is necessarily a weapon of critical attack.

I do not suggest that every page of Shaw's prose has its feet so firmly planted in a pugilistic stance, but only that he finds this stance especially congenial. The page I have been analyzing does not strike me as an unparalleled example of Shavian invective, but as one fairly easy to match in his work. His chosen role as the unwelcome sage and his image of the public as desperately clinging to soothing lies make it inevitable that he should spend much of his energy flaying complacency and disputing received opinion.

Idealists and Realists

The role of Cassandra, which Shaw finds congenial in several of his major crusades, entails a particular idea both of reality and of people. The fact that the truth is so apparent to Shaw and so obscure to others presses even his capacious ego to look for some explanation beside the superiority of his intellect. The explanation he seizes on, as I have suggested, is only a slightly less egotistical one: the superiority of his courage in facing facts. Not only in "Common Sense About the War," but in many of his social and critical writings, Shaw strikes the pose of the one uncomfortable realist among a nation of comfortable sentimentalists, and, more bluntly, the one sane man in a nation of fools. The conviction that he alone can and will tell the truth presupposes, thus, a world full of illusions and a populace that resists taking an honest look at that world.

This picture fits with something like schematic rigidity into Shaw's philosophy of Creative Evolution. Within that system man, at present, is a rather primitive experiment of the Life Force, unable to penetrate very deeply the ignorance that shrouds the secrets of life. But evolution is movement in the direction of knowledge. Art and literature, the brightest sparks yet struck by human genius, represent "the struggle of Life to become divinely conscious of itself instead of blindly stumbling hither and thither in the line of least resistance" (M&S, xxiv). Religion, too, is a step in the direction of awareness, so long as it is not sham religion. Lavinia, the would-be martyr of "Androcles and the Lion," establishes this connection between religion and the striving for truth; a Roman captain accuses her of wanting to die for "Christian fairy stories," and she replies that the approach of death has made her forget the stories, made reality become realer and realer. She is going to die for something greater than stories, but does not yet know what— "If it were for anything small enough to know, it would be too small to die for. I think I'm going to die for God. Nothing else is real enough to die for." The captain asks her what God and she answers, "When we know that, Captain, we shall be gods ourselves" (And, 138–39). Shaw believes that men will become gods, and that divinity will consist mainly in full comprehension of self and reality. Evolution, according to Don Juan, works toward "higher and higher individuals, the ideal individual being omnipotent, omniscient, infallible, and withal completely, unilludedly self-conscious: in short, a god?" (M&S, 112). But at present man is far from godlike in breadth of vision and depth of insight, and the direction of time's arrow—even the fact that it has an arrow—is hidden to all but the scattered men of genius whom the Life Force throws up from time to time as previews of what is to come. Needless to say, Shaw regards himself as one of these evolutionary anachronisms, as a man sitting on the right hand of truth. Hence the role of prophet, and hence the will to do single combat against the hordes of the ignorant. To an advanced thinker like Shaw, most of what other people think is eolithic groping, and must simply be *denied*.

If this notion of the twentieth century as an intellectual Stone Age bears part of the responsibility for the standard Shavian dichotomy of appearance and reality, a still larger share belongs to the idea that society consciously and unconsciously buries the meat of truth under a crust of lies. Ignorance is deplorable, but hypocrisy is contemptible, and it is hypocrisy, therefore, which most often places Shaw in the position of accuser. He discovered early the deceptions of society, and made them his special target. His novels, the first literary fruits of this revelation, mostly hinge on conflicts between one or more hard-headed characters and a larger number of deluded ones.

The arch-realist Conolly speaks for all of the hard-headed ones in his indictment of polite education:

> But what you call her education, as far as I can make it out, appears to have consisted of stuffing her with lies, and making it a point of honor with her to believe them in spite of sense and reason. The sense of duty that rises on that sort of foundation is more mischievous than downright want of principle. I don't dispute your right, you who constitute polite society, to skin over all the ugly facts of life. But to make your daughters believe that the skin covers healthy flesh is a crime. Poor Marian thinks that a room is clean when all the dust is swept out of sight under the furniture; and if honest people rake it out to bring it under the notice of those whose duty it is to remove it, she is disgusted with them, and ten to one accuses them of having made it themselves. She doesn't know what sort of world she is in, thanks to the misrepresentations of those who should have taught her. She will deceive her children in just the same way, if she ever has any. If she had been taught the truth in her own childhood, she would know how to face it, and would be a strong woman as well as an amiable one. But it is too late now. The truth seems natural to a child; but to a grown woman or man, it is a bitter lesson in the learning, though it may be invigorating when it is well mastered. And you know how seldom a hard task forced on an unwilling pupil *is* well mastered. (IK, 253–54)

Shaw's "unpleasant" plays, too, consist mainly in the stripping away of illusions—Trench's illusions about the innocence of interest, the Petkoffs' about war, Morell's about women and marriage, and so on. Mrs. Warren, who has most reason to doubt the saccharine Victorian world-view, gives the lie to society most convincingly, the more so because she is desperately trying to justify herself to her daughter:

> You think that people are what they pretend to be—that the way you were taught at school and college to think right and proper is the way things really are. But it's not: it's all only a pretence, to keep the cowardly, slavish, common run of people quiet. . . . The big people, the clever people, the managing people, all know it. They do as I do, and think what I think. (PPU, 1,249)

This is the social alignment against which Shaw sets himself: a few insiders with a gentleman's agreement to keep quiet, and the common run of out-siders, who have no way of disbelieving the lies that are fed them, along with a third group of comfortable middle-class hangers-on, who find it convenient to believe the lies. The poor and the bourgeoisie resemble each other in this respect; both are in darkness as to the real mechanisms of society. "Stupid or comfortably-off" (Essays, 100): these are complementary attributes for Shaw, in that they both lead to falsehood.

His language vividly reflects this preoccupation with lies and deception. A Shaw concordance would show the word "hypocrisy" and its derivatives to have unusual prominence in his vocabulary; one of the worst things he can call a man is hypocrite. A number of similar words are favorites of his too. "Humbug," "sham," "defraud," "pretence," "imposture," "farce," "deception"—these and others are the common coin of Shavian invective. A typical catalogue of sins (scientific sins, in the present instance) lumps "impostures . . . credulities, and delusions . . . brazen lies and priestly pretensions" together with "abominations, quackeries . . . venalities" (Back, lxxxviii). The former group, comprising sins of deception, seems a good deal more vivid.

Aside from the actual labels of hyprocrisy, Shaw depends heavily on less direct methods of accusation, such as the opposition of "ostensibly" and an antonym:

ostensibly for a number of capital crimes . . . but essentially for . . . (StJ, 3)

ostensibly a heroic and patriotic defender of his country . . . really an unfortunate man driven by destitution to offer himself as food for powder . . . (Essays, 100)

But such examples carry one back to the realm of style. The point to be made here is that Shaw's contempt for deception hangs like a palpable atmosphere over his writing.

And ultimately, whatever his disgust with lies told to others, his contempt for hypocrisy is greatest when it is directed toward self-deception—if indeed self-deception and deception of others are ever entirely separate. Shaw embraces Ibsenism because he sees in it the exposure of *ideals* to the cold light of day. The idealist hides from fact because he hates himself; the realist sees in ideals "only something to blind us, something to numb us, something to murder self in us, something whereby, instead of resisting death, we can disarm it by committing suicide" (QI, 34). Blindness to reality is spiritual death: the identification of the two is crucial to *The Quintessence of Ibsenism*.

The theme of reality and corrupting ideals counts for much in Shaw's plays, too. One has only to think of Candida, Bluntschli, Caesar, Undershaft, and the like to realize that many Shavian heroes are realists warring genially against the idealists that surround them.[10] And in "Man and Superman" the theme becomes virtually dominant. Don Juan's nickname for Hell is the Palace of Lies, and the main source of his disgust with it is its enthronement

---

[10] This point is developed in Chapters III and IV of Arthur H. Nethercot's *Men and Supermen; The Shavian Portrait Gallery* (Cambridge, Mass., 1954). The categories *realist* and *idealist* seem to me the most fruitful of all those that Nethercot applies to Shaw's characters.

of sentimentality and beauty. According to Juan, the earthly ideal of romantic love leads the human will to demand "love, beauty, romance, emotion, passion without their wretched penalties, their expenses, their worries." All this, the Devil answers, is realized here. "Yes, at the cost of death," says Juan (M&S, 121)—Hell is a place where people have died into their irresponsible desires. "Hell is the home of the unreal," Juan says; it differs from earth only in allowing freer license to illusions:

> Here you call your appearance beauty, your emotions love, your sentiments heroism, your aspirations virtue, just as you did on earth; but here there are no hard facts to contradict you, no ironic contrast of your needs with your pretensions, no human comedy, nothing but a perpetual romance, a universal melodrama. (M&S, 102–3)

Insofar as one can interpret the third act of "Man and Superman" allegorically, Hell is that condition of the soul which results from living out one's lies; such damnation is the only true death. Don Juan's longest piece of invective catalogues the hypocrisies of the Devil's subjects, and ends with the ultimate accusation, "liars every one of them, to the very backbone of their souls" (M&S, 129). Briefly, the man who deceives himself sins against the Life Force. Or, as Shaw puts his case when in a more pragmatic humor, "If a man cannot look evil in the face without illusion, he will never know what it really is, or combat it effectually" (JBOI, 245). The function of ideals and of religions has generally been to sugar-coat conditions that should be acknowledged and fought; Shaw's mission, as he sees it, is to write a new mythology that men can believe without such gross prostitution of the intellect.

If reality is veiled, if Life aspires upward from its present condition of ignorance to an ultimate condition of knowledge, if each step in the process involves discarding as obsolete a once-adequate creed, and if the mass of mankind (particularly bourgeois mankind) impedes the march toward truth by clinging to its comfortable old deceptions, conscience must cast the man of genius in the role of opposer. He will be, as Shaw says of himself, "born mad or a little too sane, his kingdom . . . not of this world" (Imm, xlvii).

Thus Shaw could excuse Wilde and his like for having "nothing fundamentally positive to say," because they were "at least in revolt against falsehood and imposture . . . clearing our minds of cant, and thereby showing an uneasiness in the presence of error which is the surest symptom of intellectual vitality" (Back, lxxxiv). The negative mode harmonizes admirably with the Shavian scheme of things; so much is certain. It would be unreasonable to ask a more affirmative style from a writer who finds the world sick, hypocritical, and sinful. But since the habit of saying No seems to have a life of its own in Shaw's style, over and above its utility, one may be tempted to ask whether the Shavian ethic of realism and deception is not child, rather than parent, to the posture of denial. An emotional complex like negation may well be in some sense more primary in the artist's make-up than a code of beliefs. This is a question that stylistics and criticism must refer to biography and psychology, for it cannot be answered through explication of the text. What critical investigation *can* say is that rhetorical stance and intellectual creed are consonant with one another to a degree that is surely more than chance. Questions of priority aside, the man who thinks Bernard Shaw's thoughts is recognizably the same inner man who favors the rhetoric of opposition.

A Mote in the Critic's Eye:
Bernard Shaw and Comedy

by Bruce R. Park

"What's Wrong with Shaw?"

In the introduction to his critical anthology, *George Bernard Shaw: A Critical Survey*, Louis Kronenberger writes, "what stands forth glaringly is the extent to which Shaw has *not* been written about—that is to say, by the most influential of our serious modern critics." Much has been written about Shaw, and most of those who have written about him consider the man and his work important. But little of this great bulk of commentary has been intended as criticism, and most of the commentators have either valued his work on extra-literary grounds or been signally unclear about the grounds on which they did value him.

Those few who *do* write Shaw criticism cannot place him: Jacques Barzun, for instance, finds that "There seems to be no name for his position, which, nevertheless, he is not the first to occupy. Meanwhile he eludes our grasp and measure like a man in a fog."

Those critics who do not write about Shaw place him beyond the pale. To them his work is simply not literature. Silence, as usual in literature, means contempt. But though natural, the silent contempt is not justified. There are instances in the history of English literature—*Henry IV*, *I* and Sidney's "Defence of Poesy," for example—where the object rebukes the critique. The silence says as much about modern criticism as it does about Shaw. Modern criticism has ignored Shaw because it has paid little attention to the kind of literature he writes, and it has no way to value it. Used as a touchstone to certain identifying aspects of modern criticism, Shaw's outlook reveals a curious constriction in its vision.

"A Mote in the Critic's Eye: Bernard Shaw and Comedy" by Bruce R. Park. From *Texas Studies*, XXXVII (1958), 195–210. Copyright © 1958 by The University of Texas Press. Reprinted by permission of The University of Texas Press and the author.

I am as much concerned here with the *kind* of literature Shaw writes as with the critical aphasia which blocks him and that kind of literature out; and I am more concerned with the attitude which informs Shaw's literary work than with that work itself.

Although "the most influential of our serious modern critics" have been silent, certain proxy voices have spoken for them. Ezra Pound, for one, rarely refers to Shaw, and then *en passant;* but his remarks, while passing, are never glancing. Shaw is "fundamentally trivial," "a mere louse in comparison with Hardy, Joyce, or H. James." The poets of 1946 were better mannered, but in preparing the memorial volume, *G. B. S. 90,* Stephen Winsten could find no poet willing to contribute an essay on G. B. S. as poet.

Yet Shaw insisted, "I am a poet, essentially a poet," and said emphatically to Winsten, "I am not going to let the pious people appropriate the word 'poetry' and leave me the dregs." Some of the chip-on-shoulder defiance of these and other remarks like them was just a cry for attention; Shaw could not bear indifference. Some represent Shaw's realization that "the young people" and "their" poets and critics had by their indifference placed his works on "the unreachable shelves of the classics," as he put it. But Shaw gravitated to the subject mostly because he knew *why* he was being ignored. "The one thing that might have given me satisfaction has been denied me, and that is art," he said to Winsten; and to Winsten's question, "And how do you know that you would have derived satisfaction from art?" he replied, "How does one know anything? I feel my life has been void without it. I have nothing to look back upon and nothing to look forward to. Nature despises me even more than it despises a vacuum." [1] Shaw felt the power of the word "poetry"; whatever he said at other times, he felt that it stood for the highest form of literature. It was exactly what he most wanted to be called that "the pious people" would not call him. "What's wrong with Shaw? He isn't a poet."

Shaw's perennial friend and opponent G. K. Chesterton found him lacking something more than poetry: "Any Latin, or member of the living and permanent culture of Europe will sum up all I say in one word: that Shaw has never had piety." The context of Chesterton's remark shows that he meant that Shaw was not a part of the European literary tradition. And in asserting his claim to the title poet Shaw testifies to the truth of this observation, though unwittingly: "Everything I have has come from poets: I picked up my vegetarianism from Shelley, my simplicity from Carpenter, my forthright speech from William Morris and my passion for fun from Oscar Wilde. As nobody reads these people I am regarded as 'my horrible unique self.' "

---

[1] Here Shaw's use of "art" seems to be quite general, although he was probably thinking of painting and partially referring to a period spent at the Royal Dublin Society School of Art which showed him that he was not a painter.

But Shaw is "unique" just *because* he owes these things to these people. What he got has little to do with them as poets.

The old man's realization that he stood accused of lacking "piety" and "poetry"—"art"—was just an old anxiety more strongly felt. Chesterton's statement of 1909 says much the same thing as critical silence in 1957: "Shaw is not part of the central literary tradition." Shaw execrated tradition and flung stones at art, yet he wanted to be part of both. He often said that he was proud to be a journalist, yet he constantly compiled lists of his illustrious literary and philosophic ancestors: "Shaw was full not only of Ibsen, but of Wagner, of Beethoven, of Goethe, and curiously, of John Bunyan," he wrote in *Sixteen Self-Sketches*. He claimed Shelley and Blake as his forebearers, called Michelangelo his master, and said that he was at home only among the great dead.

Shaw had always realized that the claim of art was important, perhaps because criticism had always kept it in front of him. Luigi Pirandello, writing for the *New York Times* after the Theater Guild's production of *St. Joan*, was one of the first to point out the ambiguity of Shaw's position: "There is a truly great poet in Shaw; but this combative Anglo-Irishman is quite willing to forget that he is a poet, so interested is he in being a citizen of his country, or a man of the twentieth century society." In "Bernard Shaw at Eighty" Edmund Wilson says much the same thing: "There was a poet in Shaw, still partly suppressed, or at any rate terribly overtaxed by the round of political meetings, the functions of Vestryman and borough councillor." R. P. Blackmur, in "A Critic's Job of Work," states the critical principle which seems to undergird judgments like these: "Let us say that in the nature of things—by their urgency—a writer somehow combines in his person . . . the attributes of the social reformer as well as those exclusively of the writer; that is why we call him a writer here, rather than more properly a poet—which is only what he ought to be."

Why is Shaw not a poet? Francis Fergusson, in *The Idea of a Theater*, takes us a step beyond Blackmur in writing that Euripides' dilemma was "the extremely modern one of the psyche caught in the categories its reason invents, but cut off from the deepest level of experience, where the mysterious world is yet felt as real and prior to our inventions, demands, and criticisms." One sees Shaw here, certainly. And the category which most trapped him was "the fact." He was in a sense the prototype of that "modern man" written of by Susanne Langer in *Philosophy in a New Key* who builds his attitude toward experience upon "complete submission to what he conceives as 'hard, cold facts.' " The tenor of his early relations with the Webbs in the young Fabian Society—a joyous splash in welters of blue books—is riotously factual. It is symbolically apt that the first Fabian pamphlet in which Shaw had a hand was called *Facts for Fabians*.

Shaw's sense of the term lies behind an explication he made of a principle of Wagner's aesthetic: "Wagner sought always for some point of contact between his ideas and the physical senses. . . . On all occasions he insists on the need for sensuous apprehension *to give reality to abstract comprehension, maintaining, in fact, that reality has no other meaning* [italics mine]." Shaw meant his words to paraphrase these of Wagner, which Shaw quotes: "He who after the manner of metaphysicians prefers *unreality* to *reality,* and who derives the concrete from the abstract—in short, puts the word before the fact— may be right in esteeming the idea of love as higher than the expression of love, and may affirm that actual love made manifest in feeling is nothing but the outward and visible sign of pre-existent, non-sensuous, abstract love; and he will do well to despise that sensuous function in general." The relation between text and paraphrase is odd. Clearly Shaw thought he was agreeing with Wagner when in fact he was disagreeing with him. Shaw does not seem to have understood that his "reality" was Wagner's "unreality," that he "put the word before the fact."

Shaw's "fact," then, is not "the thing in itself." Shaw seldom saw *an* object. "One tree looks exactly like another to me," he told Henderson. Shaw's rare appreciations of nature never focus on particulars—plants, flowers, animals. He saw its homogeneity—the sky, the sea, the quality of the atmosphere. What he had loved as a child in Dalkey Hill was not its flora and fauna, but its space, vistas, airiness, and light. In a way Shaw means by "fact," "Whatever cannot be gainsaid." Thus the fact is sometimes a generalization.[2]

Shaw's "factuality" leads him to interpret *The Ring* as "an allegory," a "poetic vision of unregulated industrial capitalism as it was made known in Germany in the middle of the nineteenth century by Engel's 'Condition of the Laboring Classes in England.' " Yet he told Henderson that his Uncle Walter Gurly's ribald commentaries on the Biblical stories had quite destroyed his "inculcated childish reverence for the verbiage of religion, for its legends and personifications and parallels."

This contradiction is part of the larger paradox already introduced, that Shaw coveted the prestige which the European literary tradition has accorded poetry, but distrusted poetry and poets. *The Quintessence of Ibsenism* shows both his distrust and its causes. For example, "Young and excessively sentimental people live on love, and delight in poetry or fine writing which declares that love is Alpha and Omega." "Let the Sapphos and Swinburnes sing as sweetly as they can, when we think of great poets we think of their brains, not of the concupiscences." But the crux of the matter

---

[2] Henderson observes, "Aberrations and irregularities, sexual or other, have no interest for him; they are negligible as merely trivial and personal incidents. He is concerned not with loves, but with sex."

appears in observations like this: "The idealists will be terrified beyond
measure . . . at the rending of the beautiful veil *they and their poets* [italics
mine] have woven to hide the unbearable face of the truth." Shaw distrusted
poets because they masked "facts" with beauty—biology with romantic
love, for example—because they were on the wrong side in the struggle
between truth and idealism.

The paradox is artificial. Really Shaw felt that there were true and false
poets. Shelley, Wagner, and Ibsen were true poets, and Shaw felt obliged
to defend them from the definition of "poet" he thought characteristic of
his age. He tried to rescue Wagner from the "beauty mongers"; he combated
"A beautiful and ineffectual angel, beating in the void his luminous wings
in vain" with Shelley as socialist, atheist, and vegetarian; he undertook to
rescue Ibsen from the idealist glamorizing of William Archer and those
who agreed with him. It follows that if false poets—Octavius Ramsden is an
example from the plays—were dedicated to concealing the "facts," true
poets were those who tore aside the veil. But the true poet was more than
that: "It is only the poet, with his vision of what life might be, to whom these
things [the evils of a capitalistic society] are unendurable. If we were a race
of poets we would make an end of them before the end of this miserable
century." Thus Shaw wrote in *The Perfect Wagnerite*. The poet is not only the
man who can take the hard, cold facts; he is also the man who feels he must
do something about them. Shelley and Wagner, the two "in whom intense
poetic feeling was the permanent state of their consciousness," were men
driven by the law of their nature "into open revolution against the social
evils which the average sensual man finds extremely suitable to him," Shaw
wrote in "The Religion of the Pianoforte."

So far Shaw's poet is a subspecies of the superman, in fact, a man very
like Shaw—the repository of an intenser consciousness, a more complex
organization, a greater vitality. But the poet is not only so. Shaw intimates
that there is a lesser order: "It may be that readers who have conned Ibsen
through idealist spectacles have wondered that I could so pervert the
utterances of a great poet. Indeed I know already that many of those who
are most fascinated by *the poetry of the plays* will plead for any explanation
of them rather than that given by Ibsen himself in the plainest terms through
the mouths of Mrs. Alving, Relling, and the rest." [3] There are two propositions here: first, Ibsen *is* a poet; second, there is a poet *in* Ibsen. Shaw seems
to believe that both are true, but he believes that the second *should not* be
unless the first is. The lesser poetic power is that of spinning tales and putting

---

[3] Ibsen, probably to defend himself against critics like Shaw, insisted as forcibly as Shaw
that he was primarily a poet. Aware of Ibsen's disapproval as well as that of Ibsenites
like Archer, Shaw covered himself by observing in *The Quintessence of Ibsenism,* "The
existence of a discoverable and perfectly definite thesis in a poet's work by no means
depends on the completeness of his own intellectual consciousness of it."

words together effectively, but Shaw does not think this power sufficient to earn a writer the name of poet.

To Shaw there is a poet *in* Wagner because he can handle allegory, but Wagner *is* a poet because he can *use* the allegory to project the "facts revealed by Engels." To Shaw allegory was a useful lie, and he was not fond of the lie, feeling that it was at best a concession to human inadequacy. He is vexed that Wagner had to use an allegory—what Wagner called a myth—at all. To Wagner, however, the myth was quite the opposite of a useful lie: "In the myth human relations almost completely lose their conventional form, which is intelligible only to the abstract reason; they show what is eternally human and eternally comprehensible, and show it in that concrete form, exclusive of all imitation, which gives all true myths their individual character." Shaw's lie was Wagner's truth. Even if Shaw had accepted myth as a means by which man had established himself in his cosmos, he would have viewed it as an outmoded means. Modern anthropological philosophy sees man accumulating himself in time, burying the old under the new; the individual is a kind of microcosm of the race experience. Shaw's ideal man clambers hopefully through time, travelling light, rejecting as much of the old as he acquires of the new.[4]

Modern criticism's view of language is analogous to the anthropological view of mankind: language is layered, contains all the modes of thought, feeling, and perception which the experience of ages has successively deposited; poetry is the literary species which exploits language in *depth*.[5] But to Shaw eternity was too much of a waste-basket. Thus he could not understand Wagner's "the eternally human," nor understand by "poetry" what modern criticism does. In fact, to Shaw *the best poetry is prose*.

Writing of Shaw as an Irishman, Chesterton says, "The Irish are lucid and logical. For being logical they strictly separate poetry from prose; and as in prose they are strictly prosaic, so in poetry they are purely poetical." Shaw was an Irishman. Criticizing a translation of Rilke's poem—"Again and again, however well we know the landscape of love/ And the little churchyard with its mournful names"—he said to Winsten, "In verse I am of the old-fashioned sort. I like it to rhyme. Why didn't he say: 'Again and again, however well the landscape of love we knew/ And the little churchyard with its mournful yew. . . .'"

[4] As an old man Shaw began to question the idea of time and evolution upon which he had for so long insisted. He said to Winsten, "I don't think we've discovered the proper technique for telling the truth: We write as if time is horizontal, flowing like a stream; but it is probably vertical or spiral. It isn't only a person of ninety talking to you at this moment but a boy of five and a man of fifty, fully conscious human beings. On most occasions the man of ninety is not even present."

[5] R. P. Blackmur, for example, writes in "Notes on E. E. Cummings' Language," "But when a word is used in a poem it should be the sum of all its appropriate history made concrete and particular in the individual context."

"This craze for saying the first thing that comes into your head without rhyme or reason and calling it poetry does not impress me. In my plays there is not a word I have not brooded over until it expressed the exact meaning. The fact that they are in prose shows how much care I took over them. Poetry is far too glib for my liking."

Shaw's brooding produced some good prose, probably the best of the Swiftian sort. Chesterton felt that Shaw's particular virtue was compactness. Where Chesterton emphasized how much Shaw got in, Dixon Scott, in *The Innocence of Bernard Shaw*, marked what Shaw had left out—"trailing wreaths and ropes of metaphor"—and found that "a long sentence really made up of many added items lay when finished as level as a spear, streaking past as though launched with one lunge."

Scott's metaphor of lineality is apt in distinguishing Shaw's prose—if only quantitatively—from other men's prose. But it is the conception of language denoted by this metaphor which, according to some modern writers, has most hobbled thought. Mrs. Langer writes: "All language has a form which requires us to string out our ideas even though their objects rest one within the other. . . . This property of verbal symbolism is known as *discursiveness*. . . . So long as we admit only discursive symbolism as a bearer of ideas, 'thought' in this restricted sense must be regarded as our only intellectual activity.*"*

"Modern man" conceives language as a communicative medium of one dimension, and the limits of his language are the limits of his thought. Shaw took much the same position: to a man travelling light, earlier linguistic phases are so much excess baggage. Shaw believed that truth was one, though forms are many, and the conviction was evident in his use of words. He writes, for example, of "a natural agency which the Churches call Providence and the Scientists Phlogiston, Functional Adaptation, Natural Selection, *Vis Naturae Medicatrix*, the Necessary Myth and Design in the Universe. I have called it the Life Force and the Evolutionary Appetite; Bergson called it the *Elan Vital*, Kant the Categorical Imperative, Shakespeare the 'divinity that shapes our ends, rough hew them how we will.' " Shaw believed in synonymity.

Poets do not. Shaw would never have understood fully Mallarmé's remark to Degas that poetry is made with words, not ideas, for to him there was a final *qualitative* difference between prose and poetry.[6] Mallarmé, like modern critics, thought of poetry as cutting language vertically. To Shaw language

---

[6] Shaw said to Henderson that he could write blank verse "more swiftly than prose." He could, but it was somewhat short of Shakespeare's. (See *Cymbeline Refinished*.) Shaw detested blank verse because he thought it just enough of a rhetorical discipline to make poetry. Again the Puritan Shaw emerges; poetry was *easy*, therefore less than prose. Poetry as something *in* a man was a bag of tricks with language, poetry *as* the man was an attitude of mind toward truth.

was properly horizontal and in need of rationalization.[7] To modern critics language is properly poetry; to Shaw language was properly prose.

Shaw's view of his countryman, William Butler Yeats, perfectly illustrates this cleavage. He explained Yeats to Winsten in this way:

> "There was nothing genuine about the cantilation of Yeats. I made him 'strip and go naked' when he talked to me."
>
> He went to his shelves and searched long for a volume of Yeats and read aloud:

> I made my song a coat
> Covered with embroideries
> Out of old mythologies
> From heel to throat:
> But the fools caught it,
> Wore it in the world's eyes
> As though they'd wrought it.
> Song, let them take it,
> For there's more enterprise
> In walking naked.

> "I discovered the fun of walking naked as soon as I arrived in England. Yeats remained Irish to the end. Even Ezra Pound failed to strip him of his embroideries."

The irony of the situation is apparent, for Yeats did do pretty much what this poetic manifesto declared for.

To Shaw, then, the lesser order of poets consisted of skillful rhetoricians. He meant a different thing by the term "poetry" than do modern critics. In fact, most of the problems which arise in talking about Shaw and poetry are semantic; the terms which modern critics have taken from the tradition to define poetry were to Shaw terms for the ornamentation which kept verse from being prose.

Shaw is hard to place in the literary tradition partly because his idea of literary form is pre-romantic while his idea of literary value is post-romantic; "poetry" was decoration, "prose" was organic. He might think of poetry somewhat as did Johnson, but "organic form" was as important a critical principle to him as it is to Sir Herbert Read. Shaw absorbed this idea through biological rather than literary interests—from Butler rather than Coleridge, but he applied it broadcast, first, naturally enough, to "life,"

---

[7] Mrs. Langer writes, in *Philosophy in a New Key*, that as language develops, "Speech becomes increasingly discursive, practical, prosaic, until human beings can actually believe that it was invented as a utility, and was later embellished with metaphors for the sake of a cultural product called poetry." Shaw seems to have taken much the same view she deprecates so strongly.

"a tireless power which is continually driving onward and upward—not, please observe, being beckoned or drawn by *das Ewig Weibliche* or any other external sentimentality, but growing from within." But he also applied it to many other things: to politics—"all changes from . . . mechanical agencies in government to living ones"; to society—"the social organism"; to art—"Every man has to grow his own style out of himself," says Cashel Byron of a musician; and to architecture—"Italian architecture . . . is not organic; it is flagrantly architecture for the sake of ornamentality." Shaw's long struggle against the Scribe tradition was a struggle for organic form. But perhaps Shaw's most significant application of the principle was to music: "I searched all the music I came across for the sake of its poetic or dramatic content and played the pages in which I found poetry or drama over and over again, whilst I never returned to those in which the music was trying to exist ornamentally for its own sake."

Most worthy students of Shaw have realized that his deep love for music was somehow important. Chesterton felt that music was Shaw's emotional-imaginative "safety valve," and most writers since have followed this line. Joad, for example, found Shaw's musical passion the channel for the chivalric romanticism which Stevenson had noticed in the work of the young novelist. I should put it this way: In music Shaw found the art which he had tried to reject and others had tried to take away.

There is a much quoted observation of Shaw's which Henderson, who first made it available, adduces as evidence for Chesterton's hypothesis: "In music you will find the body of and reality of that feeling which the mere novelist can only describe to you; there will come home to your senses something in which you can actually experience the candour and gallant impulse of the hero, the grace and trouble of the heroine, and the extracted emotional quintessence of their love." The same passage, however, also suggests that Shaw agreed with Pater, who wrote in a familiar passage of *The Renaissance*, "Music being the typical, or ideally consummate art . . . *all art constantly aspires toward the condition of music.* For while in all other works of art it is possible to distinguish the matter from the form, and the understanding can always make this distinction, yet it is the constant effort of art to obliterate it." Shaw was pointing toward this idea when he said to Henderson that great music had an "essentially intellectual quality"—that is, that its artistic order was free of the passions, the flesh, and their images.

But although strongly and instinctively attracted to Pater's view, Shaw was drawn away from it by an equally powerful force in the opposite quarter, and both forces are at work in the passage quoted by Henderson. Shaw was not sure whether music should be pure form or pure expression. In *The Perfect Wagnerite* he wrote, "In the nineteenth century it was no longer necessary to be a born pattern designer in sound to be a composer. One had but to be a dramatist or a poet completely susceptible to the dramatic and descriptive power of sound." And elsewhere in the same book he said, "There is not a single bar of 'classical music' in The Ring—not a note in it that has any other point than the single direct point of giving musical expression to the drama." Shaw was stretched between the musical modes of Wagner and Mozart, the composers he loved best—Wagner the dramatist in sound, Mozart the pattern designer.

Shaw's musical dilemma is the image of his dilemma at large. He was pulled in two directions at once, found "life" and "art" in conflict. From one point of view they seemed like "the market place" and "the cloister." From another they seemed, respectively, "accident" and "essence." Shaw wrote that Marx had saved him from becoming a literary man, but there are clear signs that his state of grace was sometimes bitter to him. During much of his life he seems to have wished that art would "leave him alone," and as an old man he seems to have felt that it might have been better had his wish not so far come true.

"What's Wrong with Shaw Is Right with Shaw."

By pressing his claim to art in the wrong direction Shaw played into the hands of his detractors. He was no poet as that term is defined by modern criticism. If we accept Blackmur's categories, "writers" and "poets," we must call Shaw a "writer." Shaw's sense of life was histrionic, and in the drama he found the only literary genre which could at all satisfy his demand for life *and* art. He was no poet, but he *was* a dramatist. It is quite easy for modern criticism to miss even so simple a distinction as this, for a great deal of modern criticism implies that there is just one important kind of literary art—poetry. The method of focus upon the work, of close linguistic and structural analysis, has found its most responsive material in the lyric. Thus poetry becomes "the great *Andersstreben*" of art, and works intended and recognized as "poems" seem most worthy of critical attention. Our best critical minds have neglected the drama, not by intent, but by virtue of the limitations their method sets. Unfortunately, concentration moves toward myopia; in "brightening the corner where they are," as Northrop Frye puts it, they have somewhat blinded themselves to the rest of the room. Certainly modern criticism has devoted most of its efforts to poetry; even Kenneth Burke, who assumes a kind of histrionic basis for literature, has written little about plays and playwrights.

And even when modern criticism admits to a variety of literary genres, it makes an analogous error. Having admitted that there is such a thing as drama, it finds no time, or place, for comedy. It does not deny that there are comic plays, but acts rather as though they did not exist. Tragedy becomes the *Anders-streben*, the archetype, of drama. Francis Fergusson's *The*

Idea of a Theater, certainly among the finest extended studies of drama in English, as certainly exhibits this tendency. Mr. Fergusson sees Shaw as a dramatist right enough, but he cannot grant Shaw art, mostly, I think, because he feels drama is tragedy.[8]

"The Great Tradition" of drama in our culture is tragic, and at the beginning of it are Aeschylus, Sophocles, Euripides, and Aristotle. In a sense Shaw's reputation suffers from our lack of Aristotle's treatise on comedy; certainly modern criticism has not devoted much more space to comedy than does Aristotle's surviving work. Shaw is a comic dramatist, and contemporary indifference to his work in part reflects a long European tradition of finding comedy indigestible. Criticism has always been reluctant to grant comedy literary status in its own right, while the community at large has a long-standing distrust of the comic impulse which perhaps stems from certain of the more Roman and Hebraic aspects of our legal and ethical culture.

Fergusson's criticism of Shaw is instructive in this connection. He feels that Shaw is inferior to Pirandello because he lacks "the seriousness of the artist." "[Pirandello] does not, like Shaw, see human action as rationalizing only, and the world as merely conceptualized. . . . Pirandello, in the stage itself and in our need not only to rationalize but to mythicize, has found a wider basis [than has Shaw], on which many versions of human action may be shown together to the eye of contemplation." Shaw is, that is, as we have already marked down, the modern man shadowed forth by Euripides, man "caught in the categories his reason invents."

It is possible that Mr. Fergusson is too close to the categories the psyche invents. To see the distinctive quality in Shaw he would have to think of "not only to mythicize but to rationalize." Rationalizing is suspect to modern criticism. Blackmur, for example, writes that "Knowledge itself is a fall from the paradise of undifferentiated sensation." This distrust is natural enough, a result of emphasis upon a sort of return to nature, "mythicizing," which gives a new name to the old dog beneath the skin. Shaw certainly is a rationalist. He objected violently to being so called, for he thought of rationalism as trimming the arm to fit the sleeve, but like Hume he found no substitute for the rational mode, even though he maintained that the

---

[8] This is *not* an attack on Mr. Fergusson's book at large. I owe it too much for that. But sometimes *The Idea of a Theater* suggests so much that one is not sure what it says. I sometimes wonder if I am not agreeing with Mr. Fergusson when I profess to disagree with him. I am particularly uncertain about what province Mr. Fergusson claims for his study, although he says what he does *not* claim to do, and this is really the issue in the second part of this essay. Mr. Eric Bentley, though a more fragmentary critic than Mr. Fergusson, is an exception to what is, of course, a rather oversimplified rule. He has not only written about Shaw as a literary man—a playwright—but has valued comedy highly and shown that he understands what it is and how the deepest rooted conventions of our theater and perceptions often work against it.

reason was a mere servant to the will. Shaw is a rationalist in the greatest rationalistic tradition of our culture, that of Plato.

The idea is not new. Chesterton wrote, "Bernard Shaw has much affinity to Plato—in his instinctive elevation of temper, his courageous pursuit of ideas as far as they will go, his civic idealism, and also, it must be confessed, in his dislike of poets and a touch of delicate inhumanity." Edmund Wilson puts the comparison on literary grounds: "Bernard Shaw is a writer of the same kind as Plato. There are not many such writers in literature . . . and they are likely to puzzle the critics. Shaw, like Plato, repudiates as a dangerous form of drunkenness the indulgence in literature for its own sake; but, like Plato, he then proceeds, not simply to expound a useful morality, but himself to indulge in an art in which moralities are used as motifs." Shaw's very sensibility is Platonic. Henderson calls him "essentially austere, ascetic, astringent, antiseptic." Chesterton speaks of his "dangerous and somewhat inhuman daintiness of taste which seems to shrink from matter itself." Barzun comments on Shaw's "temperamental kinship" with Shelley, "a disembodied quality in both men, which leads certain critics to find their art equally thin and bloodless."

It would have seemed to Wagner, as we have already seen, that Shaw derived "the concrete from the abstract"; but to Shaw matter itself was unsatisfactory because it was a poor approximation of the essence. Shaw's outlook was profoundly dualistic; he had a deep sense of a real, final form or essence, and a contingent, incomplete substance. The massive allegory *Back to Methuselah* articulates Shaw's Platonic sense of the nature of things. Matter is a state to be outgrown; the goal of the ancients is freedom from the flesh. In the last play of the group, *As Far as Thought Can Reach*, evolution has done away with the embarrassing conjunction of the procreative and excretory functions and substituted for sex—the symbolic antithesis to reason—the hygienic and objective egg. Shaw has put Platonism into time, made the Platonic archetype—"the vortex freed from matter"—the end of a process. Art, too, is to be outgrown; it is only, one of the ancients says, a crude attempt "to get into the rhythm of life." To Shaw, as to Plato, art is suspect and perplexing though *and because* attractive.[9] Shaw found some incompatibility between man as artist and man as citizen, and because he could not resolve that incompatibility, like Plato, he banished art. Shaw's most carefully disciplined loyalty was to the idea of man as citizen, to a community, to a *civilization*. Like Plato, Shaw was the citizen as artist.

Modern criticism has somewhat lost sight of the Platonic idea of civilization

---

[9] Shaw said to Winsten apropos of an unnamed millionaire in Park Lane, "What a dull prosaic man he was. It's the dull people who are changing the face of the earth, while the bright ones rise like balloons and burst. I have always envied dull people and tried to model my life on theirs." Artists, of course, were "the bright ones."

as a reflection of rational man. For rational man it has substituted a sort of "essential man," one whose thought is mythopoeic. The idea of myth has been very fertile, but its very fertility has led to abuse, to neglect of the part played by the conscious mind in ordering mythic themes. To primitive man myth is final—the very means of his conception; to civilized man it is protean, and he is naturally disposed to reduce it to allegory. It is too easy to forget that myths are not art, that they are secondary symbols.

As "civilization" is the place of rational man, "comedy" is the art of man as rational. Mr. Fergusson's search for *an* archetypal drama makes him wish to find it a "pure" art: "Where, in the public consciousness of the commercial city, is the art of drama to be placed? The only plea upon which it may claim to exist would seem to be—on the analogy of music and painting— the plea of 'art.' " But Fergusson's Pater-like rage for purity is frustrated by his sense of obligation to honesty: "But in the case of the theater . . . it turns out in practice, that the plea of art, though valid, is not enough. Whether this is because the theater is less pure than music, or because one cannot quite escape the fact that drama is in some sense an imitation of action, or because this art must live immediately in a public consciousness or not live at all—the fact is that some basis in reality must be established. The audience must know, with reference to something it does believe, where its make-believe, or 'suspension of disbelief' is to start."

Fergusson feels that a community is essential to drama, but he is not altogether happy with the idea of an audience. While recognizing that it is not a "theater" at all, Fergusson yearns for something like Byron's "mental theater." Thus, to a critic of Fergusson's temper, tragedy is more satisfactory than comedy, for its circumstance is more pure. The protagonist's connection with a community is tenuous; as tragic hero his vectors reach outward from inside him. But "Comedy," Fergusson writes, "in any period assumes the presence of an audience," and he says of Shaw's characters, "The secure basis of their little world, the eternity of the drawing room, is never seriously questioned. . . . Lady Brit's drawing room feels as stable and secure as the traditional cosmos of the Greeks or Elizabethans, but it is clear and small as a photograph." Edmund Wilson says much the same thing: "Shaw's comedy, for all its greater freedom in dealing with social conditions, is almost as much dependent on a cultivated and stable society as the comedy of Molière." But Fergusson's remark is deprecatory. Wilson accepts Shaw to some extent at his own valuation, as, in Shaw's words, "a classic writer of comedies" in an artistic tradition which includes Congreve, Molière, Jonson, Dekker, Plautus, Terence, Menander, and Aristophanes.

Fergusson does not seem to feel that Shaw's "emancipated parlor," as he neatly phrases it, is big enough for significant action. He has strong doubts about all parlors. To this conclusion the basis of his thinking almost invariably leads. In the introduction to his book Fergusson takes Aristotle's "imitation of an action" as a working definition of "drama." *The Divine Comedy* is to Mr. Fergusson "the very pattern of the imitation of action—mirroring the greatest height and depth of human experience, as Eliot says—in the most comprehensive scene-of-human-life to be found in our tradition." He begins the book proper with an analysis of *Oedipus Rex*, calling it "a crucial instance of drama, if not *the* play which best exemplifies this art in its essential nature and completeness" and adds that "the play is thus generally recognized as an archetype."

Mr. Fergusson writes rather as though it were *the* archetype, as though comedy were a rib of tragedy. The archetypal excellence of tragedy in Mr. Fergusson's study is *scope*. This is really the crux of the matter. The way of tragedy is the realization of a potential, the consummation and consumption of human capacity. Comedy is an image of man sustaining or undermining a rational social order. (Much of the best comedy celebrates the precariousness of civilization.) Comedy is not an adjunct of tragedy; tragedy and comedy present man's complementary—and logically contradictory—views of himself: sublime—ridiculous, godlike—animal, are two cliché examples. When a writer focuses upon the contradiction he produces irony such as Hamlet's "Oh what a piece of work is man" speech. The abstraction "scope" *can* embrace both comedy and tragedy, but it is not the proper abstraction unless one realizes that it represents only half of man's view, "the tragic sense of life," as Unamuno puts it. Rightly it is part of some such couplet as "closed"—"open," or "comprehensive"—"confined."

The parlor, emancipated or otherwise, is a symbolic scene of comic action. The comic drama does not pretend to a wider scene; often this literary mode represents a belief—seldom stated abstractly—that in this little world, "clear and small as a photograph," all that man *can* or rational man *does* know of the great world may be projected. "Civilization" *is* the comic world, with or without the sense that it is not all the world. Tragedy is an art of questioned strength, of restless and tormented siege against the unknown. Comedy is an art of asserted limitation, and comic figures meet their downfall in defection from the order by which man asserts his limitations.

Ronald Peacock, in *The Poet in the Theater*, writes, "But whilst Molière takes his fixed point from the general experience of men as rational and social beings, Shaw takes his from a rational philosophy of his own. Hence he inverts the usual method. Instead of isolating the unreasonable character, he isolates the reasonable one." Shaw's characters shrink *en bloc* in the eye of reason, whereas only Molière's hypochondriac or misanthrope does so. The tragic hero grapples half blindly with enigmatic forces outside the ken of his fellow creatures. He is alienated from society because he is bigger than any man in it. His home is the cosmos, his history is the myth. Shaw and the writers of comedy live in the city, where the stars are seldom seen.

Shaw's work has many faults, and some of his qualities *are* his defects.

But some is not all. To read plays as though they ought to be poems or comedies as though they ought to be tragedies is surely a vulgar error, and this error has been considerably encouraged by certain tendencies in modern criticism. Probably modern criticism needs to widen its conception of "literature"; certainly it needs to think more directly about literary modes and genre, and about their relationships. There is still a marked inclination to wrap them in snug bundles and distribute them between the top and bottom drawers.

Drama has a claim on literature and comedy upon drama. Like tragedy, comedy has its determinant world and its action. And like tragedy it has its central form, although that form can only be suggested here. A general definition of the central form of comedy is a kind of answer to the question which Fergusson asked in some perplexity of spirit about the drama at large: "Where in the public consciousness of the commercial city, is the art of drama to be placed?" Comedy is life perceived as theatrical in a theater conceived as art.

The Making of a Dramatist
(1892–1903)

by Eric Bentley

It was clear from the start that Bernard Shaw was a man of ideas. Later it turned out that he was a fabulous entertainer. But few have granted that the two Shaws were one. The old tendency was to allow that he was a publicist, a critic, an essayist, even a philosopher but to add: "not of course a dramatist." The later tendency was to concede that he was a great showman but to discount his thoughtful side. As Egon Friedell said, you could suck the theatrical sugar from the pill of propaganda, and put the pill itself back on the plate.

Neither in the old days, then, nor in the later ones was Shaw considered a dramatist, for even the later generations have only thought him a master of the theatrical occasion, a man with a theatrical line of talk and a theatrical bag of tricks, a highly histrionic jokester—a comedian, certainly, but hardly a writer of serious comedy. The fact is that the shock of that long career in the theatre has still not been absorbed. Shaw has not yet been seen in perspective.

In these circumstances it is interesting to go back and look what happened in the eighteen nineties. In 1891 Bernard Shaw had still not written a play, though he was 35 years old. A dozen years later, though he could describe himself as "an unperformed playwright in London," he had written *Widow-ers' Houses* (1892), *The Philanderer* (1893), *Mrs. Warren's Profession* (1893–4), *Arms and the Man* (1894), *Candida* (1894–5), *The Man of Destiny* (1895), *You Never Can Tell* (1895–6), *The Devil's Disciple* (1896–7), *Caesar and Cleopatra* (1898), *Captain Brassbound's Conversion* (1899), *The Admirable Bashville* (1901), and *Man and Superman* (1901–3).

Let us take for granted that these plays are full of ideas and jokes and ask if they do not also meet the demands of dramatic criticism as such. The drama, everyone agrees, presents character in action. Human actions become "an action" in the drama when they are arranged effectively—when, that is, they are given what we can recognize as a proper and praiseworthy

"The Making of a Dramatist (1892–1903)" by Eric Bentley. Reprinted by permission of the author.

structure. Of character dramatic critics have required many different things. One of them is emotional substance.

Let us ask, then, how Shaw, when he set about playwriting, tackled the problem of structure; and let us ask if he gave his characters' existence the requisite emotional substance.

Structure

How did Shaw put a play together? To think of questions about Shaw is to think also of the answers he invariably provided to them. In this case, he said: "I avoid plots like the plague. . . . My procedure is to imagine characters and let them rip. . . ." The quotation is from his *Table Talk* but (again: as usual) he said the same thing on many other occasions. One always has to ask not what he means (which may be clear) but what he is getting at. All Shaw's critical prose is polemical, as he freely admitted, and his writing on the theatre is devoted to the destruction of some kinds of drama and their replacement by some others (or one other). Here the enemy is the kind of play which had been dominant throughout the latter half of the nineteenth century—"the well-made play" as perfected by Eugène Scribe. In this dramaturgy the Aristotelian doctrine of the primacy of plot had been driven to an improper extreme. The plot was now, not *primus inter pares*, but all that mattered. It lost its originally organic relation to character and theme. So it became anathema to the apostles of the New Drama at the century's close. As late as 1946, when Allardyce Nicoll declared that Shaw was himself influenced by the well-made play, the old playwright went into print to deny it.

If the well-made play is defined as having no serious content, if it is defined by the relation (or lack of relation) of its plot to character and theme, then obviously Shaw did not write well-made plays. Yet Professor Nicoll had a point, and a strong one, which was that, for all the disclaimers, Shaw's plays did have plots and, furthermore, that these plots tended to be old acquaintances for those who knew their well-made play. Actually, the playwright had no need to be scandalized, for no dramatist had been more influenced by the well-made play than his own idol of those days, Henrik Ibsen. The Norwegian had begun his theatrical career by directing a large number of these plays; he made an exact imitation of them in his own *Lady Inger of Ostraat;* and he continued to the end to use many of their characteristic devices. Hence it would have been quite possible for a writer in 1890 to denounce Scribe and Sardou and simultaneously to steal their bag of tricks—from Ibsen. It is doubtful, though, if Bernard Shaw needed to deceive himself in this way. It seems more likely that he took the main situation in *Arms and the Man* from one of Scribe's most successful plays, *Bataille de Dames*.

A situation is not, of course, a plot, and the plot of *Arms and the Man* is not simply lifted from Scribe, even though parts of it may have been. Plagiarism is not the point. The point is that even when Shaw's story diverges from Scribe it remains Scribean. The play *Arms and the Man* is hung, as it were, on the cunningly told tale of the lost coat with the photograph in its pocket. The reader need only go through the text and mark the hints, incidents, accidents, and contretemps of this tale and he will be finding the layout, the plan—yes, the plot—of this play. Or at any rate the plot of what could have been a first draft of the play. Shaw, one gathers, did not write such first drafts but, supposing he had, what would be the difference between the first draft and the final one? In the answer to this question lies the secret of Shavian dramaturgy.

A corollary of the view that "plot is all" is this proposition: the cause of any incident is another incident. It is known that Scribe used to chart out a configuration of incidents and then write his play. This is to go far beyond Aristotle. It is to set no store at all by human initiative and assign to events themselves a kind of fatality: they are a network in which mankind is caught. Granted that the conception might in certain hands have its awesomeness, in Scribe's hands it had only triviality, because he manipulated the events till the issue was a pleasant one. It is curious how often that manipulation had to be arbitrary and drastic. Do events, when given their head, rush downward to disaster? To guarantee a happy ending, the well-making playwrights often needed their emergency weapon: sheer accident. Hence the Shavian complaint that well-made plays were badly made after all.

Hence also Bernard Shaw's first drama, which is an adaptation of an adaptation of a well-made play. The subject is one that Scribe and the younger Dumas brought to the nineteenth-century theatre: marrying, or refusing to marry, money. The immediate source is an unfinished play of William Archer's, *Rhinegold*. Archer's source is *La Ceinture dorée* by Emile Augier. When a young man discovers that his young lady's inherited money was acquired by her father in an immoral way, what does he do? William Archer's answer was: he pitches it into the Rhine. One presumes that Archer's action would have been set on a convenient balcony beside that river. Augier's hero is not so privileged. To preserve his honor, he would simply have to forego the pleasure of marrying the lady, if the author did not provide him and the play with an opportune accident (or money *ex machina*). The whole French economy has to meet with a crisis (war breaks out) so that our heroine's father may be reduced to poverty: it is now honorable for our hero to propose to our heroine. In the well-made play one incident leads to another with a logic that is inescapable—except when the author decides to escape it. Perhaps Shaw's objection was less to the inescapability than to the egregious, last-minute escapes.

His first play, *Widowers' Houses*, may not be great art but it is a great reversal of custom. Shaw's key decision was to refuse to accept Augier's ending, to refuse to have accident (masquerading as fate or otherwise) intervene. Such a refusal leads a man—leads a born playwright at least—back and back into the earlier stages of a story and he ends up writing an utterly different play—an utterly different *kind* of play.

Not one but two conceptions of Augier's were being rejected: not just the solution-by-sheer-accident (which condemns a play to meaninglessness) but also the autonomy-of-incidents—something, by the way, which was no part of Augier's conscious philosophy but was imposed on him by the Scribean design. Dramatists are committed to the doctrine of free will. They can say they don't believe in it: but they have to write their plays as if they did. (In this they resemble human beings in general, for your most ardent determinist acts on the assumption that determinism is false.) People in plays have got to be able to make decisions, and these decisions have got to be both real and influential: they have to affect events. I see no reason to object to Aristotle's declaration that plot is the soul of the drama, but Aristotle would have objected to Scribe's attempt to cut the soul off from the body—that is, from character.

What *does* a young man do when he finds that his bride's dowry comes from a tainted source? There are two ways for a writer to arrive at an answer. He can say: "I can think of several answers—on the basis of several different possibilities of 'theatre'. Answer A will give you Big Scene X; answer B will give you Ending Y; and so on." Or he can say: "I cannot give you any answer at all until the terms of the proposition are defined, including the term 'tainted'. Above all I need to know who these people are—what bride? what young man?" The first way to arrive at an answer would commonly be thought the playwright's way: the reasoning is "craftsmanlike" and "of the theatre" and would earn a man commendation on Broadway in 1960. The second way is only the human way. That makes it the way of the real dramatist and so of Bernard Shaw.

It could be said that we have this perfectly functioning machine of the well-made play and that a Bernard Shaw is throwing a monkey-wrench into it—the monkey-wrench of character. That is how it must seem from the Scribean viewpoint. From the viewpoint of dramatic art, however, one would say that this particular engine had been revolving all too fast and uselessly: only when a Shaw slips in the clutch can the gear engage and the vehicle prove itself a vehicle by moving.

"My procedure is to imagine characters and let them rip. . . ." The pertinence of this remark may by now be clearer: if the young man has been "imagined," the dramatist can find the decision he would make as to the young lady's money. But at this point we realize that Shaw's words leave out of account the fact that the situation confronting the young man had been established in advance of the imagining of his character. It had been established by Augier and Archer and by Shaw's own decision to use their work. Hence, Shaw's own interpretation is both helpful and misleading— or, perhaps, is helpful only if those who are helped do a lot of work on their own.

Shaw put *Widowers' Houses* together—how? He took from certain predecessors not only a situation but a story, and not only a story but that clever, orderly, and theatrical arrangement of a story which we call a plot. Then he changed the plot—or, as he would have said, let the characters change it for him. Now had he retained Augier's characters they could only have caused him to break off the action one scene earlier than Augier did: instead of the happy ending created by a national emergency, we would get the unhappy ending which the emergency reversed.

Characters in a well-made play are "conventional"—that is, they behave, not according to laws of psychology, but according to the expectations of an audience in a theatre. A type of drama in which the plot is given a free hand cannot afford any less passive or more obtrusive *personae*. Conversely, if a playwright abandons the plot-determined play, he will have to be more inventive as to character. To assume the initiative, his characters will have to be capable of it. So Shaw's first contribution to the drama was: more active characters. They were more active, first of all, in the most obvious fashion: they were violent. More important, they made decisions which affected the course of events, and they made them on the basis of their own nature, not of the spectator's. And so these characters were surprising. For a number of years they were too surprising to be acceptable. Like all surprising art, Shaw's dramaturgy was damned as non-art. The critics' formula was: Not A Play.

Augier's hero could not consider being the husband of a woman with a tainted dowry. Shaw creates a hero who has the effrontery to ask the heroine to throw up her dowry for his sake. But the Shavian joke—the Shavian reversal—is already what it would characteristically be in the future: a double one. To this demanding hero he adds an even more demanding heroine: she simply refuses to be poor to preserve her innocence. That is the nub of the first Shaw comedy. Then Shaw works his way out of the apparent deadlock, not by having the heroine weaken (that is, "improve"), but by having the hero renew his strength (that is, "deteriorate"). This the latter does by way of recovering from a shock. The shock comes from without and might be called an accident (like Augier's outbreak of war) except that it belongs to the logic of the situation. It turns out that the source of the hero's own unearned income is the same as that of his girl's father. End of Act Two. In the third and last act, our hero comes around and gets the girl by accepting the nature of capitalism. Socialist propaganda? Precisely: Shaw boasted of it. But he boasted with equal reason that he was writing comedy in the most traditional sense.

"Take what would be done by Scribe, Sardou, Dumas *fils*, or Augier and do the opposite." Is that the Shavian formula? It is certain that Shavian comedy is parodistic in a way, or to an extent, that Plautus, Jonson, and Molière were not. These others, one would judge, took a convention they respected and brought it to the realization of its best possibilities. Shaw took conventions in which he saw no possibilities—except insofar as he would expose their bankruptcy. The injunction "Do the opposite" was not whimsical. Shaw decided to "do the opposite" of Scribe in much the way Marx decided to do the opposite of Hegel—not to stand everything on its head (Hegel, he held, had done this) but to set everything back on its feet again. That was revolutionary thinking, and Shaw's art for all the polite and charming trappings, was revolutionary art. The usual relations were reversed.

Such reversals as we see in the ending of *Widowers' Houses* are relatively simple. Shaw's weakest plays are those in which he has done little more than turn the ending around: the price you pay for the brilliant ending of *The Devil's Disciple* is that of a rather dull, and decidedly conventional, first act. His best plays are those in which the principle of reversal has pervaded the whole. Such a play is *Arms and the Man.*

The idea of taking two couples and causing them to exchange partners is hardly novel and, as I have said, the little tale of the coat and the portrait is Scribean in pattern. But Shaw can justifiably plead that this is no well-made play because the artifices of the plot are not what ultimately achieve the result. Here is one of the decisive turns in the action:

Bluntschli. When you strike that noble attitude and speak in that thrilling voice,
    I admire you; but I find it impossible to believe a single word you say.
Raina. Captain Bluntschli!
Bluntschli. Yes?
Raina. Do you mean what you said just now? Do you *know* what you said just now?
Bluntschli. I do.
Raina. I! I!!!—How did you find me out?

With this last query, Raina passes over forever from Sergius's world to Bluntschli's: as a result of nothing in the Scribean arrangement of incidents but of words, words, words. It is here that, to many, the Shavian drama seems vulnerable. In drama, actions are supposed to speak louder than words. Writers on the subject invariably know their etymology—"drama" derives from a Greek verb meaning "to do"—and use it as a cudgel. Their error is a vulgar one: action need not be external. It can often be carried by words alone. Shaw used to remark that his plays were all words just as Raphael's paintings were all paint.

There is a degree of legerdemain in that remark, for Scribe too put down his plays in words. What was confusing to Shaw's readers and spectators half a century ago was that, after indicating unmistakably that he was playing Scribe's game, Shaw proceeded to break the rules. The fact that Bluntschli conquers by words gains its peculiar force from a context in which the opposite was to be expected. To look over *Arms and the Man* with an eye to technique would be to conclude that what we have here is Scribe most subtly interwoven with Shaw. Yet this formulation is inadequate, for who did the interweaving? There was a Scribe in Shaw, and there was a counter-Scribe in Shaw: what makes his works dramatic is the inter-action of the two.

The passion and preoccupation of Scribe was the idea of climax: to the Big Scene at the end—or, rather, a little before the end—all his arts are dedicated. In Bernard Shaw there was almost as great a predilection for anti-climax. It is the Shavian "effect" par excellence; no other playwright has come near finding so many possibilities in it. The bit I have quoted from Bluntschli and Raina is an apt example. *Arms and the Man* contains a corresponding scene between Sergius and Louka. Where, in a well-made play, Bluntschli and Louka would have to soar to the heights of Raina and Sergius, in the Shaw play Raina and Sergius drop with a bump to the level of Bluntschli and Louka. Such is resolution by anti-climax. It is dramaturgically effective, and it enforces the author's theme. But this is not all of Shaw: it is only the counter-Scribe. The dual anti-climaxes do not round off *Arms and the Man*. What does? Not the disenchantment of Raina and Sergius but the discovery that Bluntschli the realist is actually an enchanted soul whom nothing will disenchant. He has destroyed their romanticism but is himself "incurably romantic." This is another point that is made in "mere words"—"mere words stuck on at the end," if you wish—and yet stuck on very well, for they are firmly attached to that little tale of the coat and the photograph which gives the work its continuity and shape:

Bluntschli. —yes: that's the coat I mean. . . . Do you suppose I am the sort of fellow a young girl falls in love with? Why, look at our ages! I'm thirty four: I don't suppose the young lady is much over seventeen . . . All that adventure which was life or death to me was only a schoolgirl's game to her . . . Would a woman who took the affair seriously have sent me this and written on it: Raina, to her Chocolate Cream Soldier, a Souvenir?

Petkoff. That's what I was looking for. How the deuce did it get there?

Bluntschli. I have put everything right, I hope, gracious young lady.

Raina. I quite agree with your account of yourself. You are a romantic idiot. Next time I hope you will know the difference between a schoolgirl of seventeen and a woman of twenty three.

In this scene, plot and theme reach completion together, and the play of thesis and antithesis ends in synthesis.

The supreme triumph of Shaw's dramaturgical dialectics is to be found in *Man and Superman*, and, for all the blarney in the preface about the medieval *Everyman* and the eighteenth-century *Don Giovanni*, the method is the conversion of old materials into nineteenth-century terms, both thematic and technical. Shaw's claim to be returning to a pristine Don Juan is valid to the extent that the theme had originally been less of psychological than of philosophical, indeed theological, interest. It is also true that Don Juan had run away from his women. However, he had run away from them only after possessing them. In Shaw's play, he runs away to prevent *them* from possessing *him*. It is a comic parody of the old motif, embodying Shaw's standard new motif: the courting of the man by the woman. And where the old dramatists and librettists had used the old, "open" type of plot (or non-plot), Shaw substitutes an utterly Scribean "closed" structure.

This very "modern" and "twentieth-century" play is made up of narrative materials familiar to every Victorian theatre-goer. We have a hero who spends the entire evening hotly pursued by his foes; a clandestine marriage celebrated in defiance of a hostile father; a lovelorn hero who sacrifices himself so that the girl will go to his rival; a villain whose function is to constitute for a while the barrier to denouement and happy ending. The sub-plot about the Malone family rests upon two separate uses of the secret skilfully withheld, then skilfully released. Traditional farcical coincidence binds together Straker and Mendosa . . . The play bears every sign of careful workmanship—all of it School of Scribe.

But, as with *Arms and the Man*, as soon as we examine particulars, we find, interwoven with the Scribean elements, those typically Shavian verbal exchanges which constitute further action. Violet's marriage could have been made a secret of in any Scribe play, and Scribe could have been relied on to choose an effective moment for the release of the secret. In Shaw, what creates both the fun and the point of the news release is not the organization of the incidents but their relation to theme:

Tanner. I know, and the whole world really knows, though it dare not say so, that you were right to follow your instinct; that vitality and bravery are the greatest qualities a woman can have, and motherhood her solemn initiation into womanhood; and that the fact of your not being legally married matters not one scrap either to your own worth or to our real regard for you.

Violet (flushing with indignation). Oh! You think me a wicked woman like the rest . . . I won't bear such a horrible insult as to be complimented by Jack on being one of the wretches of whom he approves. I have kept my marriage a secret for my husband's sake.

An incident which Tanner wishes to use to illustrate his "modern" philosophy thus comes to illustrate a contrasting thesis: that Violet lives by a non-modern philosophy.

Simple? Yes, but closely linked to a point that is unsimple enough to have generally been missed: Tanner is a windbag. Indeed, the mere fact of the woman courting the man would probably not yield comedy at all, were it not for a further and more dynamic reversal: the woman, who makes no great claims for herself, has all the shrewdness, the real *Lebensweisheit*, while the man who knows everything and can discourse like Bernard Shaw is— a fool. Tanner is, in fact, like Molière's Alceste, the traditional fool of comedy in highly sophisticated intellectual disguise. Ann Whitefield, into whose trap Tanner falls, is the knave—in skirts.

While Don Juan Tenorio is Superman—or is on the road to him—John Tanner, M.I.R.C., is merely Man, and as such belongs to The World As It Is. Of dramaturgical interest is that the kind of plot Shaw evidently considers capable of giving an image of The World As It Is should be the kind that is generally considered (by himself, for instance) artificial, unreal, arbitrary, inane. Shaw the critic championed the new Naturalism, and among French dramatists especially favored Brieux, who produced dully literal theatrical documentaries. Yet when Shaw wrote an essay entitled "A Dramatic Realist to his Critics," the example of "realism" he gave from his own work was *Arms and the Man*—on the grounds that the characters respond naturally even if the situations aren't natural. We are entitled, then, to insist on his choice of "unnatural" situations. He must intuitively have understood something which, as a critic, he failed to grasp: that plot does not merely reproduce external reality. The violence and intrigue in Shakespeare, which Shaw the critic declared extraneous, provides the objective correlative of Shakespeare's feelings about life, and "idiocies" of the plot of *Man and Superman* provide an objective correlative for Shaw's sense of modern life. The very fact that Shaw despised Scribe helps to explain the particular use he made of him.

The Don Juan episode in Act Three is neither a well-made play, nor a portion of a well-made play. It stands apart as something appropriately more austere and august. It is not a traditional work of any kind, not even a Platonic dialogue, the relation between Socrates and his interlocutors being quite different. Nor is it a debate, for two of the speakers, the Commander and Ann, hardly present arguments at all: they simply represent a point of view. Do even the Devil and Don Juan *discuss* anything? A devil is scarcely a being one can convert to a Cause, and if the Don is busy convincing anyone it is himself. Certainly it is the philosophy of Bernard Shaw that he is given to speak, but is persuasion exercised—even on the audience? Rather, the contributions of the four presences come together as a vision of life— and an intimation of super-life.

Man—and superman. The comedy of John Tanner—and the vision of Don Juan Tenorio. Shaw—and counter-Shaw. Thesis and antithesis are, to be sure, of separate interest, and yet, as usual, the great Shavian achievement is to have related one to the other. Tanner seems a wise man and proves a fool. Don Juan passes for a philanderer but proves an explorer and a missionary of the truth. In our trivial, tawdry, clever, Scribean world, intellect is futile and ever at the mercy of instinct. Take away the episode in hell, and Shaw has written an anti-intellectual comedy. The episode assigns to intellect the highest role. No longer, therefore, is Ann the center and source of things—only a possible mother for superman. Here Don Juan dominates. Here (or rather in heaven) intellect is at home, and the Don is cured of that occupational disease of Shavian heroes—homelessness. He "comes to a good end"—only it is not an end, it is an episode, and from these celestial-infernal heights we must descend to earth with the shock of Shavian anti-climax, to earth and to Tanner, from Superman back to Man. One section of the play gets an electric charge from the other.

Of Shaw's "playmaking" one must conclude that he knew how to put together a Scribean plot; that he knew how to subordinate such a plot to his own purposes; and that, in *Man and Superman*, he knew how to take the resultant Shavian comedy and combine it dynamically with a disquisition on (and by) Don Juan.

Emotional Substance

If Shaw's plays are, or begin by being, a parody of the more conventional drama of his time, that parody is by no means confined to the form. We have already seen that the themes, too, tend to get turned around: these compositions not only do the opposite, as it were, but say the opposite. What of the emotions? Whatever the ultimate purpose of drama, its imme-diate impact is a strongly emotional one, and one cannot conceive of a story having an emotional effect upon an audience unless it is an emotional story and has a certain emotional structure. I may be forgiven for stating so rudimentary a principle because the Shavian drama presents us with a paradox: it has flooded a thousand theatres with emotion and yet has often been held to be emotionless.

Of course, this common opinion is absurd, bolstered though it can be with remarks of Shaw's own about being a mere "work machine" and the like. What we confront here is originality. Shaw may not have been an original thinker: he tried, rather, to make a synthesis of what certain others had thought. But he was an original person. What fitted him so well for the role of the enemy of convention was that his natural responses were not those of other people but all his own. His emotional constitution was a peculiar one, and that peculiarity is reflected in his plays.

Sex is, without doubt, the crucial issue. Comedy remains fertility worship, however sublimated, and it is fair enough to ask what Bernard Shaw made of the old sexual rigmarole—courtship and the barriers thereto. It is even fair to use any facts about Shaw himself that are a matter of public record. On the other hand, one is not honor-bound to side with "modern" opinion against "Victorian" as to what is good and bad. The very "modern" Dr. Kinsey implied that human vitality could be measured in statistics on orgasms. Our subject Bernard Shaw will not pass into any Kinseyite paradise. Though he lived to be 94 he seems to have experienced sexual intercourse only between the ages of 29 and 43. "I lived a continent virgin . . . until I was 29. . . . During the fourteen years before my marriage at 43 there was always some lady in the case. . . . As man and wife we found a new relation in which sex had no part. It ended the old gallantries, flirtations, and philanderings for both of us." This quotation is from a letter to Frank Harris, who, as a Kinseyite before Kinsey, wrote:

> Compare his [Shaw's] private life with Shakespeare's. While Mary Fitton was banished from London Shakespeare could write nothing but tragedies. That went on for five years. When the Queen died and Shakespeare's Dark Lady returned, he wrote *Antony and Cleopatra*, his greatest love story. As nothing like that happened in Shaw's life we can only get a text-booky, sexless type of play.

A remarkable blend of ignorance, invention, and arbitrary assumption! For actually Shaw concealed from Harris most of his private life; nothing whatever is known about Shakespeare's feelings for any woman; and no critic or psychologist of repute has ever argued that a man's writing has to be "text-booky" and "sexless" unless he is carrying on an adulterous romance; a more familiar argument would be that precisely the abstinent man's imagination might well be crammed with sex. But there is no settling the question a priori.

William Archer declared that Shaw's plays reeked with sex. It is a more suggestive declaration than Harris's. It reminds us that Shaw was able to recreate the sexual charm of both men and women to a degree unequalled by any English dramatist except Shakespeare. To be sure, he doesn't need bedroom scenes to do this. Morell only has to talk and we understand "Prossy's complaint." Undershaft only has to talk and we understand why he is a problem to his daughter. To say nothing of the long line of sirens from Candida to Orinthia! Few of the "sexy" ladies of Restoration comedy, by contrast, have any sex appeal at all. One thing Archer is sure to have had in mind is that the women in Shaw pursue a sexual purpose in a way absolutely unknown to Victorian literature. Of all the reversals in Shavian drama this is inevitably the most famous: the reversal in the roles of the sexes. Shaw once committed himself to the view that all superior women are masculine and all superior men are feminine. In his comedies, most often, the woman is active, the man passive. Perhaps by 1960 the theme has been restated ad nauseam; to Archer it was startling. As was Shaw's determination to rub the sore places of the sexual morality of his time. *Mrs. Warren's Profession* was for many years too "raw" a play for production in London, and it created a memorable scandal when it was produced in New Haven and New York in 1905. Like most of the major modern dramatists and novelists, Shaw mentioned the unmentionable. He even claimed to have "put the physical act of sexual intercourse on the stage" (in *Overruled*). Archer may well have felt Shaw could not give the subject of sex a rest: he may not always have been at the center of it but he was forever touching the fringes of it.

Here Frank Harris would have interjected: "he was always *avoiding* the center of it." And the interjection is called for. The impression that a man is unemotional in general and sexless in particular does not come from nowhere. Nor are the kinds of sex I have been noting what the average spectator is looking for if he demands a "sexy" show. *Overruled* does not really "put the physical act of sexual intercourse on the stage," and, even if it did, it would do so comically—depriving the act of precisely that element which people miss in Shaw, which is not sex in general but the torridity of sexual romance. At that, if this element were simply absent, Shaw might very well have got away with the omission. But it is explicitly rejected. It is not that a Shavian couple *cannot* end up in bed but, rather, that they are likely to contemplate the idea—and turn it down. If the characteristic act of the French drama of the period was the plunge into bed, that of the Shavian drama is the precipitate retreat from the bedroom door.

Harris would be right in reminding us that such was Bernard Shaw's emotional constitution. What other writer has ever created all the normal expectations in a scene between a king and his mistress (*The Apple Cart*) only to reveal that their relationship is purely platonic? *Captain Brassbound's Conversion* shows the Shavian pattern to perfection. Is there sexual feeling in the play? There is. The process by which Brassbound and Lady Cicely are brought closer and closer is positively titillating. After which, what happens? They are parted. The play has a superb final curtain. "How marvellous!" says Lady Cicely, "how marvellous!" Then with one of those quick changes of tone that marks the Shavian dialogue: "And what an escape!" Is this unemotional? No. But the emotion is not erotic—rather, it is relief at a release from the erotic. Such is the emotional content of this particular Shavian anti-climax.

As far as conscious intention goes, all Shaw's plays might bear the title he gave to three of them—plays for puritans—for that intention is to show romance transcended by a higher-than-erotic purpose. It is a classic intention—an application, really, of the traditional conflict of love and honor, with honor winning hands down, as it did in Corneille and even in one masterpiece of Racine's—*Bérénice*. We are concerned here, not with philosophic intention, but psychological substance. Where the philosopher insists that Shaw does not cross the threshold of the bedroom, the psychologist asks: why does he hover at the bedroom door?

We know from the correspondence with Mrs. Pat Campbell that Shaw liked to play with fire. Even the correspondence with Ellen Terry entailed a playfulness not quite devoid of "danger." The boy Shaw had been witness to an odd household arrangement whereby his mother's music teacher contrived to be (it would seem) almost but not quite her lover. A slightly older Shaw has recently been portrayed as the intruder into a friend's marriage like his own Eugene Marchbanks: this is speculation. Let us look at the play *Candida*, which is a fact.

It has a notable Big Scene at the end, which is characterized by an equally notable improbability. A comfortable, sensible, parson's wife doesn't let herself get jockeyed into "choosing" between her husband and an almost total stranger. People—such people at least—don't do such things. A respectable woman's choice was made before the bans were read.

Perhaps Candida is not really respectable? That is the line of interpretation taken by Beatrice Webb who declared her a prostitute. Will the play, taken as a play, bear this interpretation out? A dramatist's license to have the truth turn out different from the impression given to the audience is very limited, for it is to a large extent by giving impressions that he creates characters. Shaw has given the impression that Candida is *not* a prostitute.

Against this it can be urged that Shaw himself took Beatrice Webb's side and attacked Candida—in remarks he made about her in letters to James Huneker, Richard Burton, and others. True, but was that legitimate? He himself admitted that he had no more right to say what his plays meant than any other critic. One might add that he may have had less, for, when an author intervenes to correct our impressions of his work, he is often intervening to change or misinterpret that work.

Outside the play, Shaw is against Candida. Inside it, he is both for and against her, but he is for her effectually, and against her ineffectually, because the direct impression is favorable, while it is only by throwing logic back into the story when it is over that you can reach an unfavorable judgment. This means, I should think, that, though Shaw's intellect is against Candida, his emotions are for her.

What is it that this play has always projected in the theatre, and can always be counted on to project again? The charm of Candida. This is a reality so immediate and all-pervasive that it is hard for any other element in the play to make headway against it. Leading actresses know this and, hearing their director speak of Candida's essential badness, can afford to smile a Candida-smile, strong in the knowledge that there is nothing a director can do about this badness, once that smile has been displayed on stage as well as off.

I would say that it is a confused play but that the confusion goes unnoticed because of Candida's charm and may even be the cause of a degree of emotional tension unusual in Shaw's work. Candida is made out of a Shavian ambivalence: he would like to reject this kind of woman, but actually he dotes on her. One quickly senses that he "is" Marchbanks. One also finds he protests (too much) that he is *not* Marchbanks. "I had in mind De Quincey's account of his adolescence in his Confessions," he wrote, "I certainly never thought of myself as a model." From the empty pretence of being De Quincey, no doubt, comes the prodigious unreality of many of the lines. As a character, Marchbanks must be reckoned a failure. Shaw was hiding. What better image to hide behind than that of the kind of writer he himself was not—a romantic poet? Especially if De Quincey would do the job for him?

It didn't work, of course, except as pure histrionics. (Marchbanks, though a poorly drawn character, is always an effective stage role, and still seems to correspond to the actors' idea of a poet.) But if no one in the play can reject Candida, there is a noteworthy niche in it for the man whom she will reject. This niche Marchbanks can fill nobly, and has his dramatic moment as he marches into it: his final exit is a magnificent piece of action. Possibly everything before that (in this role) is just an improvisation. Shaw could not make us believe in the poet's poetry, but he does make us believe in his pain and his nobility, for at these points he could identify himself with Eugene completely without having to "think of himself as a model."

Dramatists usually speak of their characters individually, and that could be regarded as strange, because the drama, all through the centuries, has done much less with separate persons than with relationships. The traditional characters are, if you will, simplified to the point of crudity. What is not crude, as treated by the old dramatists, is the interaction of these characters: the dynamics of human relations are fully rendered. If what you do not get is the detailed psychological biography, what you do get is the essence of such relations as parent and child, boy and girl, man and wife.

Now modern playwrights, happily, have not departed from the classic patterns as much as they are supposed to have, and what rings true, emotionally, in *Candida* corresponds to Shaw's ability to find and recreate some of these elemental relationships. An inner obstacle, one would judge, hampered him when he tried to "do" the Marchbanks-Candida relationship, but the Morell-Candida relation is both clear and challenging. It is, as Shaw himself said, the relationship of Nora and Torvald Helmer turned around: in Shaw's play the man is the doll. But where Ibsen tells the story of a doll who finally comes to life Shaw tells the story of a seemingly-living person who turns out to have been a doll all along. (In other words, the relation of Shaw to Ibsen, instead of being direct as it might seem, is an inverse one, exactly like the relation of Shaw to other nineteenth-century drama.) Into Morell Shaw can put that part of himself (a child) which finds Candida irresistible, just as into Candida he can put that part of Woman which he finds irresistible— the Mother in her. One would have to be as naïve a psychologist as Frank Harris to consider the mother and child relation less emotional than that of lovers.

Or less dramatic. Relationships become dramatic not in the degree of their eroticism but to the extent that they contain conflict. Pure love would not be a dramatic subject at all. Love becomes dramatic when it is impure— when the loving element is submerged in a struggle for power. The axis about which *Candida* revolves is that of strength and weakness, not love and hate. And if one knows Shaw's views on the topic of the "weaker sex" in general the conclusion of *Candida* follows naturally: instead of the little woman reaching up toward the arms of the strong man, we have the strong woman reaching down to pick up her child. It is remarkable how far Shaw's thought is from the standard "advanced thinking" of his generation with its prattle of equality and comradeship. He is closer to Nietzsche.

Of the ending of *A Doll's House* it has been said: perhaps Nora has walked out in a mere tantrum and will be back in the morning. How much more savage is the ending of *Candida*! Only Strindberg could have written a sequel to it. The cruelty of the heroine—merely implicit in the present play—would have to come to the surface in any continuation of the story. Candida has chosen to let her husband discover his shame: she, as well as he, will have to take the consequences. Let the stage manager hold razors and straitjackets in readiness!

One reason why Shaw got so little credit for his treatment of the emotions is that the emotions he treats are not the ones people expect. The very fact that his favorite device is anti-climax should tell us that what he most insistently feels is "let-down." It may be retorted that, on the contrary, Bernard Shaw was the most buoyant and vivacious of men. That is also true. The axis "strength-weakness" is not more important to Shaw's content than the axis "elation-depression" is to his form. The dialogue ripples gaily along; then comes the sudden let-down. The circus has familiarized us with the pattern: it is the light of heart who take the prat-fall. Even as the fool pops up in Shavian comedy in the highly intellectualized shape of a Jack Tanner, so the prat-fall is transmuted into an anti-climax that has a positively climactic force. It has been customary to take these anti-climaxes as expressions of an idea—the idea of disenchantment. It is *the* idea of modern literature, and it is inseparable from an emotion far commoner and far more influential than romantic excitement. There seems to be no name for this emotion—and that too is significant. Let us call it desolation.

You cannot be disenchanted without having been enchanted. One is sometimes tempted to believe that our human desolation might have been avoided if only we had not started out so undesolate. It is not the fact that we don't *have* things that worries us but that we have lost them—or rather, been deprived of them. Desolation is the feeling of having been driven from paradise.

A friend of Bernard Shaw's said that when he saw *The Wild Duck* the bottom dropped out of the universe. One difference between Ibsen and Shaw is that the former produced this effect on the audience, whereas the latter produced it on the characters in a play. Just as a character in a melodrama loses a fortune, so a character in a Shaw play loses a universe. The experience may be given a playful treatment, as with Raina and Sergius. In the case of Morell, the treatment is only partly playful. It gets more serious as the play *Candida* proceeds. Morell finally loses his image of his wife and of himself. The curtain has to be rung down to save us from the Strindberg play that would have to follow.

What of *Mrs. Warren's Profession?* The starting point was a treatment by Maupassant of the theme of a girl finding out that her mother is a courtesan. In an early version of the tale Maupassant had the girl kill herself. In the later and better-known text (*Yvette*), he saves her life to engineer for himself an ironic-poignant ending: she becomes a kept woman like her mother before her. Curtain! That is the kind of inversion of a suicidal ending which Shaw did *not* go in for. Or not any more. If Shaw had shown a "surrender to the system" (in comical fashion) in the ending to *Widowers' Houses*, he was now intent on showing a rejection of the system. In the first instance, Vivie Warren's revolt represents Shaw's rational rejection of capitalism, but the play culminates in a scene that has no necessary connection with economics—a scene of family crisis, a scene in which a daughter rejects her mother. Which after all is archetypal Shaw: instead of the emotions of lover and mistress, he renders the emotions of parents and children, and particularly the emotion of the child rejecting the parent. *Major Barbara* is perhaps the grandest example of this archetype. The great last act of *Pygmalion* is the same thing in disguise, for Henry Higgins is the progenitor of the new Eliza, and that is why she must break free of him. Shaw's Joan has a father too— in heaven—and she comes at times almost to the point of breaking with Him. That she does not quite do so is the upshot of a play which, while it shows Joan's isolation from men, ends with a stretching of arms towards the heavenly father . . . Vivie Warren is already a Saint Joan in that the experience Shaw gives her is that of being desolated. It is the experience he felt most deeply—presumably because it was the experience he had most deeply experienced. In any event, the two long scenes between Vivie and Mrs. Warren are passionate playwriting such as England had not seen for a couple of centuries.

The background, however, is blurred. A Scribean climax is arranged to provide élan for the announcement that Vivie's romance is incestuous:

Crofts. Allow me, Mister Frank, to introduce you to your half-sister, the eldest daughter of the Reverend Samuel Gardner. Miss Vivie: your half-brother. Good morning.

Frank (. . . *raising the rifle*). You'll testify before the coroner that it's an accident. (*He takes aim at the retreating figure of Crofts. Vivie seizes the muzzle and pulls it round against her breast.*)

Vivie. Fire now. You may.

Direct climax (as against anti-climax) was not really in Shaw's line, and in failing to parody Scribe here, Shaw has himself tumbled into the ridiculous. Perhaps the following act was bound to be an anti-climax in a way not intended—a mere disappointment. Yet it is hard to believe that the particular disappointments it brings are simply the result of a technical miscalculation. Rather, they involve hesitations about the subject. After so strongly creating the impression of incest, Shaw shuffles the notion off in the next act in a surprisingly ambiguous way. It would be easy enough, from a technical viewpoint, to make clear that no incest had been committed. Why did Shaw leave the situation doubtful? So that Vivie could dismiss the issue as irrelevant? In that case, what is relevant? Why is she giving Frank up? One can think of possible reasons, but what reason is one *supposed* to think of?

Unclarity in the work of so careful a craftsman, a writer, moreover, who has more than once been accused of excessive clarity, surely bears witness to inner uncertainty and conflict. To think of *Mrs. Warren's Profession* in this personal way is to realize what powerful aggressions it embodies. Shaw combined the themes of prostitution and incest in order to make quite a rational point: our mad society draws back in horror from incest, which is certainly not a pressing menace and perhaps not even a bad thing, while it encourages prostitution, which is a virulent social pestilence. But both themes have a resonance far beyond the bounds of intellect. It is as if they proved to be more than Shaw had bargained for. The incest theme is sounded—all too boldly. Then the young dramatist has no idea what to do with it. He takes it back. Only it is too late. So he half takes it back. After all, what is troubling Vivie does go beyond the rationally established causes . . . Deep water! And Shaw flounders in it. Which has some interest for the student of the emotions. Even where Shaw's plays are faulty, they are not unemotional. On the contrary, it is because of a certain emotional involvement in the material, not because of incapacity for such involvement, that Shaw was not able to resolve certain problems and truly finish certain plays. *Candida* and *Mrs. Warren's Profession* could be cited in evidence. There is material in both which was not successfully "worked through."

Is there similar material in Shaw's collected plays which *was* worked through? To my mind, a good answer would be: yes, *Pygmalion.* This play might well have proved just as ambiguous as the others, for it might have seemed that Eliza must love Higgins, and therefore that her leaving him is but an over-rational afterthought of the author's, like his afterthoughts on Candida. Some people, including the author of *My Fair Lady*, think that is just what the Shavian ending is. I, on the other hand, feel—and it is feeling that is in question—that Eliza's rebellion grows organically out of what preceded. She is Higgins' creation: she cannot *be* at all unless she become independent of her creator. If he has "sex appeal," that makes the break more difficult but not less necessary. A girl's father quite normally has sex appeal for her. That is not to justify incest. Here Shaw does cope with incest, and in the best way—by avoiding it.

The ending of *Pygmalion* is the classic Shavian situation: someone is clamorously refusing to enter the bedroom. The friends of Frank Harris are thereby disgusted. That is their right. But there is a point to be made about Shaw's rendering of emotion. Refusal is emotional. There is more turbulence in conflict between Eliza and Higgins as conceived by Shaw than in romance between them as in *My Fair Lady*.

Man and Superman, on the other hand, might seem to be without emotional substance. The attempt made at a straightforward emotional climax is certainly rather unsuccessful:

Tanner. I love you. The Life Force enchants me: I have the whole world in my arms when I clasp you. But I am fighting for my freedom, for my honor, for my self, one and undivisible.
Ann. Your happiness will be worth them all.
Tanner. You would sell freedom and honor and self for happiness?
Ann. It would not be happiness for me. Perhaps death.
Tanner. Oh, that clutch holds and hurts. What have you grasped in me? Is there a father's heart as well as a mother's?

If there is capital here, it is the kind that yields no dramatic return, and indeed a criticism of this false climax would lead us to complain of the introduction of the "Life Force" in the first place. There seems no such organic relation between Tanner and Ann as there is between Vivie and her mother, Eliza and Higgins, Candida and Morell. The pair are sometimes compared to Benedick and Beatrice. The comparison is not apt. Shakespeare shows the erotically "dangerous" element in the hostility of his couple. But Tanner and Ann draw no sparks from each other. A cynic might say: here there can be no love since there is no hate. There is really no relationship at all except that she insists on having him and he cannot evade her successfully because the author won't let him. In this case, we have either to conclude that Frank Harris's kind of criticism applies—or that this is "drama of ideas" and we must not ask it to be otherwise.

Emotional substance? The farce of Tanner and Ann, taken in isolation, has very little, but oddly enough the episode in hell has a good deal, and this spreads itself over the work as a whole. Even here, though, there is a discrepancy between intention and achievement. The final effect of the Don Juan scene is not that we find the positive message inspiring. We find it at best important, at worst gallant—a brave effort to make sense of things that cannot be made sense of. It is all rather like a speech made in wartime saying that our side is bound to win because we are right. Perhaps. Perhaps. But the words that burn with irrefutability are all words expressing, not aspiration towards a better future, but recognition of a bad present. Don Juan himself is at his best when denouncing people. The speech that steals the show ("And is man any the less destroying himself . . .") is made by the Devil. Which is because it is not only a very reasonable speech but a very emotional one, a speech that springs from that very desolation which Shaw's best people experience.

This note of personal poignancy is seldom, or never, heard after *Saint Joan* (1923). So much the worse for the later plays. They have considerable merit, yet they often lack urgency even when the author makes Urgent Statements in them. And it is interesting that they lack not only dynamic and turbulent personal relationships but also close structure. There had been a connection between the emotional and the dramaturgic construction of the earlier plays; and when one went, so did the other.

I am not proposing a complete theory of the Shavian drama. Certainly, it should not be implied that this drama is dominated by the emotional conflicts of its author, much less that it ought to be. For that matter, I have had to remark that unresolved conflict sometimes resulted in unresolved art. What I am affirming is, first, that some Shaw plays communicate personal feeling of great intensity and, second, that even some Shaw plays which are less overtly emotional do embody profound feelings, though not of the kind that is usually expected.

The Conflict of Wills
in Shaw's Tragicomedy

by Norbert F. O'Donnell

In one of his play reviews written in the 1890's, Bernard Shaw outlines the crises in the life of a play which will never become "dated." First of all, he says, a play inevitably dates in its costumes and manners. If its conception of moral problems is sufficiently profound, it will survive this test, only to be confronted much later—perhaps centuries later—by another day of judgment. On this day the question will be whether or not its portrayal of the "instincts and passions" of humanity is valid enough for it to take its place as an "antique classic" in an era in which its ethical assumptions have ceased to compel assent.[1]

On the issue of the survival power of his own work, Shaw may be seen characteristically arguing with equal volubility on both sides. For one polemic purpose, he sees his plays as "petty tentatives" to be superseded by the work of some yet unborn Shakespeare—presumably because in the inevitable course of evolution their morality will become outdated. For another polemic purpose, he places his drama in a uniquely modern tradition of tragicomedy which makes the spectator "laugh with one side of his mouth and cry with the other" [2]—no doubt because the plays deal not only with transitory and ultimately soluble ethical issues but also with the permanent, or nearly permanent, problems of the world of the instincts and passions.[3] Responding to the invitation which his plays obviously offer, Shaw's interpreters have unanimously viewed them in the perspective of his abstract views of the social problems of our era. Shaw criticism has quite rightly been

"The Conflict of Wills in Shaw's Tragicomedy" by Norbert F. O'Donnell. From *Modern Drama*, IV (February 1962), 413-425. Copyright © 1962 by *Modern Drama*. Reprinted by permission of *Modern Drama*.

[1] *Our Theatres in the Nineties* (London, 1932), II, 167.

[2] Archibald Henderson, *Bernard Shaw, Playboy and Prophet* (New York, 1932), p. 615.

[3] If *Back to Methuselah* is not read simply as a fantasy for the sake of satirical comment on the present, it may be assumed to suggest that change takes place even in the world of the instincts and passions—but over a very long time span indeed.

focused on the reflection in his work of a socialist's attack on our economic and political ethics, a vitalist's reaction against the suppression of valuable human impulses by the "artificial system of morality." However, what is to be said of the plays as portrayals of the instinctive and passionate nature of man and of his relations to other men? Are they frequently not only comic but, as Shaw thought, tragicomic?

If one puts aside momentarily all of the witty social criticism which Shaw's drama contains, it becomes a portrayal of life in which the will is the key to human motives and all human relationships are, in one degree of intensity or another, conflicts of will. Since *Pygmalion*, as its title implies, is concerned with the creation of a human being, the clues which it offers to Shaw's conception of basic human nature and of human relationships are especially significant. Essentially Liza Doolittle is transformed from a subhuman flower girl into a truly human being because she shakes off her fears, develops a will of her own, and is able to meet Higgins as an equal in the strife of wills which is the human condition. After his lot in life is magically transformed by the Wannafeller bequest, Alfred Doolittle announces the psychological theme of the play when he proclaims that he can no longer assert his will to be one of the happy and "undeserving" poor because he is "intimidated"— bound by fear to a life he has not chosen. So also is Liza intimidated. At the beginning of the play, her famous cockney outcry expresses her mingled bewilderment and fear in the face of pressures on her which she cannot resist and does not understand. Even after she has successfully passed the test of the garden party, she is still not fully human—as is indicated by her attempting a "bargain in affection" with Higgins, trying to exact love from him in return for fetching his slippers and making herself generally as indispensable as possible. Her final transformation takes place only when she asserts purposes of her own which are not born of intimidation, knocking Higgins off the god-like perch from which he has viewed her only as an object, awakening for the first time his anger and his genuine human concern for her. The "squashed cabbage leaf" becomes, as Higgins puts it, a "consort battleship." The military metaphor is significant. Liza is fully human because she is now prepared to engage on equal terms with Higgins in a warfare of wills.

Ultimately, the worst thing which can happen to an individual in the strife at the psychological center of Shavian drama, as the example of Liza Doolittle suggests, is to be "intimidated" or "discouraged" by another human will. It is in this way that one experiences the humiliation of becoming merely an object in another's world, merely a means to another's personal ends. Thus in her intimidated state Liza knows the wretchedness of being nothing more than an experimental object in Higgins' scheme to demonstrate the power of speech training to bridge the gap between class and class. Thus Ann Whitefield's mother, for example, becomes merely a quaking instrument of her daughter's schemes to bewilder her elders and to trap the husband she wants. The experience is dramatized most fancifully in the form of the utter "discouragement"—sometimes leading to death—which the short-livers in *Back to Methuselah* feel in the presence of the long-livers. This discouragement obviously involves an overpowering fear, a sense of total inability to grasp the purposes of the other, and a disintegration of the will. In a world in which humanity consists of an ability to participate as an equal in psychological strife, it is the basic evil.

It is interesting to note in passing that in his non-dramatic prose Shaw thoroughly underscores his sense of the fearsomeness of the experience under discussion. He seems to have undergone it himself on only one occasion, a meeting with a strange Rabbi who, as he says, "terrified me by some power in him . . . which reduced me to a subjection which I had never experienced before, and have never experienced since." [4] Shaw was, he adds, "simply discouraged by him." To know intimidation or discouragement in any degree is to know something of degradation—hence, Shaw's violent denunciations of husbands who convince their wives or parents who convince their children that they are no more than the "property" or "slaves" of authority. "And what is a tyrant?" he asks in one of his prefaces. "Quite simply a person who says to another person, young or old 'You shall do as I tell you; you shall . . . have no will of your own; and your powers shall be at the disposal of my will.' " [5]

However, as he indicates both in exposition and plays, it may not always be possible to avoid inflicting the experience of intimidation on another. In the political context of the passage in which he mentions his meeting with the discouraging Rabbi, he regretfully concludes that those engaged in the task of making a better society may sometimes be forced to intimidate the "yahoos" of the world by natural or artificial means—this because intimidation may be the only alternative to the exercise of brute force. Shaw's heroic figures—for example, his Julius Caesar and King Magnus of *The Apple Cart*—inspire disorganization and awe in those who oppose their wills simply by the force of their original personalities. Magnus is also clever enough in a political crisis to use as his trump card such lingering power as his office has to fascinate and overawe a democratic electorate. Similarly the superior long-livers of *Back to Methuselah* must intimidate the undeveloped and unreliable short-livers who come to their realm either by the power of their own personalities or by the hocus-pocus of the Oracle's shrine. It is clear, however, that all such exceptions to the Shavian rule against even the semblance of tyranny are regrettable.

If the ultimate worst thing in the world of Shaw's drama is the experience of intimidation, the ultimate best thing is the sense of assurance which grows

---

[4] *Everybody's Political What's What?* (New York, 1944), p. 287.
[5] *Selected Plays of Bernard Shaw* (New York, 1949–57), IV, 65. Unless otherwise indicated, all references to Shaw's work assume this edition.

from an insight into the motives of others and hence an ability to control the outcome of the conflict of wills in which one is inevitably involved. Liza Doolittle "comes alive" at the moment at which she suddenly understands Higgins well enough to know that she can shake his arrogance by striking at his professional pride and his distaste for Freddy. The point is especially clear in Shaw's portrayal of his heroic figures. When the scheming Pothinus tells Caesar that Cleopatra means to use him as her entirely expendable instrument to gain an undisputed crown, he is neither surprised nor resentful. He has foreseen this—just as he foresees the consequences of the murder of Pothinus, the burning of the library at Alexandria, and even his own fate after he returns to Rome. Similarly Magnus, a Caesar in a constricted modern setting, is able to stay on his throne because he understands so thoroughly the impulses of all of the members of his cabinet, of the public, and even of his exotic Orinthia. Caesar and Magnus are skillful generals in the warfare of wills. Not, of course, that either is a tyrant. Whenever possible, both sedulously avoid using their powers of intimidation. Caesar attempts to educate Cleopatra, as Magnus cleverly tries to educate his childishly brawling cabinet. Paradoxically enough, however, the ability of the exemplary person to ameliorate the conflict of wills rests clearly upon his possession of powers which might make him a tyrant. It cannot be otherwise in a world whose fundamental principle is conflict.

A strife of wills, offering, in its most extreme form, alternatives of intimidation and tyranny, underlies Shaw's portrayal of all human relationships. It introduces a special sort of psychological tension into the famous Shavian dramatic discussions of social issues. More interesting for present purposes, it provides the substance of his version of much more intimate human encounters. He sees, for example, a great gulf fixed between children and parents. The child, he remarks in the preface to *Misalliance*, "cannot realize its parent's humanity"—cannot conceive of him as "having had youth, passions, and weaknesses, or as still growing, yearning, suffering and learning" (IV, 81). The parent, seeing his own experiences repeated by his offspring, can do much better by the child in this respect—but, as the plays make abundantly clear, is too prone to impose the patterns of his own past and present on the newest experiments of the Life Force. Shaw offers us a number of portrayals of children blithely going their way against the wills of shocked and more or less resistant parents—Vivie Warren, Gloria Clandon, Ann Whitefield, Hypatia Tarleton, and others. In this conflict it is noticeable that the rebellious youngsters are very often girls—it is the vital women who may be expected to bring home the lost dogs of the world—and that the parents are shocked and "discouraged" more often than the children. Although he had much to say about the character in his non-dramatic prose, Shaw apparently could not bring himself to put on the stage the portrayal of a truly intimidated child.

A point of interest to the as yet undiscovered biographer who will seek to show the connections between Shaw's life and his plays is that the plays never imply any special emotional bond between children and parents. The psychological strife which the relationship involves seems to be simply the strife between youth and age. Children see their parents in the same stereotypes which they apply to all older persons, and parents misunderstand their young for similar reasons. The problem of conflict between age and youth is, as one might expect, most clearly dramatized in scenes which demonstrate the consequences of a man's revealing a sexual interest in a considerably younger woman. When Jennifer Dubedat realizes that Dr. Ridgeon is in love with her, she can only exclaim in innocent but humiliating surprise, "You! An elderly man!" (I, 184). Hypatia Tarleton subjects Lord Summerhays to the most exquisite torture by reminding him with incredulous amusement that he once made advances to her:

Lord S. . . . And if you must say these terrible things: these heart-wounding shameful things, at least find something prettier to call me than an old rip.
Hypatia. Well, what would you call a man proposing to a girl who might be—
Lord S. His daughter: yes, I know.
Hypatia. I was going to say his granddaughter.
Lord S. You always have one more blow to get in.
Hypatia. You're too sensitive. . . . (IV, 144)

Neither Jennifer nor Hypatia can realize the humanity of the men to whom they are speaking—and Summerhays finds himself shocked in spite of himself by Hypatia's inability to say anything in what he considers to be a ladylike way. Although he seems to be incapable of portraying the young as seriously intimidated, Shaw, as an elderly man, may have taken a symbolic revenge on them in the latter part of *Back to Methuselah* in which the Ancients triumph over the "children" simply by rising in superior indifference above some of the usual concerns of humanity.

The strife of wills which is at the center of Shavian psychology is particularly apparent in Shaw's portrayal of relations between lovers or potential lovers and married couples. At the end of *Captain Brassbound's Conversion*, the transformed Brassbound gazes hypnotically at Lady Cicely Wayneflete and demands to know if she is in love with another man.

Lady Cicely. . . . I have never been in love with any real person; and I never shall. How could I manage people if I had that mad little bit of self left in me? Thats my secret.
Brassbound. Then throw away the last bit of self. Marry me.
Lady Cicely [*vainly struggling to recall her wandering will*]. Must I? (I, 686–687)

The guns of Brassbound's ship fire, the spell is broken, and Lady Cicely goes free. A similar scene with a different outcome is the one at the end of *Man and Superman* in which John Tanner, fighting, as he says, "for my freedom, for my honor, for my self, one and indivisible," goes down wildly talking before Ann Whitefield's fierce will to marry him. The struggle between the sexes arises, it is clear, because the sexual relationship demands a surrender of individuality. Lady Cicely Wayneflete believes that she can "manage people" because she remains to a degree selfless (i.e., impersonal) in her view of them; but Brassbound reminds her that a still greater sacrifice of self is involved in the sexual union with him which draws her. Tanner sees that he cannot remain himself, "one and indivisible," if he submits to the vital force which is thrusting him and Ann together. As Shaw's Don Juan proclaims, "In the sex relation the universal creative energy, of which the parties are both the helpless agents, overrides and sweeps away all personal considerations, and dispenses with all personal relations" (III, 637). The sexually aroused man or woman threatens to engulf two people in an ecstatic but basically impersonal encounter. The result is very often conflict—even if the conflict takes the form of the hilarious sequence in which Hypatia Tarleton chases Joey Percival up the hill and he, in turn, chases her down. Small wonder that two of Shaw's favorite Shakespearean characters were Beatrice and Benedick and that his lovers, from Leonard Charteris and his ladies to Magnus and Orinthia, are engaged in perpetually witty fencing matches. Driven toward one another by impulses which they cannot down, they are engaged in a struggle with themselves and with one another in which their individual identities are at stake.

In the world of Shavian drama, the conflict of wills between lovers continues after marriage—partly because of the transience of the impersonal magic of the sexual relationship and partly because, as critics have generally recognized, in Shaw's plays the "universal creative energy" has different ultimate uses for women and men. Tension exists between Hector and Hesione Hushabye because, despite their extraordinary efforts, they have not been able to keep alive the sexual delight in one another of which both can speak only with nostalgia:

Hector. That was confounded madness. I cant believe that such an amazing experience is common. It has left its mark on me. I believe that is why I have never been able to repeat it.

Hesione [*laughing and caressing his arm*]. We were frightfully in love with one another, Hector. It was such an enchanting dream that I have never been able to grudge it to you or anyone else since. I have invited all sorts of pretty women to the house on the chance of giving you another turn. But it has never come off. (I, 524)

Although they are able to speak frankly of the possibility of Hector's finding sexual satisfaction outside their marriage, both have suffered concealed heartbreak because the experience of marriage has revealed differences between them which were obliterated by their early electric experiences of sexual union.

Tension exists between them because Hesione, being a woman, however "modern," is prepared to find happiness in a domesticity which is an extension of childbearing, whereas Hector, being a man, yearns for the physical and intellectual adventures which create new horizons for a culture and for mankind. Hence Hesione's despairing outcry: "What do men want? They have their food, their firesides, their clothes mended, and our love at the end of the day. Why are they not satisfied? Why do they envy us the pain with which we bring them into the world, and make strange dangers and torments for themselves to be even with us?" (I, 529). Hesione and Hector are perhaps Shaw's most effective dramatization of the doctrine about relations between the sexes made explicit in *Man and Superman*. The conflict in which they are involved can be eased only, it seems, in marriages in which the sexual impulse has ceased to be vital—even as a subject of nostalgic reflection—and "spheres of influence" have been clearly established. Thus Bishop Bridgenorth and his wife, once, but presumably no longer, deeply "in love" and beyond regret of love's passing maintain a satisfying relationship in which most of the time he goes his intellectual and she her domestic way. Kings Magnus and Charles II are deeply attached to and happy with their rather shadowy wives, perhaps because both are free to devote much of their energy to political interests and to philandering. It is no doubt significant that the Bishop and the two kings are all three very clever tacticians in the Shavian war of wills—and that they and their wives are not young.

The moments of true feeling which are the basis of the Shavian tragicomedy emerge naturally from the conflicts which provide the psychological undercurrents of the plays. They may be distinguished as moments of "nakedness," moments of "disillusionment," and moments of "conversion"— each reflecting a character's defeat or victory in the struggle of wills. The characters who experience moments of nakedness suddenly find themselves outraged and sometimes fearful, aware that they are bested in conflict but for the moment unable to relinquish the feelings and ideas which have led them to defeat. Liza Doolittle undergoes such an experience at the time of her first appearance in Higgins' home—outraged and fearful in the face of her treatment as merely an object for experimentation, she can only bristle, wail, and finally allow herself to be literally stripped and scrubbed. The epitome of such moments is the one in which Mangan, the businessman— shamed, frightened, and angered by the intellectual frankness he meets everywhere in Heartbreak House—cries: "Let's all strip stark naked. We may as well do the thing thoroughly when we're about it. We've stripped ourselves morally naked: Well, let us strip ourselves physically naked as well, and see how we like it" (I, 584). Mangan has been defeated in his every encounter with the people of Heartbreak House, especially in the scene in which, in a presumed hypnotic trance, he has heard Ellie Dunn and Hesione Hushabye discuss him as an unattractive object of which they feel sure that they have the power of disposal. He has heard one or another of his fellow guests challenge every one of the pretenses upon which his power in the world of business and government depends—and has even been betrayed into revealing his own knowledge of the hollowness of the pretenses. Yet he can only rage against his nakedness, refusing to let go of the attitudes which have produced his psychological defeat and which ultimately lead to his death. He reminds us of Mrs. Warren at the end of her play, reduced to her melodramatic declaration of her intention to continue to do evil; of Dr. Ridgeon, gabbling and sputtering in the face of the revelation of his failure to play God successfully; of the anguished Elderly Gentleman through most of his encounters with the long-livers; of some of the perpetually agitated cabinet members in *The Apple Cart*. These are people on the verge of total intimidation, their only virtue being their refusal to acknowledge defeat. They are guilty not only of the "crime of being intimidated"—which might be paralleled with the "crime of poverty" so eloquently discussed in *Major Barbara*—but also of the crime of remaining static, of resisting the pressure to change which is the Shavian law of both social and psychic life.

The moments of disillusionment which Shaw's characters undergo are more hopeful because, in the shock of defeat in psychological struggle, the characters who experience them are willing to relinquish old attitudes and to grope toward new ones. Although she is empty of any real purposes, Liza Doolittle is much more promising as a human being at the moment at which she throws Higgins' slippers at him in a burst of disillusioned anger than she was when she brought them into the room with the intention of pleasing him. At the moment at which she throws the slippers, she has given up her illusory hope of a "bargain in affection" born of her intimidation and is in a position to form new and less humiliating purposes. Near the end of his play, Captain Brassbound makes explicit the feelings which underlie many a moment of disillusionment in Shaw's plays. Robbed of his fancy that he is a romantic avenger and his uncle a sanctimonious devil, he cries out to Lady Cicely:

> Now everything is gone. You have taken the old meaning out of my life, but you have put no new meaning into it. I can see that you have some clue to the world that makes all its difficulties easy for you; but I'm not clever enough to seize it. Youve lamed me by shewing me that I take life the wrong way when I'm left to myself. . . . I see that now; for youve opened my eyes to the past; but what good is that for the future? What am I to do? Where am I to go? (I, 683–684).

It is in precisely this painful mood of emptiness and groping that Major Barbara listens to Bill Walker's ironic gibes in the Salvation Army shelter just after her father's theatrically written check has "bought" the Army. It is this sort of disillusionment which leads Ellie Dunn, in her heartbreak over her misjudgment of Hector Hushabye and Boss Mangan, to contemplate a mercenary marriage to Mangan (a gesture parallel to Liza's throwing the slippers at Higgins). It is a similar but even more painful sort of disillusionment which leads the Elderly Gentleman in *Back to Methuselah* to prefer death at the hands of the long-livers to a return to life in the world from which he comes, the Preacher in *Too True To Be Good* to announce himself finally as a man permanently without a cause worthy of the exercise of his gifts.

Most often the disillusionment which Shaw's characters meet does not, as for the Elderly Gentleman and the Preacher, lead to death or to the surrender of the future. Rather it leads to emotional moments of hope, moments of "conversion" in which new purposes suddenly become clear and the Shavian characters return with new energy to the struggle of wills which is their destiny. Liza Doolittle rises in furious anger against Higgins: she will teach phonetics, she will marry Freddy. Brassbound, thanks to his near-success in hypnotizing Lady Cicely into marrying him, finds that he has at last discovered "the secret of command." Major Barbara enthusiastically joins Cusins in the social mission represented by his acceptance of responsibility for the munitions factory. Seizing him with both hands, she cries: "Oh, did you think my courage would never come back? did you believe that I was a deserter? that I, who have stood in the streets, and taken my people to my heart, and talked of the holiest and greatest things with them, could ever turn back and chatter foolishly to fashionable people about nothing in a drawing room? Never, never, never, never: Major Barbara will die with the colors" (I, 445). Her use of military metaphors, however appropriate to her character as a former officer in the Salvation Army, has a deeper significance. She has recovered from her disillusionment to join once again in the strife of wills in which all vital human beings are involved. Similarly, in the face of somewhat the same twentieth-century realities which produce the despair of the Preacher in *Too True To Be Good*, Ellie Dunn throws off the mood of disillusioned rejection of her true nature in which she has decided to make a calculating marriage with Boss Mangan. Having made old Shotover her "spiritual husband and second father," she devoutly hopes that the bombers which come over Heartbreak House at the end of the play will come again, destroying the corrupt and stupid world she knows and bringing her something of the experience of elemental struggle which the ancient captain found on the bridge of his ship in a storm. We should remember that even at the end of *Too True To Be Good*, as the Preacher delivers his disillusioned closing speech, the Patient and her mother, both of whom have experienced "conversions" of a sort, are off to found a sisterhood which may restore the sense of purpose in life whose loss the Preacher so bitterly mourns.

Whether or not we agree that the patterns of psychological strife and of moments of true feeling discussed here produce a tragicomic tone in Shaw's plays depends, of course, on our participation in his attitude toward the strife he portrays and toward its emotional crises. His attitude toward the world of human conflict which he dramatizes seems to be very much like that of some of his heroes with whom he is closely identified. Such figures as Caesar and Magnus appear to be surrogates for their creator, and their sense of life is clearly tragicomic—for significant reasons. Caesar understands Cleopatra very well and is sympathetically concerned that she cease to be the aggressive little barbarian he finds upon his arrival in Egypt. He is truly moved that human strife should have produced the wanton murder of Pothinus, which makes him visualize with horror a future in which "murder shall breed murder, always in the name of right and honor and peace, until the gods are tired of blood and create a race that can understand" (III, 457). Yet he maintains a certain amused detachment, a certain impersonality, in all of his dealings. When Pothinus asks Cleopatra if Caesar does not love her, her reply is instructive:

Cleopatra. Love me! Pothinus: Caesar loves no one. Who are those we love? Only those whom we do not hate: all people are strangers and enemies to us except those we love. But it is not so with Caesar. He has no hatred in him: he makes friends with everyone as he does with dogs and children. His kindness to me is a wonder: neither mother, father, nor nurse have ever taken so much care for me, or thrown open their thoughts to me so freely.

Pothinus. Well: is not this love?

Cleopatra. What! When he will do as much for the first girl he meets on his way back to Rome? Ask his slave, Britannus: he has been just as good to him. Nay, ask his very horse! His kindness is not for anything in me: it is in his own nature (III, 439).

Presumably Caesar's impersonality, like Lady Cicely Wayneflete's, is the secret of his ability to "manage people." Similarly, King Magnus is deeply sympathetic to the tempestuous people with whom he has to deal, including his especially tempestuous Orinthia, but retains his power because he keeps a certain humorous distance from them, because his whole self is never entirely committed. It is noticeable that both Caesar and Magnus keep their balance because they have a sense not only of the stresses and strains of the individual human conflicts they observe and in which they are involved but also because they believe strongly in the objective importance of the historical roles they play. They are sympathetic but ultimately impersonal in their attitudes toward the people with whom they deal because they see them in the perspective of vast social conflicts which are of primary importance to all of mankind. So it is with Shaw as a dramatist. He understands and sympathizes with his characters in the more or less permanent psychological strife in which they are involved, but he preserves a certain detachment toward them in that he sees them as a part of social conflicts which are more important than individual destinies. Insofar as he preserves a degree of feeling for individuals in their lonely struggles to assert their wills, he is a tragedian. Insofar as he feels compelled to regard these struggles with the amused impersonality of one who sees large historical forces at work upon them, he is a comedian. The result is that he creates a drama which is very frequently a tragicomedy.

It is obviously beyond the scope of this essay to consider whether or not this tragicomedy is, as Shaw thought, a uniquely modern phenomenon. It is possible to observe, however, that the psychology which provides its tragic undercurrents is very much present in the work of at least two of the latter-day heirs of romanticism—August Strindberg and D. H. Lawrence. The parallel is particularly evident in the portrayal which both Strindberg and Lawrence offer of relations between the sexes. The essential clue to Strindberg's attitude is in the famous scene at the end of the second act of *The Father* in which the Captain explains that he first loved Laura as a mother and then attempted to win her as a wife:

Captain. . . . I thought you despised my lack of virility, so I tried to win you as a woman by proving myself as a man.
Laura. That was your mistake. The mother was your friend, you see, but the woman was your enemy. Sexual love is conflict. And don't imagine I gave myself. I didn't give. I only took what I meant to take. Yet you did dominate me . . . I felt it and wanted you to feel it.[6]

The Captain and Laura are locked in an inevitable struggle of wills in which she is ultimately the victor. In, for example, *Miss Julie* and *Creditors*, men are the victors in a similar struggle. The drift of Strindberg's portrayal of relations between the sexes in all of his plays, however, is in Laura's line, "Sexual love is conflict." Sexual love is also conflict, though not such a desperate or hopeless one, in the novels of D. H. Lawrence. In Lawrence the sexual relationship may yield the best that is to be known in life, but it is complicated by the determination of some lovers to control those whom they presumably love by absorbing them totally to their own personalities—and by the determination of others to control by remaining detached and, so to speak, "above the battle." Lawrence visualizes the happiest relationship as the one in which the partners achieve "polarity," a true communication without the sacrifice of the individual integrity of either lover. Thus Paul Morell in *Sons and Lovers* feels that Miriam Leivers wishes to control him by consuming his identity; Gerald and Gudrun of *Women in Love* wish to control one another by remaining powerful through detachment; and Birkin and Ursula in the same novel know something of "polarity." Although each

---

[6] *Six Plays of Strindberg*, tr. Elizabeth Sprigge (New York, 1955), p. 42.

has a different reason for his view, Shaw, Strindberg, and Lawrence all imply a common attitude: human relationships are a strife of wills.

Bertrand Russell suggests that a basic tension in romantic literature is that between the absolute value which the romantic sets on the realization of individuality and the social claims imposed by any human relationship. This tension, he feels, becomes especially apparent in portrayals of sexual love, in which assertions of individuality must inevitably meet counter-assertions—the result being conflict.[7] Whether or not this is an accurate interpretation of all romantic portrayals of love, it casts some light on Strindberg, Lawrence, and Shaw. It seems most accurate as a guide to understanding the conflict of wills in Strindberg's plays, in which individuals clash and one or another goes down to terrible defeat, even destruction. It also has a certain applicability to Lawrence's portrayal of human relationships, though Lawrence asserts passionately that some few people who understand life sufficiently can find escape from the law of conflict in a kind of private human communication which suspends it. Furthermore, in view of the tragic, or nearly tragic, tone of the work of both Strindberg and Lawrence, Russell's generalization helps to explain the position of Shaw as a tragicomedian. Like his heroes, he understands and sympathizes with individuals involved in the war of wills which he himself cannot avoid. In the end, however, his work takes on its markedly comedic tone because he sees life in terms of social problems which he believes transcend those of the individual. Because in our loneliness we are a part of the struggle of wills which arises from our instincts and passions, we should not forget, his tragicomedies imply, that we are also a part of the comedy of real and potential sociability.

[7] *A History of Western Philosophy* (New York, 1945), pp. 681–682.

Shaw's Challenge to Liberalism

by Louis Crompton

Major Barbara, together with *Man and Superman* and *John Bull's Other Island*, forms part of a trilogy of philosophical comedies, all of which deal with the bankruptcy of nineteenth-century liberalism in the face of the brute facts of sex, nationalism, and poverty. This propagandistic purpose has been from the start a bone of contention. It is not by chance that critics holding a formalist position, from Shaw's friend A. B. Walkley down to Francis Fergusson[1] in our own day, have denounced the play as a kind of literary monster, while philosopher-critics[2] have regarded it as one of the few dramas with anything serious to say on the subject of politics. Indeed, *Major Barbara* raises the central issue of modern aesthetics as squarely as any piece of writing can. This question—putting it in the simplest possible terms—I take to be whether art is to be regarded as autonomous and *sui generis* or whether it is to be judged in relation to some ulterior standard of reality, that is, as a form of science or knowledge. But even if you accept this second view of the nature of art—which is certainly Shaw's view—you will still have to ask yourself whether your conception of this ulterior reality corresponds to Shaw's. Thus the play presents a double challenge—first to the dominant literary theory of our day, and second to our political and social ideals.

Only the inordinate length of *Man and Superman* kept Shaw from publishing his three philosophical comedies together in a set, as he did the *Plays Pleasant and Unpleasant* and the *Three Plays for Puritans*. For his German edition, Shaw suggested that they be grouped and given the title *Comedies of Science and Religion*. Like the grouped plays of the other cycles, these plays share, besides their common theme, a common mood and a common dramatic structure.

It is this latter feature—their unique dramatic form—which has first of

"Shaw's Challenge to Liberalism" by Louis Crompton. From *Prairie Schooner*, XXXVII, No. 3 (Fall 1963), 229–244. Copyright © 1963 by the University of Nebraska Press. Reprinted by permission of *Prairie Schooner*.

[1] See Walkley, *Drama and Life* (1907); Fergusson, *The Idea of a Theater* (1949).

[2] Charles Frankel, "Efficient Power and Inefficient Virtue" in *Great Dilemmas in Literature*, ed. R. M. MacIver (1956).

all confused, puzzled, and exasperated critics. What Shaw does is to mix together in each play a Molièresque comedy and a Socratic dialogue. Each play begins by presenting us with a high-minded idealist, who takes himself with earnest seriousness and looks upon himself as an enlightened reformer. He is then made the subject of a comedy in the style of Molière, not with the idea of unmasking his hypocrisy, but of exposing the comic contradictions within his ideals and temperament. The problems raised by this character, which appear originally in a farcical-satirical light, are treated more and more seriously until they are shown to be bound up with what Shaw calls "the destiny of nations," and the audience which has settled down for a night of fun finds it must either transform itself from an audience of pleasure-seekers into a "pit of philosophers" or founder hopelessly in the dream sequence of *Man and Superman* or the last acts of *John Bull's Other Island* and *Major Barbara*. An impossible procedure you will complain. But not, Shaw would answer, to someone who believed that "Every joke is an earnest in the womb of time," and that the prophet who did not make his audience laugh would suffer, at worst, the fate of Socrates and Christ, and at best that of Rousseau and Tom Paine.

The idealistic liberals who are the butts of the satire are Roebuck Ramsden in *Man and Superman*, Tom Broadbent in *John Bull's Other Island*, and Lady Britomart Undershaft in *Major Barbara*, but since our subject is the latter play let us look at Lady Britomart as a representative of her species. The character of Lady Britomart, like most of those in *Major Barbara*, was drawn from a real person. It is a well-known fact that Shaw based Adolphus Cusins, his professor of Greek, on Gilbert Murray, but it is less well-known that he based Lady Britomart on Murray's real-life mother-in-law, Lady Rosalind Frances, Countess of Carlisle. (Indeed, Shaw jokingly told Murray in a letter that he was at work on a play to be called "Murray's Mother-in-Law".) The Countess of Carlisle was, like Lady Britomart, a Whig peeress; her father was the Liberal whip in parliament, and she was herself a crusading temperance reformer and the leader for eighteen years of the national Woman's Liberal Federation. Since her husband was more interested in art than in estate management, she ran the extensive family estates like a personal fiefdom, attending in minute detail to the farmers' personal welfare—and to their moral characters. Castle Howard and her house in Kensington were salons for the Liberal intelligentsia. Murray himself has paid tribute to her crusading enthusiasm and to the heartening quality of her formidable benevolence.

The clue to Shaw's treatment of the comic contradictions in Lady Britomart's character may be found in a remark by James Froude, Carlyle's biographer, on the subject of Lady Rosalind. Froude, who disapproved of her politics but admired her character, said that though she professed to be a Liberal, she was by temperament better fitted to be an "empress." Hence if Shaw had chosen to make her the central figure of the play he might have imitated Molière's "Bourgeois Gentleman" to the extent of calling it "The Imperious Liberal." By family tradition and personal conviction Lady Britomart is an avowed believer in free speech and a democratic franchise, but every speech that she utters shows her native aristocratic spirit and natural masterfulness at odds with these ideals. Where Lady Britomart's moralism is not an aristocratic Mrs. Grundyism, a Queen Victoria-ism so to speak, it is merely a rationalization of her class prejudices and privileges, "right" and "propriety" being whatever furthers the Stephenage family interests and "wrong" or "impropriety" being whatever conflicts with them. For the central issue of the first act, and indeed of the play as a whole, is who will inherit the armament factory owned by Lady Britomart's husband, Andrew Undershaft.

The question of the Undershaft inheritance has caused a rift between the husband and wife: according to the tradition of the firm, the inheritance must go not to a son of the owner but to some promising adopted heir. This condition, utterly at odds with aristocratic belief in birth and blood, so offends Lady Britomart that it is useless for Andrew to argue that the Roman Empire was run successfully on this scheme and that it brought to the throne Marcus Aurelius. She is so used to thinking of the Stephenages as governors by natural right that when Andrew had refused to break the firm's law of succession in favor of his son Stephen the resulting quarrel led to a legal separation. Lady Britomart's way of putting this is to declare that nothing can bridge fundamental "moral" disagreement.

We have only to spend two minutes in Stephen's presence to realize the soundness of his father's decision, for Stephen is a conscientious, thoroughly well-intentioned prig and moral pedant, tediously prating about "right" being "right" and "wrong" being "wrong." His sister Sarah lacks his pretentiousness, but also his starchy character, and is, in fact, no more than a fashionable nonentity. Only in their third child, Barbara, has the Undershaft-Stephenage marriage justified itself as an evolutionary experiment in the crossing of types and classes, for Barbara has Lady Britomart's genius for leadership and mothering, with none of her class limitations. So little is she concerned with mere propriety and decorum and so intensely does she identify herself with the religious spirit of the race that she has joined the least snobbish of the reforming religious sects of the day, the Salvation Army.

As the play opens we learn that Sarah and Barbara have both become engaged, Sarah to Charles Lomax, an amiable aristocratic noodle as empty-headed as herself, and Barbara to a man as complex and subtle in his moral and intellectual perceptions as Lomax is silly. Shaw shows us in Cusins a representative of the humane conscience in its most tender and perceptive form. In writing to Gilbert Murray, Shaw pointed out that he had taken pains to make his professor "the reverse in every point of the theatrical strong man":

> I want him to go on his quality wholly, and not to make the smallest show of physical robustness or brute determination. His selection by Undershaft should be a standing puzzle to the people who believe in the strong-silent still-waters-run-deep hero of melodrama. The very name Adolphus Cusins is selected to that end.[3]

In choosing Murray as his model, Shaw had in mind a type of liberal in strong contrast to the active, bustling Lady Britomart. Cusins is the academic, cloistered, sympathetic, skeptical, ironic, supercivilized liberal who shrinks instinctively from what E. M. Forster has called the world of "telegrams and anger."

Murray's liberalism sprang from several sources—from the radicalism of Castle Howard, from his Irish rebel background, and from a strain of Shelleyan humanitarianism that made him, like Shaw, a vegetarian and a hater of all forms of cruelty. The other side of the picture was his Hellenism. For Murray, Greek literature was a living force having direct bearing on modern politics, morals, and culture. Here is how he writes of Euripides, the Greek playwright to whom he felt especially drawn:

> His contemporary public denounced him as dull, because he tortured them with personal problems; as malignant, because he made them see truths they wished not to see; as blasphemous and foul-minded, because he made demands on their spiritual and religious natures which they could neither satisfy nor overlook.[4]

In short, Murray regarded Euripides as standing in relation to the golden age of Athens as the "New Drama" of Shaw and Ibsen stood in relation to the age of Victoria and Edward VII. (Shaw returned the compliment by hailing Murray's translations of Euripides as modern masterpieces that had earned their place on the contemporary stage in their own right.) In *Major Barbara* Shaw makes Undershaft give Cusins the nickname "Euripides," thus implying that he looks on human affairs with the same mixture of ironic pessimism and pity as his Greek predecessor.

Lady Britomart has invited her estranged husband to her West End mansion with the eminently practical intention of extracting dowries from him for the two brides-to-be, her estimate of the earning power of a feckless man-about-town and a classics professor being realistically small. But her attempt to bring up once more the matter of the inheritance meets flinty resistance from Undershaft. Indeed, only the unexpected interest Undershaft shows

---

[3] October 7, 1905; printed in Murray, *An Unfinished Autobiography* (1960), pp. 155–156. This whole letter is of great interest for the play.

[4] *A History of Ancient Greek Literature* (1897), p. 250. See also *Euripides and His Age* (1913).

in Barbara's novel religious aspirations saves the family reunion from shipwreck. It is an immense puzzle to both the naïve and the sophisticated members of the family group that Undershaft should show such a concern with her new faith, particularly since he is resolutely unashamed of his destructive trade and even seems to glory in it, declaring, "Your Christianity, which enjoins you to resist not evil, and to turn the other cheek, would make me a bankrupt. My morality—my religion—must have a place for cannons and torpedoes in it." Barbara challenges him to maintain this faith after visiting her East End Salvation Army shelter. Her father accepts the invitation, and issues a counter-challenge: she shall in return pay a visit to his arms factory and face the temptation offered by a religion of "money and gunpowder."

The scene at the Salvation Army shelter is a remarkable piece of low-life melodrama, equalled in English only by the works of O'Casey. The refugees at the barracks include a cynically smart young man and an old crone, both posing as redeemed sinners, and Peter Shirley, who is brought in in a state of semi-starvation. Turned out of his job as overage, Shirley finds the necessity of accepting charity all the more bitter because he holds the faith of a secularist, in contrast to the others who believe in nothing but their right to bilk and exploit capitalist society as it has bilked and exploited them. Finally, Bill Walker enters, a half-drunk, blustering bully in a very mean mood, who bawls angrily for his girl, and curses the Army for taking her from him.

This scene ends with Barbara's struggle for Bill's soul. This is a fight which comes very near to success and only fails through a stroke of diablerie on the part of her father. The latter frustrates her simply by demonstrating that although the Salvation Army can afford to refuse to sell the blackguard his salvation for twenty shillings, it cannot, no matter how scrupulous it affects to be, refuse to sell the millionaire his for, say, five thousand pounds. Barbara had refused to accept her father's tuppence in the collection plate because the money was earned through the creation of destructive forces far more brutal in their effect than anything the slum ruffian might aspire to. But when the Army commissioner comes to plead for money to carry on the Army's work in a hard winter, she is forced to accept Undershaft's proffer of the aforementioned thousands despite his sardonic emphasis on the terrifying nature of his enterprises. The ruffian, when he sees the rich man's gift accepted where his own conscience money was rejected, turns on Barbara with cynical scorn, and Barbara, facing at once the failure of her attempt at salvation and a realization that the Salvation Army, if it is to exist at all, can only exist as the pensioner of the distillery and cannon industries, utters her bitter and heart-rending cry of despair, "My God: why hast thou forsaken me?"

It is at this point that the play takes the most surprising of its many surprising turns. For at the moment that Barbara's God, the God of Evangelical Christianity, appears to have failed her, the professor of Greek hails as a new deity the very man Barbara now fears as anti-Christ, her diabolical-seeming father. Cusins, in a transport of ecstasy, declares himself to be possessed by the spirit of Undershaft, whom he addresses as the new "Dionysos." Barbara in the pain and confusion of her loss can, of course, see nothing in this behavior but a piece of perverse irony.

It may be well at this point to ask what Shaw means by his idea of a "new" Dionysos. What has the ancient Greek god to do with modern society? The answer is to be found in the meaning Dionysiac religion had in the Greek world. Historians and philosophers, of whom Nietzsche is the most famous, have repeatedly emphasized the strange disparity between the serene rationalism of Greek society as we usually conceive it and the wild barbarity of the Bacchic cult which entered Greece from Thrace and Macedonia in the tenth century before Christ. Nietzsche traces the birth of dramatic tragedy itself to this irruption of frenzied rites and ecstatic orgies into the calm order and moral rationalism of Greek life, which the new religion challenged with its worship of super-normal psychic energy and its identification of the worshipper both with the new God and with the life processes of the animal and vegetative world. Cusins had earlier praised the services of the Salvation Army as the "true worship of Dionysos," finding in the Army's ecstasy and enthusiasm (literally, a standing outside oneself and possession by the divine will) an analogue of the uncouth religion that shocked the cultivated Greeks as the Army shocked the conventional Anglicanism of the West End. In its stirring religious music he had seen the primitive dithyramb reborn, its trombones, timbrels, and drums being the antithesis both of tepid hymns sung in fashionable churches and of the salon music of the fashionable drawing room. Even its symbols, Blood and Fire, Cusins points out, are Dionysiac symbols. Its joy and happiness are those of the God-possessed, as Barbara's later grief is that of the God-forsaken.

Thus Dionysianism is what Bergson calls a "dynamic religion," [5] with its basis not in conventional morality or institutionalism but in a mystical union with the divine will. It breaks down social barriers, taking the intellectual into University Settlements in the slums, and pitting him actively against evil. It carries its devotees beyond the bounds of logic and reason. Aroused and lacking rational direction, it finds its expression in the frenzy of the revolutionary mob. Cusins is a sophisticated intellectual who has joined the Army, as Lady Britomart puts it, to worship Barbara. (No bad object of worship, Shaw would insist.) As a student of comparative religion and a disciple of Sir James Frazer, his view of the Army is, to say the least, not that of a fundamentalist. But Barbara's obvious religious genius attracts him strongly, and her evangelicalism, on its practical side, is not at all incompatible with his own religion of love, pity, and forgiveness. Indeed, for

[5] *The Two Sources of Morality and Religion* (1935).

all his sardonic irony, he faces a crisis of his own beliefs at the same moment Barbara faces hers. As we have already seen, Cusins, in his skepticism and humanitarianism, is akin to the young Euripides who casts doubts on the traditional Greek attitudes to such questions as patriotism, religion, women, and slaves.

But the Greek playwright's later development has a strange and unforeseen twist to it. For Euripides, who first turned the Greek drama away from its roots in Dionysiac religion toward a critical and skeptical direction, does return to Dionysos at the end of his career. In what is generally regarded as the last work of his old age, *The Bacchae*, the humanistic and humanitarian playwright does come face to face with the religion in which the drama had its origin. It is probably no exaggeration to say that *The Bacchae* is, by a good margin, the most terrifying, unedifying, and enigmatic of all Greek tragedies. You will recall that in this play Dionysos visits in disguise the city of Thebes where his rites have been forbidden by the moralistic King Pentheus and works a horrifying revenge. The problem Euripides' drama poses, put in the briefest terms, is this: what attitude are we to adopt to this new force in society, at once so terrible and so fascinating? Does Dionysos' ghastly triumph over Pentheus signify the rebirth of vital religion or does he symbolize some dark, demonic power from which we are to recoil in dread?

Now, like the Greeks of Euripides' day, Cusins has also been brought face to face with a brutal, primitive force of life and death which the cultivated, sensitive side of him recoils from, but which the clear-headed student of society is forced to take into account. And Shaw, to emphasize the fact that he has had the parallel with Euripides' drama in mind all along, has Cusins quote some twenty or thirty lines from the play in the Salvation Army scene, in what Cusins identifies as his "own" (that is, Murray's) new translation.[6]

It is no exaggeration to say that Shaw's Undershaft has created the same bafflement in critics as Euripides' Dionysos, whether the critic be as naïve as the *Time* reviewer who accused Shaw of making a "complete about-face" and firing on his own socialist ranks, or as sophisticated as Mr. Francis Fergusson who for all his learning and intelligence, denounces *Major Barbara* as a tissue of "unresolved paradoxes."

What then *are* we to make of this man who has so puzzled Shaw's commentators? It may perhaps be best to turn first to the living models from whom Shaw may have obtained hints for his millionaire munitions maker. One was a neighbor at Ayot Saint Lawrence, Charles McEvoy, a quiet and gentle man, who had manufactured torpedoes for the North during the American Civil War. But I should like to suggest that Shaw, in drawing the sardonic side of Undershaft's character, seems to have had in mind the Swedish arms maker Alfred Nobel, the inventor of nitroglycerine. During the closing decades of the nineteenth century, Nobel's success in creating more and

[6] The lines are quoted from page 126 of Murray's *Euripides* (1904).

more powerful explosives had sent a wave of panic around the world. A leading figure in European business and international finance, Nobel was also a man of an intellectual and literary cast; like Undershaft, he belonged to a munitions dynasty. In thought and sentiment, he was a Shelleyan radical and humanitarian, but this did not limit his hardheadedness in business, and he sold his patents indiscriminately to autocratic and liberal states alike. (In a manuscript draft of *Major Barbara* Shaw makes Undershaft boast that he has sold a new rifle to the Swedish, Italian, and German governments without any compunctions on the score of politics.[7]) Nobel's motto, "My home is where my work is, and my work is everywhere" might well have been Undershaft's. And, of course, one of the last deeds of this complex and enigmatic man was his endowment of the Nobel Peace Prize, which challenged the humanitarian liberals among his personal friends to solve the problem his discoveries had created. The Peace Prize was first awarded in 1901, four years before Shaw began his play.

This will perhaps explain, in part, one of the paradoxes of *Major Barbara*— that it is a dealer in lethal weapons who plays the role of Socrates in this socialist drama. But what of Undershaft's peculiar commercial ruthlessness, that specifically cold-blooded side of his personality that has so shocked and baffled critics and audiences? To unravel this puzzle we must begin by considering his background. Undershaft is a slum boy, reared in that wilderness of desolation that was East London in the middle of the nineteenth century. He has, like all the members of his dynasty, assumed the name of the firm's founder, an abandoned orphan reared in the parish of St. Andrew Undershaft in the city.[8] Determined to escape from the indignities of poverty, he has taken for his own the stern old Scots slogan: "Thou shalt starve ere I starve."

Here the second paradox appears, for as a socialist we expect Shaw especially to condemn this spirit. But he condones it and even insists that for a poor person it is indeed the only possible "manly" attitude. (Undershaft's Christian name, "Andrew," means "manly.") For Shaw, the great cardinal virtues are courage and self-respect, and he believed that if the poor in a democracy let themselves be exploited, starved, and snubbed, it is only because of their own inveterate abjectness. Hence the cutting remarks which Undershaft, the ex-slum boy, addresses to Peter Shirley, the down-trodden, long-suffering worker, in the Salvation Army shelter:

Shirley (angrily). —Who made your millions for You? Me and my like. Whats kep us poor? keepin you rich. I wouldn't have your conscience, not for all your income.
Undershaft. —I wouldn't have your income, not for all your conscience, Mr. Shirley.

[7] British Museum additional MS 50616B, folio 53. The passage is cancelled. This draft of act one is dated "Sandgate 4/4/05."
[8] The odd epithet "Undershaft" was applied to the church because of the custom of setting up a maypole outside its doors.

Undershaft is driving home the point that the play makes over and over
again, that a mere conviction of moral superiority is in itself the hollowest
of consolations, the last resource of the weak and cowardly, and the treach-
erous quagmire in which true worth and manhood are lost.

Honor, justice, and truth are indeed part of Undershaft's religion, but
he stresses that these can be had only as the "graces and luxuries of a rich,
strong, and safe life." Any liberal like Cusins who preaches these virtues to
the poor without taking into account economic realities is a fool. Undershaft can even declare that his determinedly ruthless conduct satisfies the
Kantian test, since the world would be an immeasurably better place if all
the poor behaved exactly as he has. But first we must rid ourselves of the
liberal belief that moral virtue by itself is ever capable of becoming a significant force in the world. Shaw made this point abundantly clear in a speech
of Undershaft's in the unpublished Derry manuscript of the play:

> Come, come, my young friends; let us live in the real world. Your moral world
> is a vacuum; nothing is done there, though a good deal is eaten and drunk by the
> moralists at the expense of the real world. It is nice to live in a vacuum and repeat
> the fine phrases and edifying sentiments a few literary people have manufactured
> for you: but you know as well as I do that your morality is tolerated only on the
> assumption that nothing is to come of it. Your Christmas carols about peace and
> goodwill to men are very pretty; but you order cannons from me just the same.
> You ring out the old, ring in the new: that is, you discard muzzleloaders and
> introduce breechloaders. Barbara converts laborers whose conversion dont
> matter, because they have no responsibility and no power; but she does not con-
> vert the Secretary of State for war. Euripides abhors war, he says; but he will not
> stop it by Greek verses. It can be stopped only by a mighty power which is not
> in his class room.[9]

Undershaft soon makes it clear that this power is the power of bombs.

Liberal intellectuals frequently distrust power and decry the use of force.
In so doing, they overlook that the authority of governments in liberal de-
mocracies rests on the police and army as surely as in any authoritarian state.
Shaw, speaking through Undershaft, defines a government as a body of men
with the courage to kill. Stephen, the conventionally-minded parliamen-
tarian, must himself be as ready to kill his political opponents as Caesar,
Cromwell, Washington, Lincoln, and Stalin were to kill theirs. Being a totally conventional young man with his head stuffed full of moral clichés and
a conviction of the divinely righteous nature of upper-class British interests,
he will kill stupidly and senselessly. How little his high-mindedness represents anything in the way of real scruples we see when the Undershaft party
arrives at the factory. Stephen, who has earlier expressed priggish horror
at his father's business, is now all admiration for this triumph of industry.

[9] British Museum MS 50616D, folios 35–36. This first "Irish" version is dated "Derry
8/9/1905."

But for the intellectual humanitarian and the former Salvationist the reconciliation to the factory of death is not so easy. The last scene of the play is at once an intellectual argument and a religious wooing of the souls of Cusins and Barbara by Mephistopheles-Dionysos-Undershaft. Cusins may admit that force is the basis of present-day society and that a capitalist state exists for the sake of protecting the rich man's dividends, just as the Salvation Army inadvertently plays into the hands of the rich by diverting the attention of the poor from revolution. But perhaps the answer is not to use force against force but to abandon force completely and to appeal for social justice on the grounds of Christianity, love, and mercy. No: Undershaft inexorably insists, government and rule mean killing: all political progress (not to mention political conservatism) rests ultimately on the willingness to kill.

Let us see if we can determine exactly what Undershaft means before we raise the cry of "unresolved paradox." I think that Shaw's intention is clear enough if we give full weight to what Undershaft says in the final scene, but since these relatively straightforward statements have been for most people as music to the deaf and sunsets to the blind, we may profitably take another look at the unpublished manuscript version of the play in the possession of the British Museum. Here Undershaft does not, I think, depart from any of the positions he maintains in the final version of the play, but he is perhaps more explicit:

Undershaft (grimly). —Why do [the poor] starve? Because they have been taught that it is their duty to starve. "Blessed are the poor in spirit"—eh? But now mark my highest claim, my proudest boast. To those who are worth their salt as slaves I give the means of life. But to those who will not or cannot sell their manhood—to those who will not stand tamely by and suffer their country to be ravaged by poverty and preyed upon by skulkers and idlers—I give the means of death. Poverty and slavery have stood up for centuries to sermons and Bibles and leading articles and pious platitudes: they will not stand up to my machine guns. Let every English citizen resolve to kill or be killed sooner than tolerate the existence of one poor person or one idler on the English soil; and poverty and slavery will vanish tomorrow.

Barbara. —Killing! Is that your remedy?

Undershaft. —It is the final test of conviction, the sole lever strong enough to lift a whole people. It is the right of every man who will stake his own life on his faith. It is the only way of saying Must.[10]

Here it is perhaps natural to ask whether Shaw, in giving Undershaft these speeches, was expressing his own political philosophy or merely presenting an idea, so to speak, dramatically. Any doubts on this subject may be resolved by consideration of another British Museum manuscript, that

[10] British Museum MS 50616D, folio 18.

which contains Shaw's notes for a lecture on Darwin delivered to the Fabian Society in 1906, the year after the production of *Major Barbara*:

> Revolutions, remember, can only be made by men and women with courage enough to meet the ferocity and pugnacity of the common soldier and vanquish it. Do not delude ourselves with any dream of a peaceful evolution of Capitalism into Socialism, of automatic Liberal Progress, of the conciliation of our American bosses, and South African Landlords and British county society and Pall Mall military caste by the Fabian Society. The man who is not a Socialist is quite prepared to fight for his private property, or at least pay someone else to fight for him. He has no doubt whatever of the necessity and morality of such warfare. . . .
>
> We must clear our minds from cant and cowardice on this subject. It is true that the old barricade revolutionists were childishly and romantically wrong in their methods; and the Fabians were right in making an end of them and formulating constitutional Socialism. But nothing is as constitutional as fighting. Rents cannot be collected now without force, nor are they socialized—to the small extent to which they are already socialized—without force.[11]

Shaw is here appealing to history to verify Undershaft's statement that "the ballot paper that really governs us is the paper that has a bullet wrapped up in it." The Commune of 1871 had demonstrated the willingness of the proprietorial class to fight for their property rights. Later in this same Fabian lecture Shaw argues that the classic instance of non-violent change, the passage of the Reform Bill of 1832, is really an instance in favor of his view; for the Reform Bill passed only when the temper of the English nation reached the point where it was clearly a choice between passing the bill and facing a revolution.

I have called the last act a religious wooing of souls. Undershaft, seeing in Cusins the brains and sensitivity he thinks necessary in anyone who is to run a factory of death (or let us say, a democratic, or any other kind of state) offers him the management of the munitions work. The intelligentsia is to undertake the responsibilities of political power, that is, the power of life and death over millions. Cusins finds himself in the position of a famous predecessor of academic fame; Mephistopheles has once again put in a bid for a professor's soul, and though Cusins, wiser than Faust, realizes that he has already sold his soul for his professorship, this does not make his dilemma less cruel.

For Barbara's engagement to Cusins is both a love match and something more again. Their marriage is to be a religious marriage in a sense of devoting them to something beyond themselves, to "larger loves and diviner dreams than the fireside ones." Their understanding is that unless their marriage can foster this religious side of themselves they are to part and seek other mates, or join the legion of the world's celibate saints and philosophers.

---

[11] British Museum, MS 50661, folios 81–82.

If Cusins elects to sell his soul to Undershaft he thus jeopardizes his relation with Barbara, who is first of all a "salvationist" (in an unsectarian sense) and only secondly a fiancée.

At this point Shaw turns to an episode from real life to solve the dilemma. When an idealistic student[12] of Murray's set out for the Greco-Turkish War in 1897, Murray had given the young man, not a copy of Plato's *Republic*, but a revolver. Shaw ascribes this incident to Cusins, and makes Undershaft seize upon it to demonstrate to the professor that he is, for all his hatred of war, committed to the side of the industrialist. Cusins is forced to concur, and declares that he will choose the "reality and power" of the factory of death, even if it means losing Barbara.

But Barbara, for all her talk about turning her back on wickedness, can no more turn away from life than can Cusins. Now she will be able to preach to the well-fed, self-respecting men and women in Undershaft's model factory-town and know that, when they abandon their snobbishness and self-ishness for higher ends, they are not simply being tempted by the bribe of bread. She has regained her faith and courage: the enthusiasm of the new Dionysianism possesses her and she goes "right up into the skies," saved for-ever from the fate she has most dreaded, the boredom and triviality of the genteel drawing room.

[12] The young man was H. N. Brailsford; see *An Unfinished Autobiography*, p. 97.

Bernard Shaw:
The Face Behind the Mask

by Robert Brustein

Behind Shaw's concern with the Superhuman—the whole complex of messianic Shavianism—is a profound and bitter existential revolt. . . . For Shaw is not simply dissatisfied with certain human activities; he sometimes seems to be in rebellion against the very nature of human existence. The bodiless character of Shaw's Superman—not to mention Shaw's own vegetarianism, teetotalism, and abstention from sexual intercourse after his marriage—indicates a kind of Swiftian disgust at the human body and its functions. And though, like most comic writers, Shaw is often able to transform these personal feelings into ironic amusement at the dualistic nature of man, he is, as a Utopian philosopher, apparently unable to accept man's animality as a permanent fact of life. Strindberg, finally coming to terms with the same feelings, was able to universalize his revulsion at "the dirt of life" in the excremental vision of his art. But Shaw, concerned with a "higher purpose" than this, will neither explore his existential rebellion nor even acknowledge it. Nevertheless, it probably determines the shape of his Utopia in *Back to Methuselah;* and his outrage at human limitation undoubtedly determines the characteristics of his Superman. Thus, despite his pretense at destroying illusions, Shaw cannot accept the reality of his own feelings. And thus, he refuses to see what Arnold called "the object as in itself it really is."

He is, in fact, subject to the granddaddy of all illusions—one, ironically, that he had already described in *The Quintessence of Ibsenism:*

> The king of terrors, Death, was the Arch-Inexorable: Man could not bear the dread of that. He must persuade himself that Death can be propitiated, circumvented, abolished. How he fixed the mask of personal immortality on the face of

death for this purpose we know. . . . Thus he became an idealist, and remained so until he dared to begin pulling the masks off and looking the spectres in the face—dared, that is, to be more and more a realist.

If Shaw is too much of a "realist" to don the mask of personal immortality, he is too much of an "idealist" to face the "dread" of the "Arch-Inexorable." And so he tries to propitiate, circumvent, and abolish death through a mask of his own invention—voluntary longevity. Philosophy, according to Montaigne, consists in learning how to die; but death has no place in Shaw's philosophy, since it calls an end to progress, and mocks all human aspiration. The ageless Ancient proceeds from the imagination of a man unable to look his "spectres in the face," lest he be forced back into existential despair.

Shaw admits as much by the imperative nature of his phrasing. "We can and *must* live longer." "Professional science *must* cease to mean the nonsense of Weismann and the atrocities of Pavlov." We "*must* renounce magic and yet accept miracle." Such imperatives suggest how Shaw continually reverts to the consoling and the necessary, rather than to the true. If he *must* believe that all the theories, opinions, and facts which contradict his doctrine are "delusions," he cannot prove that the delusions are not his own. Temperamentally unable to contemplate a permanent state of imperfectibility, Shaw is finally forced back into simple expressions of faith:

> We must either embrace Creative Evolution or fall into the bottomless pit of an utterly destroying pessimism. . . . Discouragement does in fact mean death; and it is better to cling to the hoariest of the old savage-creators than to abandon all hope in a world of "angry apes," and perish in despair like Shakespear's Timon.

This is as close to an admission of emotional desperation as Shaw is likely to come. Confronted with the Arch-Inexorable (Shaw, significantly, identifies discouragement with death), he must turn away his face and seek out utilitarian illusions by which to survive.

Shaw's determination to keep his mask firmly fixed over his anguished features can be clearly observed in his remarks about *Too True To Be Good* (1932). In all other respects a pleasant light comedy, this work is intermittently suffused with the author's almost nihilistic bitterness on the subjects of the cruelty and madness of World War I, the futility of the Geneva negotiations, the aimlessness of the young, and the spiritual dislocation caused by Einstein's universe ("All is caprice; the calculable world has become incalculable"). And the last speech of the play, the concluding sermon of Shaw's protagonist, Aubrey, is a moving confession of messianic bankruptcy:

> I am by nature and destiny a preacher. I am the new Ecclesiastes. But I have no Bible, no creed: the war has shot both out of my hands. . . . I must have affirmations to preach. Without them the young will not listen to me; for even the young

grow tired of denials. . . . I am ignorant; I have lost my nerve and am intimidated; all I know is that I must find the way of life, for myself and all of us, or we
shall surely perish. And meanwhile my gift has possession of me: I must preach
and preach and preach no matter how late the hour and how short the day, no
matter whether I have nothing to say—

The tone of personal disillusionment is strong, and the autobiographical note
is unmistakable; but when critics made the obvious connections, Shaw
vigorously repudiated them, declaring that Aubrey's despair "is not my
despair," and that he had never lost his messianic beliefs: "I affirm, on the
contrary, that never during my lifetime has the lot of mankind seemed more
hopeful, and the beginnings of a new civilization more advanced." Shaw
can look for a moment into the bottomless pit, but it is not long before he is
whistling up his spirits again. His messianic rebellion is his last refuge, his
Utopian idealism his last escape, from the tragic impasse of modern existence.

It is for the same reason that Shaw ignores the more depressing implications of nineteenth-century thought. His embrace of Creative Evolution
seems like the last desperate gamble of a Victorian rationalist confronted
with a mechanical and determined world. Since Shavianism assumes an
ordered, reasoned, and coherent universe, Shaw must adopt mystical and
irrational principles in order to maintain his assumptions; and despite his
affectation of a "scientific method," Creative Evolution is neither scientific
nor methodical. Thus, he rejects Darwin not on empirical evidence, but on
the grounds that Darwinism inspires pessimism: "What damns Darwinian
Natural Selection as a creed," he declares, "is that it takes hope out of
evolution and substitutes a paralysing fatalism which is utterly discouraging.
As Butler put it, it 'banishes mind from the universe.' " Still fleeing from
discouragement, Shaw puts mind back in the universe in the form of the
Life Force—that amiable fiction which seems to be occupied exclusively
with human betterment and social perfection, and which resembles nothing
so much as the smiling God of Voltaire's Doctor Pangloss.

Shaw is just as unable to accept the concept of a malevolent or determined
man as to accept the concept of a determined and mindless universe. Though
he follows Ibsen in twitting the liberals and ridiculing their sentimental
ideals, Shavianism is itself based on a familiar Liberal illusion: "It is quite
useless," Shaw declares, using his characteristic utilitarian phrasing, "to
declare that men are born free if you deny that they are born good." Ibsen
was forced to modify his subjective faith in the will, and acknowledge the
power of fate. But Shaw, still riding the first crest of Romanticism, can
tolerate no limitation on human possibility—which is why he repudiates
the religious concepts of imperfectibility and predestination, and the scientific concepts of aggression and determinism. Thus, in the century of Darwin,
Shaw's characters are never victimized by their biological inheritance. And
thus, in the century of Freud, they are totally free from any real anguish,

suffering, or neurosis. The Shavian soul is generally a sunlit soul—empty of menace, without fatality. If the unconscious exists in Shaw's writings, it exists largely as a subject for discussion. Made self-conscious—reduced to analytical terms—it loses all its darkness and its threat.

This is not to say that Shaw completely ignores the aggressive side of man. It is one of the major subjects under discussion in the Hell sequence of *Man and Superman;* and the Devil's descriptions of human greed, ruthlessness, and cruelty are among the most eloquent in literature. Still, like his protagonist, Don Juan, Shaw is inclined to attribute such things not to human evil, but to human cowardice, stupidity, or prejudice; and he almost never shows them in action. "Crime, like disease, is not interesting," he affirms in the preface to *Saint Joan,* proceeding to dramatize (through the repentance of "mad-dog" De Stogumber) his conviction that whatever passes for human cruelty is really the consequence of ignorance. Shaw's kindness is one of his most appealing qualities, but it makes him incapable of appreciating human defect, while his need to believe in limitless possibilities for mankind continually binds him to the darker, more unredeemable side of human character.

Thus, as late as 1944, during the most terrible war in the history of man, Shaw is still insisting that the "pessimism" of Ecclesiastes, Shakespeare, and Swift is based on a misreading of the human soul:

> [Reformers] all agree that you cannot have a new sort of world without a new sort of Man. A change in heart they call it. But the Bible tells us that the heart of Man is deceitful above all things and desperately wicked. . . .
>
> Nevertheless if this book is to be worth writing or reading, I must assume that all this pessimism and cynicism is a delusion caused, not only by ignorance of contemporary facts but, in so far as they are known, by drawing wrong conclusions from them. It is not true that all the atrocities of Capitalism are the expression of human vice and evil will; on the contrary, they are largely the product of domestic virtue, of patriotism, of philanthropy, of enterprise, of progressiveness, of all sorts of socially valuable qualities. . . . With such human material, we can produce a dozen new worlds when we learn both the facts and the lessons in political science the facts can teach.
>
> (*Everybody's Political What's What*)

Here, again, we can observe how Shaw's ideas are motivated by a utilitarian imperative ("if this book *is to be worth* writing or reading, *I must assume*"), and how this imperative forces him into wishful thinking. For the "contemporary facts" which Shaw would have us understand would now have to include the Nazi extermination centers, saturation bombing, and Soviet slave labor camps (Hiroshima and the spectacle of two mass powers threatening each other with nuclear extinction are still to come); yet, he is still affirming the essentially philanthropic nature of man. One can see why Leon Trotsky expressed the wish that "the Fabian fluid that ran in [Shaw's] veins might have been strengthened by even so much as five per cent of the blood of Jonathan Swift." Despite his Marxist orientation, Shaw cannot accept Marx's analysis of the darker human motives behind capitalism. For although he is wont to expend considerable indignation against the "system," he invariably exempts the system-makers from his indictment,[1] providing them with the same "socially valuable qualities" which he hopes to utilize in his new world. In short, Shaw *must* believe in human decency. Without this belief, his hope in the future is misplaced; and all he can look forward to is apocalypse.

We can sympathize with Shaw's dilemma, since we share it. If Shaw has illusions, they are the illusions of mankind in an appalling world; and, as a social philosopher, they permit him to function in a productive manner. Yet, the function of the social philosopher is quite different from the function of the artist, since the *modus vivendi* of the one is often a form of dishonesty to the other. Shaw's need to believe in the possibilities of redemption rob his drama of an essential artistic office: the ruthless examination of all illusions, no matter how unpleasant. Eric Bentley, defending Shaw's optimism, asserts that no other philosophical attitude is possible: "If man is not a moral animal, let us all shoot ourselves. If he *is* a moral animal, then pessimism is an irresponsible pose"—but this is to adopt Shaw's utilitarian posture. The function of the artist is not to console, not to adopt a "responsible" pose, not to support "optimism" or "pessimism"—but to reveal, relentlessly, the truth that lies in the heart of man and in the heart of the universe. Some of the greatest works of art, in fact, have achieved greatness by exposing things which *might* tempt us to shoot ourselves, while elevating us with the prospect of human courage and nobility in the face of a terrible reality.

Such works—*Oedipus, King Lear, Rosmersholm, The Dream Play, The Ice Man Cometh*—are generally tragic dramas, and it would seem that I am chiding Shaw for failing to be a tragic artist. I am not. But I am suggesting that Shaw's failure to penetrate his own existential rebellion has robbed him of a tragic vision, without which his philosophy is trivial and even his comedy seems too narrow and restricted. Without a "sense of horror," as Bentley concedes, Shaw is excluded from the company of such great comic drama-

---

[1] Although Shaw attacks prostitution, slum-landlordism, professional imposture, and capitalism, he very rarely attacks prostitutes, slum landlords, professional impostors, or capitalists—probably because the only motives he seems to accept as valid are economic ones. In *Mrs. Warren's Profession*, for example, Mrs. Warren is a brothel madam purely out of financial need. And in *Getting Married*, Shaw declares that prostitution has no other source than "the underpayment and ill-treatment of women who try to earn an honest living." This is in direct conflict with all studies of prostitutes and prostitution. In Shaw's world, however, there are very few psychological or emotional determinants, which is why he can continue to believe that an equal distribution of wealth will automatically eradicate all such social evils.

tists as Ben Jonson and Molière, neither of whom ignored the less consoling aspects of human character. And his insensitivity to the metaphysical side of man even excludes him from the company of the great modern dramatists of revolt. Too often, Shaw's reformist impulses and imperative needs dull his apprehension of Necessity, so that, like Arthur Miller, he sometimes tends to identify tragedy with social exploitation.[2] For like Arthur Miller, Shaw envisions a reconciled society in which there will *be* no more tragedy— or mystery either, since all human problems will be already solved. Looking forward to what will be, Shavianism can neither understand nor come to terms with what already is.

Thus, while Shaw exalts, exploits, and publicizes the rebel movement, he is totally unable to accept its darker side. The gospel of Shavianism channels the energies of revolt into social-political philosophical uplift. The irony of Shaw's sense of "higher purpose" is that it imposes crucial restrictions on his art, since it usually prevents him from examining the bitter rebellion in his own heart. Although he finds "the true joy of life" in being "a force of Nature instead of a feverish selfish little clod of ailments and grievances complaining that the world will not devote itself to making you happy," it is just this note of personal discontent that we miss in his work—for through this, we could better understand the unhappiness of all men. Shaw's perpetual cheer and optimism do not come easily to him, but they have become, in recent years, his most irritating qualities. If, at the same time that his fame is rising in commercial circles, he seems to be receding from our consciousness, this is perhaps because his buoyant mood is no longer a suitable response to the actualities of our time. In Shavianism, we can see— just as clearly as in the technological vision of H. G. Wells—the utter bankruptcy of the progressive Victorian temper in an age of confusion, upheaval, and ominous threat.

Shaw's messianic philosophy has alienated him from us; the myths of Shavianism neither console nor convince; his "scientific religion" has come to look neither like science nor religion; and his own illusions seem just as pronounced as the ones he sets out to expose—but there are still areas of Shaw's work which remain perfectly valid. Shavianism may seem just as quackish as Swedenborgianism—but like Swedenborgianism, it can some-

---

[2] "True tragedy," Shaw declares, is "being used by personally-minded men for purposes which you recognize as base"—in short, tragedy is the result of social exploitation. Compare Miller, who writes: "I think the tragic feeling is evoked in us when we are in the presence of a character who is ready to lay down his life, if need be, to secure one thing— his sense of human dignity. From Orestes to Hamlet, Medea to Macbeth, the underlying struggle is that of an individual attempting to regain his 'rightful' position in society." Miller's sociological definition is much more simpleminded than Shaw's, and Shaw never falls into Miller's sentimentalization of common humanity—but neither writer is able to understand the metaphysical basis of tragedy.

times be turned to imaginative use. If we regard Shavianism as a source for Shaw's dramatic metaphors (somewhat like the theosophical concepts of Yeats), then its quackeries seem less important; and if we regard it as a technique for demonstrating the spiritual and moral inadequacy of traditional creeds, then it even serves a valuable illustrative function. Actually, Shaw handles his hatred of reality in two distinct ways. As a revolutionary reformer, he registers his revolt against the real by pursuing the ideal in politics (Socialism) and philosophy (Creative Evolution). But, as an artist, he registers this revolt by recreating reality in the ideal form of art. Shaw may disapprove of those dramatists whose rebellion does not work towards positive goals, but his own rebellion is most compelling when it is least constructive. As Shaw himself understands, "Construction cumbers the ground with institutions made by busybodies. Destruction clears it and gives us breathing space and liberty." Like most artists who construct redemptive systems (Lawrence, for example), Shaw is convincing only in the act of denial. Behind the affirmative yea-sayer is a man who knows how to say no; behind the evangelical quacksalver stands a gifted diagnostician of modern maladies.

As a matter of fact, only a small part of Shaw's creative energies are channeled into Shavianism; one can hardly say that the bulk of his drama is dominated by a philosophical purpose. Accounting for the absence of ideology in his early plays, Shaw says: "Like Shakespear I had to write potboilers until I was rich enough to satisfy my evolutionary appetite (or, as they say, give way to my inspiration)," and he includes among such "shameless potboilers" *Pygmalion*, *Fanny's First Play*, and *You Never Can Tell* (he might have added *The Philanderer*, *Arms and the Man*, *The Devil's Disciple*, and *Overruled*). For a messianic prophet with such serious intentions, Shaw certainly enjoys a large number of holidays in his work; and one begins to suspect that his Puritan disapproval of the "mere artist" may reflect his self-disapproval as a writer of frivolous light comedies. Most of these comedies are still quite delightful; but they are generally free from any radical questioning, since their form is not hardy enough to support much philosophy. Like Oscar Wilde and W. S. Gilbert, Shaw bases his comic technique on the inversion of Victorian conventions, but while he is often outrageous, he is seldom much more: nothing in his work will bring a blush to the cheek of the young person.[3] Similarly, while Shaw is relentless in his ridicule of

[3] Richard M. Ohmann, in *Shaw: The Style and the Man*, demonstrates, through a study of Shavian style, that the author often cultivates outrage for its own sake, and owes much of "his enormous popularity" to this ritualized unconventionality: "His denunciations of the old social order burned the ears of the pre-World War I generation, but they stirred the blood, too, and offered forbidden amusement to the more adventurous Victorians and Edwardians. . . . He was still crying the same blasphemies twenty, thirty, forty years later, though, and unconventionality is a garment that can wear thin." Ohmann's book, though primarily a semantic analysis, is one of the most intelligent of recent books on Shaw.

"Sardoodledom," the great majority of his comedies revolve around a love plot borrowed from the well-made play—usually resolved conventionally, if for unconventional reasons. The artist in Shaw is sometimes so far from being a revolutionary that he seems to be a "mere" entertainer, creating works which are rescued from Boulevard conventionality only by a dazzling style and lively ideas.

Shaw's more serious plays, on the other hand, do embody Shavian principles; but these are usually treated in a highly ambiguous manner. Politically, for example, his dramas are surprisingly neutral. As Eric Bentley observes: "The fact is that while Shaw is a socialist in his treatises, and perhaps chiefly a socialist, he realizes . . . that neither socialism, nor capitalism, nor feudalism, nor any other ism can be the basis of an art, even so social an art as comedy. . . ." [4] Shaw may believe that his plays are written to "influence public opinion," but these works are usually too complicated to evoke a simple response, for like the plays of all the better rebel dramatists, they involve the author's revolt in a shifting dialectic of attitudes. In a letter to the Marxist, Hyndman, Shaw clearly defines this dialectic:

> You are an economic revolutionary on a medieval basis of chivalry—Bayard educated by Marx. I am a moral revolutionary, interested, not in the class war, but in the struggle between human vitality and the artificial system of morality, and distinguishing, not between capitalist and proletarian, but between moralist and natural historian.

In another place, Shaw affirms that, as a dramatist, he deals "in the tragicomic irony of the conflict between real life and the romantic imagination." In both cases, he is partly describing the clash between his own rebellion and reality. If we assume that the "romantic imagination" he speaks of is his own Utopianism—and the "artificial system of morality" he refers to is the system of Shavianism—then we can see that he is usually dramatizing his own inner conflicts: the Platonist versus the Aristotelian, the revolutionary idealist versus the pragmatic realist, the Socialist versus the Vitalist, the Romantic versus the Classicist. Shaw once told Stephen Winsten that he would never have written plays if he had not been "a chaos of contradictions," for these contradictions, bothersome to an ideologist, are made to order for the drama. In consequence, no matter how wishful, fantastic, or visionary Shavianism may be, Shaw, in his drama, usually disciplines his "romantic imagination," confronting it with an unchanging, and sometimes unchangeable social order.

---

[4] Contributing to a symposium on the problem play, Shaw observes: "To this day your great dramatic poet is never a socialist, nor an individualist, nor a positivist, nor a materialist, nor any other sort of 'ist,' though he comprehends all 'isms,' and is generally quoted and claimed by all the sections as an adherent."

Take *Man and Superman*. Surrounded by an extensive preface on one side and a full-length revolutionary manifesto on the other—embodying a long "Shavio-Socratic dialogue" in the midst of the play, and a good deal of polemicizing throughout—the work would seem to be a shotgun blast of pure Shavianism, scattering ideology in all directions. Yet, unlike *Back to Methuselah*, where Shaw's "romantic imagination" is unfettered and unrestrained, *Man and Superman* brings his rebellion in conflict with flesh-and-blood reality, balancing the idealism of the philosophical moralist against the neutrality of the "natural historian."

The Epistle Dedicatory lays down the line that the play is *supposed* to follow. Dared by the aesthete-critic, Arthur Bingham Walkley, to write a Don Juan play, Shaw has decided to take up this mischievous suggestion, but he will turn it to his own ends; characteristically, he is preparing to invert (and domesticate) the traditional Don Juan character. From the Tirso de Molina *Burlador de Sevilla* to the Mozart–Da Ponte *Don Giovanni*, Don Juan has always been represented as a libertine and seducer who is finally punished by supernatural powers for his various sexual crimes. Shaw, on the other hand, is more attracted to the philosophical implications of the Don Juan story. Since Juan, while pursuing his own desires, inadvertently breaks moral, canon, and statute law, Shaw elects him as the agent of revolutionary Shavianism, envisioning him as a kind of Faustian rebel against God. Transformed into a messianic idealist and metaphysical saint, Shaw's Don Juan, therefore, both anticipates and predicts the coming of the God-defying Superman.

By this subtle trick, Shaw manages to ignore the sexual aspect of Don Juan entirely, for in Shaw's mind this totally unselfconscious libertine takes on the character of a contemplative rebel hero who has progressed past his childish passions to a love of "purpose and principles." Though he manages to extract the amoral, promiscuous element from the legend, however, he does not totally extract its sexual quality, for he transfers Don Juan's amorousness to "Doña Juana," the husband-hunting female. Changing a legend of rape and seduction into a story of courtship and marriage, therefore, Shaw has the opportunity to reflect on a subject close to his heart—the character of the modern "unwomanly woman." Observing that "Man is no longer, like Don Juan, victor in the duel of sex," Shaw adds:

> Woman must marry because the race must perish without her travail. . . .
> It is assumed that the woman must wait, motionless, until she is wooed. Nay,
> she often does wait motionless. That is how the spider waits for the fly. But the
> spider spins her web. And if the fly, like my hero, shews a strength that promises
> to extricate him, how swiftly does she abandon her pretense of passiveness, and
> openly fling coil after coil about him until he is secured for ever!

All this talk about the spider-woman, treacherously lying in wait for a male quarry and imprisoning him for her own purposes, sounds dangerous. And in the work of Schopenhauer and Nietzsche, where it was first formulated, and Strindberg, where it was first dramatized, the idea *is* dangerous. But Shaw swiftly takes the horror out of the perception. His spider-woman is not the dominating, amoral, and conscienceless *belle dame sans merci* of the Romantic agony, but rather the independent, intelligent, and well-mannered gentlewoman of the Victorian imagination, whose "unwomanliness" consists mainly in her active pursuit of a husband. Thus, Shaw adapts the Don Juan legend to the legend of Venus and Adonis, examining not the ruthless exploitation of the woman by the libertine seducer but rather "the tragicomic love chase of the man by the woman." Lest the reader suspect that this purely Romantic subject is to be treated in a purely Romantic manner, Shaw adapts both legends to Shavianism, arguing that the whole comedy is played out for a higher purpose, the eventual evolution of the Superman through eugenic breeding. The marriage of John Tanner and Ann Whitefield, therefore—though a perfectly conventional conclusion of Romantic comedy—becomes another myth of the Life Force. Through such marriages man will breed that political capacity which will save him from the ruinous failures of democracy.

In his Epistle Dedicatory, in short, Shaw is single-mindedly devoted to advancing the gospel of Shavianism, elevating his comedy into a "play for a pit of philosophers." The Don Juan in Hell sequence—inserted into Act IV as the dream of Tanner and Mendoza—serves a similar function in a more double-minded way. By turning the Conan Doyle brigand, Mendoza, into the wily, hedonistic Devil, and Tanner into a contemplative Don Juan, Shaw initiates a debate on the virtues of Shavianism, elaborating on the various issues raised in his preface—reality and the ideal, man and woman, reason and emotion, man and Superman. The central device of the sequence is a Blakean inversion of the traditional concepts of Heaven and Hell. But where Blake used this device to express his diabolism and sensualism, concluding that "the tigers of wrath are wiser than the horses of instruction," Shaw imagines his hero trying to escape the sensual pleasures of the Devil's palace into a paradise of pure thought. The difference between the Devil and Don Juan rests mainly in their divergent interpretations of the universe. The Devil—assuming a universe without mind or purpose—holds that emotions rule men's lives and that history takes the form of an eternal recurrence. Ruling out progress, therefore, he has become a "romantic idealist," who posits physical pleasure and the cultivation of the arts as the highest goods. Don Juan, on the other hand, believes in a purposeful universe ruled by the Life Force: "That is, the working within me of Life's incessant aspirations to higher organization, wider, deeper, intenser self-consciousness, and clearer self-understanding." Like the "masters of reality" in Heaven, therefore, he has become a confirmed Shavian, one who believes in free will, the power of the mind, and the capacity of man to transform himself and his environment. If the Devil is right, then evolution is an illusion, marriage serves no particular purpose, and man's essentially destructive nature will climax in his self-destruction. If Don Juan is right, then evolution is a fact, marriage is an instrument of the Life Force, and man's malleable nature will eventually respond to reason. Because of Don Juan's concern with what will be and the Devil's concern with what is, we are not always sure who is the master of reality and who the Romantic idealist. But though Shaw uses loaded terms to suggest his own sympathies, he does not resolve the debate; and the Devil's diagnosis is made just as persuasive as Don Juan's hopes for the future. At the end, Don Juan—asserting his belief that "To be in hell is to drift, to be in heaven is to steer"—goes off to join the other heavenly pilots in their contemplation of a higher life, while the Devil returns to his duties. But while each antagonist remains unconvinced by the other, one person is converted to the "Life to come"—Doña Ana. Echoing Nietzsche's admonition to women ("Let your hope say: 'May I bear the Superman' "), she goes off to seek a father for the Higher Man.

If one were only to read the Epistle Dedicatory and the dream debate—not to mention *The Revolutionist's Handbook*, with its Nietzschean apothegms, Wildean epigrams, and Marxist admonitions—one might easily assume that the play proper was simply a dramatic illustration of these Shavian questions. Almost the opposite, however, is true. Since the play is concrete, contemporary, and ironic, rather than discursive, visionary, and abstract, it has a different quality altogether than the imposing material that surrounds it. The banter of Shaw's comedy, and its exuberant lightheartedness, contrast strongly with the more earnest tone of his prose; and many of the characters are peripheral to his central philosophical theme, being stock Shavian comic types. Roebuck Ramsden, for example, embodies Shaw's perennial satire on the Liberal Briton, the personification of dead conventions and outmoded ideals; 'Enry Straker, the class-conscious automobile mechanic, is a satire on the engineering hero of H. G. Wells; Mendoza, the lovelorn brigand, who turns to Socialism out of unrequited passion, is a satire on amoristic idealists; and Hector Malone, Sr., is a satire on the Irish-American millionaire, revenging himself on the English by buying up their hereditary titles and stately mansions. As for the Violet-Malone, Jr., subplot, this, as Eric Bentley tells us, has a structural function, being an inversion of the main plot (Violet begins with her man and must acquire her fortune; Ann begins with her fortune and must acquire her man)—meanwhile permitting Shaw to recapitulate his old idea (first advanced in *Widowers' Houses*) that a sound marriage must rest on a practical economic foundation.

The central action does develop some of Shaw's philosophical themes, but in a highly circumscribed and limited manner. John Tanner, though based on the gentleman Marxist, H. M. Hyndman, is much more occupied with the doctrine of the Life Force than with Marxist politics, and so he is the prime agent of revolutionary Shavianism. Still, as a rebel, he seems very tame. Considering Shaw's attitude towards libertinage, we are hardly surprised to find that his Don Juan is not only indifferent to women, but actively afraid of them. But if Tanner is no Don Juan, then neither is he that Faustian insurgent and God-killer whom Shaw speaks of in his preface. Shaw concedes as much when he tells Walkley that he has not bothered to put all the "tub-thumping" of the Epistle Dedicatory into the play: "I have only made my Don Juan a political pamphleteer, and given you his pamphlet by way of appendix." Shaw's dramatic instinct is quite sound. The atmosphere of the play proper is much too frothy to bear much "tub-thumping." And while Tanner's ideas may seem revolutionary in the appendix, the most radical thing he is capable of in the play is a willingness to tolerate premarital pregnancy—something designed to shock only the most conventional Victorian figures like Ramsden and Octavius.

Actually, Shaw is less occupied with advancing the cause of Shavianism, in *Man and Superman*, than with etching ironic contrasts between idea and character. "I shatter creeds and demolish idols," boasts Tanner, but he is, at heart, an eminently respectable gentleman of the upper middle class, differing from Ramsden in degree rather than in kind. Tanner implies as much when, defending his character against slander, he cries: "Thief, liar, forger, adulterer, perjurer, glutton, drunkard? Not one of these names fits me. You have to fall back on my deficiency in shame"—which is to say, his only rebellious characteristic is his intellectual impudence. Yet, this impudence remains strictly verbal; even Tanner is easy to shock. For all his talk about the predatory instincts of women—so glibly communicated to that cardboard lover, Octavius—Tanner behaves according to the strictest Victorian sexual standards. Though he is inclined to describe Ann's designs in the language of Schopenhauer and Strindberg (he is always commenting on her hypocrisy, bullying, lies, coquetry, and amorality, besides comparing her with such male-devouring insects as the spider and the bee), he is continually surprised when she does not act like the most conventional Victorian maiden.

Ann, too, seems unconventional only by contrast with an extremely outmoded ideal of feminine behavior. She is hardly the "dutiful" daughter that Ramsden thinks her, but neither is she that "Lady Mephistopheles" that Tanner speaks of. One has only to compare this charming coquette with Strindberg's Laura or Ibsen's Hedda or Chekhov's Arkadina to see that she has been created not by an antifeminist or a realist or a "natural historian," but rather by an archfeminist with a powerful admiration for women. Certainly, Ann's "unwomanliness" is not a fault but a virtue: she tells lies merely in order to win the man she loves. Despite the countless speeches in the play about the ruthlessness of sexual relations, therefore, *Man and Superman* confronts us not with a tragic combat between "the artist-man and the mother-woman" but rather with a classical opposition between two gifted sex antagonists who, like Benedick and Beatrice or Mirabel and Millamant, are ideally suited for the marriage which inevitably will come. Shaw lets his characters discuss the one action, but actually dramatizes the other. This gives the play intellectual depth and makes for ironic contrasts as well.

Reduced to its action, then, *Man and Superman* is too lightweight to support Shaw's doctrines. Rather than "a play for a pit of philosophers," it is a Classical comedy on the order of *Much Ado About Nothing* or *The Way of the World*. The presence of Shavianism in the play, however, does account for the wit inversions and satiric humor. Obviously, John Tanner functions not only as a mouthpiece for Shaw's theory of the Life Force, but also as an independent character with foibles of his own. While Octavius, worshiping women as the living embodiments of the Romantic ideal, is Tanner's butt, Tanner, worshiping life in its perpetual struggle upwards, is Shaw's. The doctrine of the Life Force is another form of Romantic idealization, and one of Shaw's purposes in the play is to show how all ideals are invariably mocked by life. The joke on Tanner, of course, is that all the time he is theorizing about the Life Force, he is being ensnared by it, until he is finally enmeshed in that machinery whose cogs and screws he has so accurately described. Thus, Shaw demonstrates how the self-conscious theoretician is caught up, against his will, by an unconscious, irrational force. Tanner's understanding of the transcendent principles of the universe is not defense against their actual workings. His "romantic imagination" is surprised by "real life."

Shaw is actually playing a practical joke on his own "romantic imagination" here. By distancing himself from the Shavian Tanner, he can demonstrate how Shavianism, being mainly intellectual and theoretical, is really inadequate to the thing it describes. For while Jack preaches Vitalism, it is Ann who personifies the Vitalist truths, precisely because she is motivated by instincts and unconscious will. As she tells Tanner, "You seem to understand all the things that I don't understand; but you are a perfect baby in the things I do understand"—one has the intelligence of the head, the other of the heart. And like the Reverend Morell in *Candida*, this windy preacher must be taught the lesson of life. For this reason, Tanner is always being punctured by Ann during his rhetorical flights, a deflation Shaw suggests through his use, in stage directions, of images of escaping air (Tanner "collapses like a pricked balloon," he falls "in ruins," he is "heavily let down," et cetera).[5] At the conclusion of the play, when Tanner, having

---

[5] The puncturing of the rhetorical male by the unwomanly female is a favorite device of Shaw's, as the author admits in the parenthetical remarks with which he concludes *Too True To Be Good:* "The author, though himself a professional talk maker, does not

yielded to the inevitable, is trying to regain control of his fate by making a stump speech on the evils of bourgeois marriage, Ann contributes Shaw's final satiric thrust with her famous "Go on talking, Jack," and the sound of a punctured gasbag is smothered in "universal laughter." Shavianism, too, has been partly smothered in this laughter. For if Shaw, like Tanner, lacks a "negative capability" before the mystery of existence, he is too much of an artist not to satirize himself for it. His aim in *Man and Superman* is not so much to affirm or deny the principles of Shavianism as to show them in collision with reality—to confront a principle of change with the unchanging principle of life.

Unlike *Back to Methuselah*, then, *Man and Superman* has a double function: the prose portions of the work vindicate Shaw's philosophical ideals, while the drama places these ideals in the way of a gentle, mocking humor. The Don Juan in Hell sequence may take the form of a "consoling myth" (Shaw is later to call this section "a dramatic parable of Creative Evolution"), but his command of dialectic is sure enough to let him credit the arguments of the opposition. At this point in his career, Shaw is still able to control his rebellion, keeping the desperate illusions of his Utopian imagination under strong creative restraint.

The joyous exuberance of *Man and Superman* suggests Shaw's confidence at the time it was written. But when he sits down to compose *Heartbreak House* in 1913, England is on the verge of war, and when he completes it, in 1916, the English are committing suicide on the battlefields of France. Unnerved by the war hysteria at home and abroad, and shaking with frustrated bitterness towards pugnacious jingo patriots, Shaw is now inclined to examine human qualities that he had scanted before. Still not prepared to believe in evil, he is no longer so sanguine about man's philanthropic nature; and the brutality, barbarism, and bloodlust emerging from the war have made his distinction between human cowardice and human malevolence a little academic. Undoubtedly, the Devil's arguments—that all of man's ingenuity issues only in instruments of greater destructiveness—are ringing in his ears with more force; and there is real danger that man will exterminate himself before the Superman is able to evolve. For the first time in his career, Shaw is half-inclined to say, Let it come down.

For *Heartbreak House* is permeated with a powerful prophetic fury: the pessimistic tone of the Preface and the black mood of the play suggest that Shaw has come as close as he will ever come to discouragement and despair. In the face of the reality of war, Shaw's Romantic imagination has momentarily been balked; and his Utopianism is in real danger of disappearing

---

believe that the world can be saved by talk alone. He has given the rascal the last word; but his own favorite is the woman of action, who begins by knocking the wind out of the rascal, and ends with a cheerful conviction that the lost dogs always find their way home. So they will, perhaps, if the women go out and look for them."

altogether. Still, he has not repudiated Shavianism, for he is still urging political responsibility on the upper classes, who have been wasting their rightful inheritance in the pursuit of pleasure and amorous dalliance.

It is this group, the leisured, cultured amorists, which Shaw identifies with Heartbreak House—a palace of inertia, built on the stones of deterministic science and loss of will:

> Heartbreak House was far too lazy and shallow to extricate itself from this palace of evil enchantment. It rhapsodized about love; but it believed in cruelty. It was afraid of cruel people; and it saw that cruelty was at least effective. . . . Heartbreak House, in short, did not know how to live, at which point all that was left to it was the boast that at least it knew how to die; a melancholy accomplishment which the outbreak of war presently gave it practically unlimited opportunities of displaying.

The war, in fact, has come about as a consequence of this irresponsibility, for the Heartbreakers, while engaging in useless private amusements, have permitted "power and culture" to fall into "separate compartments." Born to rule, educated and sophisticated (their libraries contain works by all the latest authors, including Wells, Galsworthy, and Shaw), they have handed the government over to the incompetents and the marauders: the Horse-backers (which is to say, the stupid imperialist classes) and the Practical Businessmen (which is to say, those "who become rich by placing their personal interests before those of the country"). The result, according to Shaw, has been an orgy of blood, pugnacity, and lunacy.

Shaw's response to this is to withdraw, partially, from his public concerns into a more personal, private, and poetic form of expression: in certain passages of the play, the existential roots of his rebellion are finally exposed. Certainly, the work seems peculiarly unplanned, as if it had been snatched from the top of the author's unconscious without much effort at order or organization. The plot is crammed with implausible things, proceeding by fits and starts—new entrances, abrupt reversals, and the most peculiar recognition scenes—almost as if in a dream. The characters, too, possess a dreamlike quality—sometimes they lose their individuality in allegory—and occasionally the atmosphere turns mystical, even phantasmagoric, as at the end of the first act, when Shotover and his family gather together for a weird ritual chant (a foretaste of the kind of choral technique T. S. Eliot will use in *The Family Reunion*) on the loss of heroism in life. Frustrations and resentments fill the air, mingled with a general feeling of aimlessness. As Shaw told Archibald Henderson, *Heartbreak House* "began with an atmosphere and does not contain a word that was foreseen before it was written." Certainly the haunted, almost tortured atmosphere of the play—where, instead of the expected Shavian wit, the dialogue is heavily charged with overtones, breaking out of the usual rhetorical balances and Latinate antitheses into an ambiguous, highly charged dramatic poetry—is something totally new to the Shavian drama.

The new mood, the new structure, and the new techniques of *Heartbreak House* owe something to Shaw's new models: turning away from the rationally ordered Ibsenite drama and the compact problem play, Shaw, as he announces in the first paragraph of his Preface, has adopted the more open forms of the Russians. Shaw feels certain intellectual affinities with Tolstoy, who took a moral attitude towards Heartbreak House, and who "was not disposed to leave the house standing if he could bring it down about the ears of its pretty and amiable voluptuaries." Shaw's Tolstoyan moral judgments on his characters are often apparent in his play; and his cataclysmic conclusion shows a similar desire to raze the walls of the house. Still, Shaw could have found Tolstoy's moral and apocalyptic tendencies in Ibsen. The really new element in the play comes from Chekhov—the "fatalist" who "had no faith in these charming people extricating themselves." Growing disillusioned with long-range Shavianism, Shaw is losing faith in his usual forms of revolt. And instead of a consoling myth, revolving around characters with a high sense of purpose, he is here providing a Chekhovian myth of fatalism, revolving around characters with no sense of direction at all—with the result that we are no longer quite so certain of Shaw's convictions about the possibilities of ethical reform.

In short, Shaw remains Shavian insofar as he still continues to judge his characters; but he is also Chekhovian insofar as he is now permitting them an independent life of their own, while "exploiting and even flattering" their charm. Shaw's subtitle—"A Fantasia in the Russian Manner on English Themes"—suggests a certain misunderstanding of Chekhov's technique. For while the "fantasia" (defined by the *Oxford English Dictionary* as "an instrumental composition having the appearance of being extemporaneous . . . in which form is subservient to fancy") describes the structure of *Heartbreak House* and Shaw's later disquisitory plays, it is not an accurate way to characterize Chekhov's carefully hidden plotting. Nevertheless, Shaw has successfully imitated a number of the more superficial Chekhovian characteristics. His new concentration on the group picture, for example, recalls Chekhov's method of discouraging audience identification with a single hero; and like Chekhov, Shaw is now permitting the exposition of plot and character to proceed at a very leisurely tempo. The scene in the garden, at the beginning of Act III, where the pace is retarded by the sleepy reflections of the characters, recalls the second-act opening of *The Cherry Orchard*, permeated with yawns, coughs, and guitar sounds; Ellie Dunn frequently reminds us of Chekhov's young and innocent heroines; and the relationship between Hector and Ariadne—two bored and unloving creatures toying with each other's emotions—is reminiscent of the relationship between Astrov and Yelena in *Uncle Vanya*. Finally, of course, the weird drumming in the air, variously interpreted by Shaw's characters, is very similar to the ominous sound of the broken string in *The Cherry Orchard;* and in both cases, the noise embodies a feeling of doom and finality.

On the other hand, Shaw's moralism remains much more dominant than Chekhov's; and his characters are infinitely more self-conscious and self-aware—so much so, in fact, that they frequently pass judgment on themselves. One could not imagine Astrov saying, as Hector Hushabye says: "We are useless, dangerous, and ought to be abolished." Still unable to suppress his subjective revolt, Shaw is still unable to suppress his comment. For the same reason Shaw includes a quite un-Chekhovian author's surrogate in the person of Captain Shotover—superficially similar to such clownish old men as Sorin and Serebryakov, but really indigenous to the Shavian world. Through Shotover, Shaw is able to express his personal feelings about the wastefulness, idleness, and irresponsibility of his characters, while exhorting them to learn their business as Englishmen and navigate the ship of state. Through Shotover, too, Shaw can communicate his anger at the vileness of the contemporary world and at destructive mankind—the dynamite hoarded by Shotover is meant "to blow up the human race if it goes too far." On the other hand, Shotover is not Shaw, for he is also drifting, vainly trying to stave off his terrible fatigue with life. Stranded between memories of the past and illusions of the future, this half-demented old man takes refuge from the present in idle dreams. Seeking the seventh level of concentration, he can find it only in rum, and drinks in order to build his resistance to the seductive pleasure of pure passivity.

As for the play, it is an extended nautical metaphor in three acts. Built in the shape of a vessel, Heartbreak House represents the ship of state; the ship is foundering, and about to go on the rocks. The Captain is a drunken old man with a dissolute crew who have not yet learned to navigate: England is drifting into a destructive and futile war. Aside from its allegorical meaning, Heartbreak House also suggests the Bohemianism of the cultured classes of England, wallowing in a disorder of their own making. While breaking each other's hearts, they have permitted their house to tumble down—the masters are eccentric, the servants are spoiled, and even the burglars act unnaturally. Actually, Heartbreak House is another version of the Shavian Hell. But unlike the Hell of *Man and Superman,* whose inhabitants at least enjoyed themselves, the Hell of *Heartbreak House* is peopled with will-less, exhausted sensualists. Hector Hushabye, for example, might be Don Juan before he has reached the philosophical stage of evolution. Unlike John Tanner, who has developed "moral passion," Hector has not yet progressed beyond eroticism; and he is floating, against his will, in a sea of vacuity and discontent. A lover without conviction, a husband who stays at home, he is the victim of the slavery of men to women, moping about like "a damned soul in hell."

Towards Hector and his seductive wife, Hesione, Shaw is alternately indignant and indulgent. Towards those who have usurped their political prerogatives, however, he shows little sympathy at all. If nobody recognizes that upright equestrian, Ariadne Utterword, then this is because she does not exist. Incapable of any strong emotion except a passion for respectability, she lacks even the self-awareness of the Heartbreakers; and as a member of the Horsebackers, she is dedicated to that imperialist approach to government that Shaw abhors. As for Boss Mangan, the practical businessman, he is one of the most unredeemable characters that Shaw ever created. Vulgar, greedy, sentimental, selfish, and faceless (Shaw provides him with "features so commonplace it is impossible to describe them"), Mangan personifies everything that is vile about the commercial world. Shotover, reflecting on Mangan's type says, "There is enmity between our seed and their seed," and announces that the purpose of his dynamite hoard is "to kill fellows like Mangan." Shaw's instinct, too, is to annihilate Mangan, an impulse so murderously strong that he must continually remind himself that Mangan is also human: "It comes to me suddenly," says Hesione, "that you are a real person; that you had a mother, like anyone else." Most of the time, however, Mangan is not a man but a "Boss." And for those who think that Shaw capitulated to capitalism in *Major Barbara*, this character stands as proof of his abiding distaste for the self-seeking businessman.

The existential quality of Shaw's revolt in *Heartbreak House* is mainly expressed through the gradual disenchantment of Ellie Dunn, who is divested of her illusions one by one through a kind of spiritual striptease, until she stands naked and defenseless against the terrors of reality. Having been brought up on Shakespeare by her romantic father, she is ripe for a broken heart at the very beginning of the play. And when Hector proceeds to break her heart, she decides on a practical marriage of convenience with Boss Mangan. Although, in his earlier work, Shaw might have supported such a marriage, here it is insupportable; and Mangan's money turns out to be as much an illusion as Hector's romantic fabrications. When she contracts a spiritual marriage with Captain Shotover, and learns that his wisdom and purpose proceed primarily from the rum bottle, she can protect herself against total despair only through the vision of "life with a blessing." Since this is a vision of the future, however, the only thing that sustains her now is her expectation of Armageddon from the skies.

Armageddon is about to come, for driven to fury by the failure of men, Shaw, dropping all pretense at comedy in the last act, prepares for that total conflagration which Ibsen envisioned: the torpedoing of the entire Ark. Hector had warned, earlier in the play, "I tell you, one of two things must happen. Either out of that darkness some new creation will come to supplant us as we have supplanted the animals, or the heavens will fall in thunder and destroy us." But now the Superman seems a long way off, and Shavianism

just another of Ellie's illusions. The drumming in the air proves to be the
sound of approaching enemy bombers; and "the smash of the drunken skip-
per's ship on the rocks" is heard in the explosion of enemy bombs. Having
lived badly, the Heartbreakers prepare to die well. Hesione, comparing
the noise to Beethoven, finds the prospect of destruction glorious; Hector
turns on all the lights to guide the bombers on their way; and Shotover
prepares for the Last Judgment. Yet, at the last moment, Shaw relents in
his fury. The two pirates—Billy Dunn, the water-thief, and Boss Mangan,
the land-thief—are blown up while seeking safety; and the rectory has been
turned into "nothing but a heap of bricks." But the Heartbreakers are still
alive to take advantage of the warning. By killing off capitalism and the
Church, Shaw demonstrates that his hopeful Utopianism is still more powerful than his existential fatalism; and the play ends with his "romantic
imagination" once more dominating his despairing sense of "real life."
Still, the bombers will return. And Ellie awaits them with such radiant
expectation that, if only for a moment, Shaw's revolt is absolute, finding its
consummation in a flaming vision of total destruction.

The negative power of Shaw's rebellion in *Heartbreak House* brings the play
closer to an authentic art of revolt than anything in the Shavian canon.
Yeats has defined rhetoric as proceeding from the quarrel with others, poetry
from the quarrel with ourselves—in this sense, *Heartbreak House* breaks out
of rhetoric into genuine dramatic poetry, since there Shaw is disputing the
entire philosophical basis of his work. There, too, it is possible to see that
when Shaw drops the cheerful mask of the ethical reformer, the sorrow,
bitterness, and strength of the existential rebel is deeply etched in his features.
But he dropped his public mask too seldom; and if he is fading from us
today, then this is because he stubbornly refused to examine, more than
fitfully, those illusions he held in common with all men. Shavianism was
that "mighty purpose" which kept Shaw writing when his heart said no;
and though he continued to say no with wit and vigor, he could never quite
sacrifice his delusionary yes. As a writer of high comedy, Shaw has no peers
among modern dramatists; but his ambitions are larger; and he lacks, as a
rebel artist, the stature of the men he admired and wished to join. If Strindberg thought he failed to be the man he longed to be, then Shaw's failure
is the opposite: pursuing his ideal role, he failed to face the man he actually
was. Yet, we measure this failure only by the highest standards, and it is
because of his generous mind and talents that these standards continue to be
applied to his art.

Shaw's Integral Theatre

by G. Wilson Knight

When a thing is funny search it for a hidden truth.
Back to Methuselah, v.

I

Bernard Shaw combines the offices of critic, humorist and visionary. His thinking may be related economically to Marx, metaphysically to Goethe and Lamarck, and dramatically to Wagner, Ibsen and Nietzsche. Nietzsche's works he regards as the Bible of the modern consciousness (*The Quintessence of Ibsenism*, 1913; "An Ibsen Theatre"). He is as much Continental as British, his Irish humour bridging the gap; in terms of humour he engages in a daring which British audiences would not otherwise have allowed. His obvious attacks are levelled against middle-class values and professions; doctors and science, politicians and British democracy. *Widowers' Houses* (1892) and *Mrs. Warren's Profession* (1893) handle the evils of slums, prostitution and tainted money. *The Philanderer* (1893) lays the basis of Shaw's advanced sexology. Like other satirists, he regards self-deception as more dangerous than open criminality. He has the usual sympathy with energies, with the satanic, his Preface to *On the Rocks* (1933) stating that dangerous *thoughts* are allowable though they must be distinguished from the corresponding *actions:* a helpful comment to students of drama. His thought varies from satanism, through attacks on hypocrisy, to religious mysticism: he has strong religious sympathies, and is an admirer of Bunyan. Comedy, so often limited to the sexual, is brought by Shaw to bear on the subjects *generally regarded as the domain of tragedy:* statesmanship and world affairs, wars, and such great persons as Caesar, Napoleon, and Saint Joan. His is a large-scale comedy like Aristophanes'; and like Aristophanes' it touches vision. Comedy is often our best approach to the mysteries.

"Shaw's Integral Theatre" (original title: "Shaw") by G. Wilson Knight. From *The Golden Labyrinth* by G. Wilson Knight (New York: W. W. Norton & Company, Inc., 1962), pp. 342–354. Copyright © 1962 by G. Wilson Knight. Reprinted by permission of W. W. Norton & Company, Inc., J. M. Dent & Sons Ltd., and the author.

His considered philosophy is evolutionary. He believes in the Life Force, affirming an optimistic recognition of its miraculous nature as it travails to create a greater humanity, of which certain great men of history are the precursors. Its power is strong in women, who are impelled by it, as *Man and Superman* (1903) shows, to win a husband and bear children. In *Back to Methuselah* (1921), where man is shown gradually evolving towards a spiritualized and immortal being, the personification of the bisexual Life Force is Lilith, a female figure who speaks the epilogue. Women are central powers and man's prided intellect often childish in comparison. Shaw's Life Force corresponds to the Living God of the Bible.

II

Such is the context in which we must understand Shaw's dramatic socialism. Reform is not easy. In *Major Barbara* (1905) the Salvation Army heroine finds that in her work for the poor she is forced to accept assistance from both a whisky magnate and her millionaire father, Undershaft, who has himself created an ideal little society of his own from the proceeds of his armament factory. Shaw has his eyes on the real lines of force, involving money: good and evil do not in practice exist apart from their context, and Undershaft, the great industrialist, has the necessary drive and wealth. Such powers we must respect, expanding the evil into good:

> Yes, through the raising of hell to heaven and of man to God, through the unveiling of an eternal light in the valley of the Shadow.   (iii.)

Advance depends on such men as Undershaft, we need more and not less of them, and the revolutionary who thinks otherwise impedes progress. In "The Revolutionist's Handbook" appended to *Man and Superman* we are reminded that "what Caesar, Cromwell and Napoleon could not do with all the physical force and moral prestige of the State in their mighty hands, cannot be done by enthusiastic criminals and lunatics," and that "whilst Man remains what he is there can be no progress beyond the point already attained" (vii); so "national Christianity is impossible without a nation of Christs" and "man" must be replaced by "superman" (ix). *Back to Methuselah* dramatizes the evolution.

Shaw's dramatic socialism contains strong aristocratic sympathies. The aristocratic connections of so central and admired a person as Lady Cicely in *Captain Brassbound's Conversion* (1899) are intrinsic to her dramatic stature. In *Misalliance* (1910) democracy and aristocracy are regarded as interdependent. *On the Rocks* delights in relating a modern attempt at "Platonic communism" to the ruling class, a duke and leading figures of the services and of finance embracing the change while the voices of proletarian socialism reject it. Under the proposed system the police will "have a status which they feel to be a part of the status of the Duke here" (II): the aim might almost be called a "royalistic communism." *The Apple Cart* (1929) is a dramatic essay on aristocratic and royal valuation. King Magnus regards his royal office as a safeguard of the long-range and eternal values as opposed to the politics of ephemerality and expedience (I). As we see him turning the tables on his socialist cabinet we watch a flowering of the great man from its symbol, which is royalty: even the old supposed divinity of kings housed a truth, since man has a "divine spark" in him (I), and it is this human and divine reality within the political order that the crown symbolizes. The next step is to use the divine spark in actuality. That is the task of the great man, the leader.

This greatness is a matter of integration. Power must be bisexual. In the preface to *Good King Charles's Golden Days* (1939) it is suggested that votes should be given not for the individual but for man-with-woman, called "a bisexed couple"; or bisexuality may be found or felt within the individual, and perhaps that is why Mrs. Basham in this same play is found regretting the use of "abandoned females" in place of the far more convincing boy actors who "could make you believe"—as the others could not—"that you were listening to real women." Shaw regularly counterbalances male traditions by forceful women: as bearer of the Life Force woman is an almost impersonal power in *Man and Superman*, and Mrs. George in *Getting Married* (1908) is a medium who in trance speaks inspiredly of sexual relations, covering both the female and the male contributions. The more obviously feminine qualities do not exhaust feminine potentiality: Candida in *Candida* (1894) and Lady Cicely in *Captain Brassbound's Conversion* are both natural commanders. Such women intuitively recognize the folly of men: they are always realists and in some sex as such may be surpassed. "How could I manage people," says Lady Cicely, "if I had that mad little bit of self left in me? That's my secret" (III). Sexual principles may be fused within the individual and this sexual blend, or integration, has much to do with what we call "genius." In *The Philanderer* membership of The Ibsen Club is limited by the exclusion of any manly man or womanly woman (I). "All good women" are "manly" and all "good men" are "womanly" (*The Quintessence of Ibsenism*, "What is the New Element?"). "Genius" is part-feminine and a poet naturally has the "temperament" of "an old maid" (*Man and Superman*, Epistle Dedicatory; also IV).

We accordingly have a number of part-feminine men. The artist Dubedat in *The Doctor's Dilemma* (1906) is "pretty" but not "effeminate"; "a man in his thoughts, a great poet and artist in his dreams, and a child in his ways"; and he is "one of the men who know what women know" (II; III; V). Such artist types are preferred to the normal appetite-driven and convention-bound man, though women may have the strength either of their sex or of its surmounting, or both. In *Misalliance* the boy Bentley is one of those "who from seventeen to seventy" preserve the appearance of age in mind and of youth in looks. He is a mixture of emotionalism and insight, an artistic type, contrasted with his brother's normality, and at the conclusion he masters his nervousness to face danger with Lina, the Polish acrobat, a woman of action called "a man-woman or woman-man," averse from love-making. Bentley, also, will "never marry"; they follow the thought pattern of *The Philanderer*. Bentley is of similar make to the "effeminate" (i) yet disturbing eighteen-year-old poet Marchbanks in *Candida*, who renounces his love and realizes his true power and destiny, a "secret" (iii) akin to Lady Cicely's. In *Saint Joan* (1923) we have the saintly heroine in male dress making a man of that beautiful study in querulous non-masculine sensibility, the inadequate yet fascinating Dauphin, the understanding between them as underlined in the Epilogue being one of the most attractive themes in the play. Highly developed types may be older, like the Irish mystic Keegan in *John Bull's Other Island* (1904) and old Captain Shotover in *Heartbreak House* (1916), who has no family emotions, thinks being married "up to the hilt" is "hell" and yearns for a land with "no women," for "strength" and "genius" flower from independence (ii). Keegan, despite his years, has the face of a young man (ii) and the aged Shotover believes in "youth," "beauty," and "novelty" (i). Both have the secret of enduring vitality.

The complications of Shaw's sexology make of his Don Juan in the Interlude in *Man and Superman* (iii) what might be called a kind of esoteric justification of Restoration comedy. This Don Juan, descended from Charteris in *The Philanderer*, repudiates marriage vows in terms obliquely reminiscent of Etherege's Dorimant as illogical and impractical, while putting trust in an astringent philosophic quest leading to the superman. The Life Force, he says, impels sexual unions, coming as a sudden invasion from without; but he has no mystique of sexual union: there is just a sudden irruption for the purposes of procreation strangely antithetic to his astringent philosophy. This—we find it again in *You Never Can Tell* (1896; iii)—may be unsatisfactory, though in *Getting Married* Mrs. George, as spokeswoman of sexual intercourse, does something to right the balance. In contrast to Don Juan, the Devil and Hell stand for conventional values and pleasures, for sentiment and romance; for all the more obvious, though superficial, positives. Our various esoteric types are precursors of the Ancients in *Back to Methuselah*.

Integration conditions male leadership. If we are not to be left with the plea advanced at the conclusion to *Too True To Be Good* (1931) for the "woman of action" to solve our difficulties, the female powers and insights of a Lady Cicely must somehow be functioning within the man. Napoleon in *The Man of Destiny* (1895) shows promise and tries to "act like a woman," but is indecisive and worsted by a woman in boy's dress. King Magnus in *The Apple Cart* is near integration; his wife is now mainly a loved companion and his relations with his dream mistress Orinthia are "strangely innocent." He is beyond dangerous desires: "I never resist temptation, because I have found that things that are bad for me do not tempt me." Orinthia regards him as either a "child" or a "saint," with the "makings" of a "woman": "There is more of you in me than of any other man within my reach. There is more of me in you than of any other woman within your reach" (Interlude).

Our firmest realization of an integrated leader is Caesar in *Caesar and Cleopatra* (1898). He addresses the Sphinx:

> I am he of whose genius you are the symbol: part brute, part woman, and part god—nothing of man in me at all. Have I read your riddle, Sphinx? (I.)

Though ageing, Caesar has a "child's heart" (I) and is called "boyish" (III). He makes friends everywhere, and "has no hatred in him" (IV). But his unattachment can be maddening: Cleopatra means little to him; at the close he has forgotten her. Like Byron's Sardanapalus and Ibsen's Julian in Gaul—and Magnus who hated death-warrants—he is clemency personified; slaying in hot blood he can forgive but he loathes judicial punishment (V). Clemency he regards as a matter of practical common sense and it is suggested that his views foreshadow Christ (IV). Shaw is aiming to create a personality in whom *Christ's teaching becomes political wisdom*. Though kindly, Caesar is strong and master of every situation. He is an artist in action. When the aesthete Apollodorus compliments him on being an artist as well as a soldier, the very contrast angers him. Told that Rome produces no art, he replies:

> What! Rome produce no art! Is peace not an art? is war not an art? is government not an art? is civilization not an art? All these we give you in exchange for a few ornaments. You will have the best of the bargain. (V.)

The reply is unanswerable.

Shaw likes soldiers. Bluntschli in *Arms and the Man* (1894) is highly original and Private Meek in *Too True To Be Good* is a genius. Soldiers may be associated with religion. The Salvation Army title *Major Barbara* makes a sexual blend which typifies the ideal that gave us Saint Joan. Anthony Anderson in the last act of *The Devil's Disciple* (1897) is a pastor turned soldier, and the relationship of the Roman captain to the Christian Lavinia in *Androcles and the Lion* (1912) is beautifully developed. In Caesar we have hints of that "soul of Christ" demanded by Nietzsche. That the treatment is light marks, in Shaw, no lack of purpose: rather the reverse.

The approach may be mystical. In *Getting Married* Mrs. George is a woman of promiscuous sexual experiences and also a "clairvoyant" who speaks poetically in "trance" of woman's surrender to man and what it does for him. She is a medium, a "pythoness"; ecclesiastics are doubtful whether to call it demoniac "possession" or "the ecstasy of a saint." She taps the creative powers, as a human analogue to Lilith in *Back to Methuselah*. We first meet Keegan, the Irish patriot-mystic of *John Bull's Other Island*, in a "trance" by sunset (II). Though ageing, he has "the face of a young saint." He loves all animals, like St Francis, and talks to a grasshopper (II) as Caesar talks to the Sphinx. Formerly a Catholic priest, he has since derived wisdom from a dying Hindu who explained earthly suffering to him by the great law of Karma (IV). To him this world seems to be Hell. What he craves is a state where priest and worshipper, work and play, human and divine, are one (IV). Beside Keegan we have Captain Shotover in *Heartbreak House*, whose wisdom is similarly given exotic support; he was once married to a West Indian negress who "redeemed" him and is said—though he has his own version—to have sold himself to the Devil in Zanzibar, getting in return a "black witch" for a wife (I; II). He is supposed to possess uncanny powers of divination and clairvoyance (II); he is a man of "vibrations," "magnetic" (II), striving to attain "the seventh degree of concentration" (I). His powers have natural sanction: like Timon, he is averse from humanity and challenges society in the name of vast nature and Heaven's "dome" as "the house of God" (I). Man is, or should be, free: "The wide earth, the high seas, the spacious skies are waiting for you outside" (II). England he sees as being driven on the rocks by crass inefficiency. "Navigation" alone can save her: "Learn it and live," he says, "or leave it and be damned" (III). But he is not himself now a supporter of forceful government (III), his interests having become more purely psychic. When he sees the Church as severed from "God's open sea" (III), he may mean that it has lost contact with the natural psychic powers, but they exist as strongly as ever and he is labouring to invent a psychic ray as a defence against human iniquity and stupidity; a "mind ray" able to explode his enemy's ammunition (I), like Prospero's weapon-negating magic. His mind varies from thoughts of destroying his fellow creatures to a dislike of force. He is a figure of *spiritual* force. He is as frightening as Oedipus in the *Oedipus Coloneus;* a "supernatural old man" (I). In *Heartbreak House* we are on the edge of the numinous and strange psychic forces, of explosions and death. We end with an air-raid, in which each member of the mixed but well-defined community has an allegorical fate. To some the drumming in the sky is Beethoven music; suicidally they make the house lights blaze, embracing danger after paralysis (III). Shotover himself only knew the true intensity of living when risking his life at sea (II). On death's brink we touch life. We are reminded of the mystique of risk and courage in *Misalliance*.

The mystical insights of *Saint Joan* are obvious enough: the miracles, the sense of power, the voices and clairaudience, and best of all the wonderfully composed Epilogue, where Joan's spirit talks to the earth people who are travelling in the astral while their bodies sleep. Joan contains nearly all

Shaw's favourite qualities: bisexuality, soldiership, occult powers, saintliness, common sense, efficiency.

The other-worldly metaphysic follows the teaching of Spiritualism. The visual and musical directions to the Don Juan Interlude in *Man and Superman* are exquisite realizations of the etheric dimension; music is used as a language, and the account of Heaven and Hell, where we hear that the state beyond death corresponds so exactly to what we are that Heaven would be no pleasure for one unfit for it, is closely spiritualistic. In *Back to Methuselah* the superman quest is given a cosmic and mystic range. Adam and Eve, like Joan, hear voices. Adam chooses death rather than an unbearable eternity of himself and Eve embraces procreation as an alternative. Cain, prototype of soldiership and force, is given, as in Byron and Ibsen, a case; but man must mature; he must live longer; and we see this happening, in different stages, until at the last we watch him graduating through the artistic intelligence to the stature of the Ancients. The artists are beyond the sexual, and must next, like Ishak in *Hassan*, pass beyond art. The attempt at a living sculpture recalls Shakespeare and Ibsen. The Ancients themselves correspond to Prospero, as Shotover to Timon. They are nearly sexless, the She-Ancient having a man's breast; their life is mental, beyond sex and art and even food and sleep, with mesmeric and magnetic powers corresponding, like Shotover's, to Prospero's magic. Their experience cannot be described except by analogy; telepathy replaces language; they can create and re-create and change their bodies by mental or spiritual power. Though sounding cold it is an "ecstasy" one moment of which would strike the lower people dead (v). It corresponds point by point to accounts from higher planes in and beyond the etheric as received today through trance mediumship. We are in a world of new sense-powers and "ears with a longer range of sound than ours" (v). The Ancients refer to the "astral body" in which earlier men believed and their own destiny is "to be immortal" in a world not of people but of "thought," which is "life eternal" (v). Lilith, the bisexual creative power torn asunder for creation, speaks the Epilogue, recapitulating the whole story from the Fall when man refused "to live for ever": "They did terrible things: they embraced death, and said that eternal life was a fable." So man chose death and mutual slaughter, but through the labours of creation he will at last "disentangle" his "life from matter." This will be the true "life"; "and for what may be beyond, the eyesight of Lilith is too short. It is enough that there is a beyond." This great work is one long concentration on the breaking of the opacity shutting man from the immortality, or eternal life, which is his birthright.

Shaw has used Spiritualism to fill out his evolutionary statement, and we can always ourselves use it, should we so choose, to make sense of superman claims: they, and Ibsen's "third empire" too, may be unrealizable in this dimension, and point to another. Both processes are rational; more, they converge. For, as Shaw says in his Preface ("The Artist-Prophets"), "We aspire to a world of prophets and sibyls." His aim is never for long limited to the religious or occult. His desire is to blend inspiration with sociology, politics and, above all, with great men. That is why he compares himself to Shakespeare, to awake us to his true message, which exists strongly within the unfurling humanism of Renaissance drama.

III

Shaw's dramas are shot through with comedy. His humour is bright, kindly and exciting. He contrasts with Ibsen in his peculiar forwardness; dramatic revelations from the past do not interest him. He refuses to take old compulsions and clogs seriously: Shotover is angry at one who probes into "old wounds" (*Heartbreak House*, III) and Caesar would let the race's memories be destroyed and build the future on their ruins (*Caesar and Cleopatra*, II). The trial in *Saint Joan* opposes prophecy in Joan to tradition in the Inquisitor, and tradition, as the Epilogue demonstrates, loses. Jesus, dramatized before Pilate in the Preface to *On the Rocks*, is all for newness:

> The beast of prey is not striving to return: the kingdom of God is striving to come. The empire that looks back in terror shall give way to the kingdom that looks forward with hope.

The mysterious "lady" who visits the Prime Minister in *On the Rocks* (I) introduces herself, by a profoundly Shavian paradox, as a "ghost" not from the "past" but from the "future." Believing in a beneficent cosmic process Shaw allows scant respect to ingrained evils, to hereditary and ghostly compulsions. What he likes best is to show a false and backward-looking valuation rendered ridiculous by the ever-new and up-bubbling Life Force. True humour derives from the overthrowing of superficialities by the orgiastic, or some derivative in the realm of facts and forces; sex, its usual theme, is as "sex" only part of Shaw's concern, but his humour obeys the same law, with the Life Force as feminine and cosmic agent.

Vengeful and judicial retaliations are accordingly repudiated, as in *Thus Spake Zarathustra*. The embittered and revengeful Gunner in *Misalliance* is comically bested by one woman and mothered back to sense by another. The avenging pirate in *Captain Brassbound's Conversion* finds his melodramatic outbursts constricted by the trying on of his newly mended coat by his captive Lady Cicely, who has been tidying him up. Here neither the Pirate with his revenge nor later the Judge with his law is allowed respect; both think in terms of retribution and our only trust is in Lady Cicely, whose controlling function recalls Shakespeare's Portia. Shaw pays no respect to horrors. The Crucifixion, symbol of that whole gamut of sin and torture throughout our blackened world which he tends to regard as unnecessary folly, he naturally repudiates, complaining that we have turned Christianity into "Crosstianity" (Preface to *On the Rocks*). Following Byron and developing the humour of Ibsen in *The Pretenders*, he likewise repudiates that prodigious symbol of retribution, Hell. In *Man and Superman* we are startled to hear from the Devil that anyone can go to Heaven who wishes to, though if we are not fit for it, it will be as boring as classical music to the uninitiated. Laugh after laugh is raised by replacing the traditional by a more spiritualistic eschatology, and much the same happens in the Epilogue to *Saint Joan*. No intellectual argument could disprove the traditional threat of Hell; but humour acts differently; it dissolves it. Whatever our beliefs, we must recognize that, insofar as we respond to the fun, some deeper health in us has already ratified the reversal.

Superficialities of all sorts are overturned, *including many of Shaw's own most cherished allegiances*. The advanced Shavian opinions of Tanner on unmarried love are toppled over at the brilliant climax of the first scene of *Man and Superman* (I). Despite Shaw's Marxist interests, Mrs. Tarleton in *Misalliance* takes Gunner's communist terms such as "capitalist" and "bourgeoisie" as swearing: "All right, Chickabiddy: it's not bad language; it's only socialism." Shaw's humour often appears suicidal. After all the accumulated profundity, bitterness and scorn of Keegan's denunciation of England in *John Bull's Other Island*, the very crassness of Broadbent's typically British impenetrability and capacity for adjustment wins unconditionally with nine words: "I think these things cannot be said too often" (IV). That is great humour, depth beyond depth. In *Candida* the Christian socialist Morell is a stuffed dummy beside the esoterically conceived Marchbanks, and yet even this, Shaw's inmost and cherished sanctity, the "secret" of Marchbanks and Candida, does not escape. In *Too True To Be Good* Colonel Tallboys speaks to Private Meek, the soldier-genius:

Tallboys. No doubt you are an extraordinary soldier. But have you ever passed the extreme and final test of manly courage?
Meek. Which one is that, sir?
Tallboys. Have you ever married?
Meek. No, sir. (III.)

Is the Christian and Nietzschean celibacy to be our highest ideal or not? Is it, after all, a retreat? That "No, sir" raises as deep a problem of racial destiny as any two words in our drama. Such strokes indicate that Shaw's real message is *in the humour itself*. When in *Androcles and the Lion* we enjoy the muscular Christian convert's shame at having let himself go against the gladiators in the Roman arena instead of turning the other cheek, we recognize that in spite of what we mumble in church we did not want him to restrain himself; we exult in his comic fall from grace; and from that paradox is momentarily born some flaming sight of a Christianity not humble but triumphant.

Nietzsche's Zarathustra insisted on humour as necessary henceforth to the highest wisdom; the conclusion to John Cowper Powys's study *Rabelais* (1948) develops the attendant philosophy and Shaw is our grand exemplar in practice. Keegan's way of "joking" is "to tell the truth," for "every dream is a prophecy" and "every jest is an earnest in the womb of time" (*John Bull's Other Island*, II; IV). "When a thing is funny," says the He-Ancient in *Back to Methuselah*, "search it for a hidden truth" (V).

Such humour startles us into unexpected possibilities which on reflection may be found reasonable. Shaw's dramatic technique throughout relies on startling; comic surprise replaces the tensions, suspense and expectancies of tragedy. In *Misalliance* an aeroplane containing a Polish woman acrobat suddenly crashes into the conservatory of a middle-class Surrey house: nothing could have been more unlikely. *Heartbreak House* is called "a house of surprises" (I), and they certainly occur; the entry and amazing message of the American ambassador in *The Apple Cart* is a typical example and so is the irruption of a twentieth-century cleric from Rome in the Epilogue to *Saint Joan*. Joan's miraculous powers give us the comic climax to her first scene, though these very same powers raise tears in her third. Shaw's use of humour and surprise is of a piece with his beliefs; all events, natural or miraculous, come from the one Life Force, the normal expressions of life "ever renewing itself" being a "continual miracle" (*The Apple Cart*, I). Our dramatic surprises, functioning variously in terms of farce, high comedy, philosophy and the sacred, come from the inexhaustible stores of futurity, and to this we must trust. The humour is never cruel: the laughter raised by the extraordinarily funny incident of the pig in *John Bull's Other Island* only confirms the sensitive Keegan in his belief that our earth itself is Hell (IV). Never in Shaw are man's physical and cosmic instincts degraded, but only, as in Byron's *Don Juan*, his mental follies. Hence our sense of well-being, of a sun dispelling fogs, of a golden quality. Yet there is little of the warmth we feel in O'Casey's humour; Shaw's is rather made of light, it is like mountain air, or the golden asceticism of Flecker's Samarkand; and by its light we see colour.

Shaw's prose style may be bare but his total drama is colourful. Setting and costume may be as important today as was poetry to the Elizabethans, and to read Shaw for his "ideas" without visualizing his stage directions is like reading Shakespeare in a prose paraphrase for children. Shaw loves contrasting stuffy interiors with the wide-open spaces of God's creation. The sea-captain Shotover and Lina the Polish acrobat both long for open spaces. At a crisis the wise King Magnus deliberately arranges to meet his cabinet out of doors. *Too True To Be Good* takes us from neurosis and a sick-room to a north African sea-beach with a coloured pavilion backed by mountains.

The Simpleton of the Western Isles (1934) is all South Sea expanse, ready for the descent of the Angel of Judgement who after being shot at by a terrified humanity lands safely and proceeds to shake the bullets out of his feathers. Localities are many: Balkan highlands, Moroccan castle, African desert, the Sierra Nevada, tropical jungle (in *Buoyant Billions;* 1947), Hindhead in Surrey. Settings include the Sphinx, a Roman arena, Rheims Cathedral, Covent Garden, The Hague; and there is a wide range of costume. The wise Keegan and Shotover have travelled widely and are associated with warm lands: Jerusalem, India, Zanzibar, Jamaica. Shotover's black wife serves an imaginative purpose; Shaw's religious anti-self gives us *The Adventures of the Black Girl in her Search for God* (1932). This exploitation of geographic colour— not colour for its own sake as in O'Casey—reaches an extreme in the exotic orientalism of *Buoyant Billions*. But colour is not limited to foreign lands: when the action is in England Shaw does his best with terraces, deck-chairs, gardens and views. *Caesar and Cleopatra* is richly inlaid, its directions are little poems: against a "vivid purple" sky changing to "pale orange" a colonnade and a vast image of the god Ra show "darklier and darklier" (IV); and Caesar's ship is "so gorgeously decorated that it seems to be rigged with flowers" (V). *Heartbreak House* has its first setting designed as the poop of an old-style sailing ship, but for the air-raid we are outside with hammocks lit by "an electric arc" like "a moon." These effects are of man, his civilization and the cosmos; of earth contact as such we find less, though it is finely established by Keegan's talk to the grasshopper and the beautiful direction describing Roscullen (*John Bull's Other Island*, II), where colour is felt in depth. Or we may touch other dimensions, as when in *Man and Superman* (III) the Spanish setting at nightfall melts into an etheric world of violet light and ghostly music. Newton in *Good King Charles's Golden Days* rates above his scientific labours "the elixir of life, the magic of light and colour, above all, the secret meaning of the Scriptures." Costumes alone are of an extraordinary richness and variety. The colourlessness of Shaw's prose dialogue acts as a transparency through which we view a wider range of geographic and other colours than has been deployed by any other of our major dramatists.

Back to Methuselah: The Poet and the City

by Margery M. Morgan

None of Shaw's plays has been more strongly disliked than *Back to Methuselah*. On the most superficial acquaintance it invites the charges of untheatricality, verbal incontinence and incoherence of form; its vision is found repellent; and the teasing, if naïve, question of whether Shaw means what he says, when he is evidently talking nonsense, is more sharply provoked than by any of his other works.[1] Serious study of the play raises central problems of Shavian criticism. Is the glorification of mind only a cowardly flight from emotion?[2] Are his reversals of convention simply mechanical, useful for liberating adolescent thought, but unsatisfying to grown men? Does his puritanism express a false understanding of human nature (including his own nature)? If it does, his art can have no universality. Does this puritanism (like Tolstoy's) involve an essential devaluing of art, destructive to the integrity of any work in which it is found?

Granville Barker showed himself aware of the relevance of such considerations to the last part of *Back to Methuselah*, when he wrote to Shaw in 1921, upon the publication of the play:

Part V . . . raises one question—How far can one use pure satire in the theatre? For satire scarifies humanity. The theatre uses it (*humanity*) as a me-

"*Back to Methuselah:* The Poet and the City" by Margery M. Morgan. From *Essays and Studies 1960* XIII, 82–98, published for The English Association by John Murray (Publishers) Ltd., London. Copyright © 1960 by Margery M. Morgan. Reprinted by permission of the author.

[1] Even Shaw's most perceptive critics tend to fall foul of this play. Chesterton (*George Bernard Shaw*, Second Edition, 1935) wrote of "those bloodless extravagances, which Bernard Shaw meant to make attractive," "bloodless Struldbugs (*sic*) who kill people for purely sociological considerations." Eric Bentley (*Bernard Shaw*, 1950) judges Shaw to be "at his worst as a playwright" in the later sections of *Back to Methuselah*. Edmund Wilson (*The Triple Thinkers*, 1938) considers it a frightened play, bleak and inhuman, with "nothing genuinely thrilling except the cry of the Elderly Gentleman."

[2] T. S. Eliot has written of Shaw's rejection of poetic values as sub-adolescent. (See "A Dialogue on Dramatic Poetry," *Selected Essays*, 1932, pp. 43–58.)

dium and must therefore be tender to it. . . . If you degrade the token . . .
you falsify your case. . . .[3]

It is doubtful if great satire is ever "pure" in the sense that Barker gives to
the word: ever totally divorced from compassion. Gulliver is himself a
Yahoo, and the redemptive element of Yahoo-nature is at work in the horror
of his self-contemplation. The Shavian version of Gulliver among the
Houyhnhnms comes in Part IV of *Back to Methuselah:* "The Tragedy of an
Elderly Gentleman." Once we cease to be deluded by the fable of longevity
into seeing the whole cycle as a straggling chronicle-play, this part emerges
as the emotional centre of gravity which holds the rest in balance. From
the mouth of its hero comes Shaw's own acknowledgement of the peril
attending too complete an objectivity:

> I think that a man who is sane as long as he looks at the world through his own
> eyes is very likely to become a dangerous madman if he takes to looking at the
> world through telescopes and microscopes. Even when he is telling fairy stories
> about giants and dwarfs, the giants had better not be too big nor the dwarfs too
> small and too malicious. . . .

From one part to another, and often abruptly within a single scene, the
author adjusts his dramatic technique as if he were altering the range and
focus of scientific instruments. If the reader or audience is able to receive
the impact of the five parts as a whole,[4] the play takes on the character of
a hall of mirrors directed upon human nature from many angles and all
distorting in various ways. "Have you been sent here to make your mind
flexible?" a Guardian inquires of the Elderly Gentleman; and the question
travels on into the auditorium. But such flexibility would be merely frivolous
apart from some absolute standard of reference. This is supplied whenever
the tone of the dialogue deepens and the drama builds up to some emotional
intensity. The Elderly Gentleman, who is disclosed weeping by the side of
the ocean, and then flings himself into an absurd butterfly-dance in top hat
and frock coat, is the only heroic figure in the entire play; for the true
Shavian hero, as has occasionally been observed,[5] is the romantic fool:

> I accept my three score and ten years. If they are filled with usefulness, with
> justice, with mercy, with goodwill: if they are the lifetime of a soul that never
> loses its honor and a brain that never loses its eagerness; they are enough for me,
> because these things are infinite and eternal. . . .

[3] A longer extract from the letter appears in C. B. Purdom, *Harley Granville Barker*
(1955), pp. 198–99.
[4] Only once has the entire play been performed on a single day: at the Arts Theatre
in February 1947. The performance started at 2.30 p.m.
[5] This is plainly implied by Katherine Haynes Gatch, "The Last Plays of Bernard
Shaw: Dialectic and Despair," in *English Stage Comedy*, ed. by W. K. Wimsatt, Jr. (1955),
pp. 126–47, especially in the concluding quotation from Thomas Mann on modern tragicomedy and the grotesque style.

Gulliver begs to be allowed to remain among the horses, though he can never be as they are; the elderly Joseph Barlow, O.M., otherwise Iddy Toodles, clings to the idea of truth, whatever it may cost:

The Elderly Gentleman. They have gone back to lie about your answer. I cannot go with them. I cannot live among people to whom nothing is real. I have become incapable of it through my stay here. I implore to be allowed to stay.
The Oracle. My friend: if you stay with us you will die of discouragement.
The Elderly Gentleman. If I go back I shall die of disgust and despair. I take the nobler risk . . .
. . . *She looks steadily into his face. He stiffens; a little convulsion shakes him; his grasp relaxes; and he falls dead.*

Like *Heartbreak House, Back to Methuselah* was a fruit of the war. Shaw read a draft of Part II, "The Gospel of the Brothers Barnabas," to a group of friends in 1918.[6] This part remains most nearly akin to his pre-war plays in dramatic style. The scale of character-drawing and action is as close to the naturalistic as Shaw gets in the whole play-cycle. The setting represents an ordinary middle-class Edwardian drawing room; the passage of time on the stage matches the passage of actual time; Bill Haslam and Savvy, Conrad and Franklyn Barnabas would not be out of place among the types of conventional drawing-room comedy; even Burge and Lubin are exaggerated little enough beyond the images of themselves that men project from a political platform. The action follows a simple dialectical order of thesis and antithesis. First, the professional statesmen and then the philosophers expound their political principles and programmes. The analogy of a political meeting, modified by the drawing-room comedy elements, is sustained in the recurring pattern of accusation and counter-accusation through which the rival candidates move, in heckling interruptions and in the way that Burge and Lubin refer every topic to the measure of electoral appeal. These two figures are animated caricatures of Lloyd George and Asquith. Their responsibility for the war is brought under review, but the severest indictment is introduced non-satirically, when the statesmen and the Brothers Barnabas have left the stage to Savvy and the young curate:

Haslam. Lubin and your father have both survived the war. But their sons were killed in it.
Savvy. [*sobered*] Yes. Jim's death killed mother. . . .
Haslam. . . . To me the awful thing about their political incompetence was that they had to kill their own sons. . . .

[6] Granville Barker was among them (see Purdom, op. cit., p. 192). The version read to them almost certainly included the section later discarded and published separately in *Short Stories, Scraps and Shavings* (see below, p. 87).

This horror is the common ground of experience on which Shaw approaches his audience of men, in order to turn them into an audience of philosophers. The critical decision reached by Adam and Eve in Part I of the cycle was to exchange eternal life for continuance through generation. From the disturbance of the natural succession of sons to fathers, by the carnage of 1914–18, the drama proceeds in strict logic to the reversal of that fabled decision: individual life must now be prolonged, until at last men are ready to accept the burden of eternal life that Adam found too heavy. The title of the last part of the drama, "As Far as Thought can Reach," gives a broad hint that the length of life which is Shaw's serious concern is that which the individual mind can encompass—which it is stretched to encompass, as the action proceeds. It is of major significance that Part V is to be presented with costumes and décor resembling *"Grecian of the fourth century B.C.":* the age of Plato. If its atmosphere is found a little chilling, this but corresponds to the impression that philosophic thought makes on the unreflective human being.

Samuel Butler reports an Erewhonian belief in a race of men whose foresight more than equalled our acquaintance with the past, but "they died in a twelvemonth from the misery which their knowledge caused them." He comments:

> Strange fate for man! He must perish if he get that, which he must perish if he strive not after. If he strive not after it he is no better than the brutes, if he get it he is more miserable than the devils.

This misery of the man whose vision outruns his capacity for action makes its appearance in *Back to Methuselah* as the disease of Discouragement, which threatens the Shortlivers and even the Youths of Part V. Its torments are known to Franklyn Barnabas:

Lubin. Why do you fix three hundred years as the exact figure? . . . I am quite prepared to face three thousand, not to say three million.
Conrad. Yes, because you don't believe you will be called on to make good your word.
Franklyn. [*gently*] Also, perhaps, because you have never been troubled much by vision of the future.

In fact, Shaw's play in its entirety derives its power from the conflict inherent in the human situation which Plato expressed for later ages in terms of the rational and appetitive faculties, being and becoming, guardian and subject. The twentieth century has come to prefer doctrines of the whole man to the theory of the divisions of the soul. Yet the older fashion of thought is fundamental to puritanism, the religion of Jonhobsnoxius (to which the Elderly Gentleman was a victim); and it is also essentially dramatic. Shaw took from the *Republic* some of the principal symbols and concepts on which *Back to*

Methuselah is based. They are the more meaningful and forceful in their new context because he was able to identify them with the warring forces of his own personality: accessibility to emotion and fear of it; deprivation of family affection avenged by attacks on the family and a care "more for the Public Thing than for any private thing";[7] revolutionist principles in conflict with authoritarian inclinations.[8]

The antithesis between reason and the sensual soul is most clearly represented in Part V, in the relation of the Ancients and the Youths. This is repeated in variant forms in the Longlivers and Shortlivers of Parts III and IV and, in Part II, in the counterbalancing of the myopic chauvinism of Burge and Lubin with the philosophical farsightedness of the Brothers Barnabas. Shaw uses the repetition of similar elements in different parts as a device for unifying the play-cycle. He profits in this way from the theatrical necessity of reducing the cast-list by allowing for the doubling of rôles. So, as in a Harlequinade, Savvy Barnabas appears again as Zoo and yet again as the Newly Born; Burge and Lubin merge into the Burge-Lubin of Part III and the Badger Bluebin of Part IV; Conrad Barnabas turns into Accountant-General Barnabas; Cain reappears as Napoleon, Emperor of Turania; Archbishop Haslam and Mrs. Lutestring change into the He-Ancient and She-Ancient.[9] The discarded fragment, originally intended for Part II and published in *Short Stories, Scraps and Shavings* as "A Glimpse of the Domesticity of Franklyn Barnabas," contains the major character of Mrs. Etteen, who shows recognizable affinities with Eve's portrait of Lua, Cain's wife, and with Ecrasia, the aesthete of Part V. This is one way—a visual means— whereby Shaw demonstrates his notion of the disguises in which ideas find expression. "You are Eve, in a sense," declares Conrad Barnabas to his niece, "you are only a new hat and coat on Eve."

It is in Part III, "The Thing Happens," that Shaw tests most severely the capacity of his dramatic technique to hold the stage. This section is a disquisitory play, in which action is unimportant, almost non-existent, and the situation appears to be a mere excuse for the characters to range, apparently at random, over diverse topics. The fantasy of a Britain of A.D. 2170, effectually governed by a Civil Service of Chinese and negresses, satirically reverses the Imperialist argument of the unfitness of "native" populations to govern themselves. Three divisions of what we must call the "action" are discernible: a general exposition; the revelation of a precise situation in the debate of two groups over a table; and finally a conversion of the central character.

---

[7] The observation is Chesterton's.

[8] Discussed by Edmund Wilson, loc. cit.

[9] The main productions (Theatre Guild, Birmingham Repertory Company and Arts Theatre) between them exploited all these resemblances—except, surprisingly, that between Savvy and the Newly Born—and some others.

The general exposition consists of a succession of duologues between President Burge-Lubin and, first, Accountant-General Barnabas, then the Chief secretary, Confucius, and finally the negress who is Minister of Health. Burge-Lubin is a complete figure of fun; fat clown facing thin and miserable Harlequin, when the screen is withdrawn to disclose Barnabas sitting opposite him in an identical office; stupid clown playing stooge to clever clown, when he sets up the commonplaces of English history for Confucius to overturn them.[10] Sensuality has decayed into frivolity of mind in this elected representative of the people, who flirts with the televised image of the negress and protests:

> My relations with her are purely telephonic, gramophonic, photophonic, and, may I add, platonic.

The curious dramatic flatness of these first episodes is not inappropriate, indeed. For this is Shaw's Laputa, the home of false science and false philosophy. It has its American "projector," who has invented a method of breathing under water; like the tailors and architects of Swift's Laputa, Accountant-General Barnabas insists that actuality and human life should conform to his calculations. Abstraction reigns, "the dupe of appearances";[11] its symbol is the large television screen on the wall, a variant of the Platonic mirror that man can turn upon all things in the illusion that he is the creator of everything it reflects.[12] The He-Ancient of Part V, looking back over the progress of human understanding, describes the barrenness of this condition:

> . . . when the marble masterpiece is dethroned by the automaton . . . when the body and the brain, the reasonable soul and human flesh subsisting . . . stand before you *unmasked as mere machinery* . . . you . . . would give worlds to be young enough to play with your rag doll again, since every step away from it has been a step away from love and happiness. (*My italics.*)

The imagery draws attention to the fact that in "The Thing Happens" Shaw is attacking one of his own attitudes, the realistic attitude of *The Quintessence of Ibsenism:*

> The masks were [*man's*] ideals, as he called them; and what, he would ask, would life be without ideals? Thus he became an idealist, and remained so until he dared to begin pulling the masks off and looking the spectres in the face. . . .[13]

The duologue of Burge-Lubin and Confucius does not forward the action in any obvious way; it anticipates no change in the situation and thus lacks

---

[10] This scene is Gilbertian in its repetition of the one trick of surprise.

[11] Cf. "A Glimpse of the Domesticity of Franklyn Barnabas": *Immenso Champernoon.* Like all men of science you are the dupe of appearances.

[12] "The Book of the Machines" in *Erewhon* has certainly contributed to this satire of the mechanization of life and the de-humanizing of men.

[13] *The Quintessence of Ibsenism*, original edition (1891), p. 20.

both suspense and urgency; an immediately evident reason for its inclusion is that it gives opportunity for a necessary scene-shift behind the curtain. In fact it is here that the dramatist makes his central statement of the link between his general theme of man and narrower theme of politics. The argument of the *Republic* is still his source: as reason should rule over appetite and passion in the soul, so should the Guardian (who is the philosopher) rule in the state. The double reference is contained in the idea of self-government:

Confucius. . . . You could fight. You could eat. You could drink. Until the twentieth century you could produce children. You could play games. You could work when you were forced to. But you could not govern yourselves. . . . You imported educated negresses and Chinese to govern you. Since then you have done very well. . . . People *like* you. . . . Nobody likes me: I am held in awe. Capable persons are never liked. I am not likeable; but I am indispensable.

The alienation of sympathy from his personifications of reason, in all sections of *Back to Methuselah*, is certainly part of Shaw's design.

(This is an appropriate place to recall Cain's introduction of himself:

I am the first murderer: you are only the first man. . . . To be the first murderer one must be a man of spirit.

If we recognize in him the type of the spirited, irascible faculty, his presence in Part I, as the third figure with Adam and Eve, is philosophically justified. Certainly he is the usurper: the false superman and self-deluding idolator, who "cannot love Lua until her face is painted." In Cain, the theme of war, the force behind the killing of the sons, first takes its place among the characters).

The central episode of Part III is dominated by Mrs. Lutestring. She is the Barnabas's parlourmaid transformed into the Domestic Minister, a silk purse made out of a sow's ear by an additional 250 years of life. She and Archbishop Haslam are god-like beside the others, and their dignity is largely a matter of deeper tones. It is possible that Shaw, in gracing her with the name of a moth (taken from Weismann?), also had her impressive style of speech in mind;[14] false etymology may have suggested to him the plangent quality of the lute:

Mrs. Lutestring. There was one daughter who was the child of my very heart . . . She was an old woman of ninety-six, blind. She asked me to sit and talk with her because my voice was like the voice of her dead mother.

[14] Brewer's *Dictionary of Phrase and Fable* defines "lutestring" as: "A glossy silk fabric; the French *lustrine*," and discusses the expression, "speaking in lutestring," which is taken to refer to: "Flash, highly polished oratory." It compares the Shakespearian "taffeta phrases and silken terms" and the use of "fustian," "bombast" and "shoddy" (which Shaw adopts as a pseudonym in *Back to Methuselah*)—"a book or speech made up of other men's brains."

An unexpected grim pathos, working up to indignation, sounds in her recollections of the lives of the poor in the early twentieth century: the "miserable pittances for worn-out old laborers to die on," and "the utter tiredness of forty years' unending overwork and striving to make a shilling do the work of a pound." Burge-Lubin's conversion, in the last scene, is presented as an automatic reaction to the knowledge that he may have three hundred years to live, and it takes burlesque form in his treatment of the negress (the false ideal, a coloured mask of beauty). He remains an inflated paper-bag of a character, incapable of feeling. And the *experience* of conversion is communicated to the audience only through the emotional resonance that Mrs. Lutestring has given to the dry doctrine of labour and production which is under discussion.

Shaw's drama is most gripping when the free development of feeling, "from grave to gay, from lively to severe," demands constant modulations in the actors' delivery.[15] This quality is most marked in the Elderly Gentleman section of the present play, which can rapidly draw from an audience a very considerable and subtly varied range of response. The musical form and texture of *Back to Methuselah* (always excepting the Burge-Lubin scenes) are very notable. Part I is essentially an overture in two sections: the first, a sonata, in which the leading themes of the play to follow are sounded and lightly interwoven by Adam and Eve, then by Eve and the Serpent, and then by all three in a final development punctuated by the harsh laugh of the Serpent—the anticipatory spasm of the Comic Spirit. The second Act is a noisy and vigorous operatic trio, Adam (tenor), Eve (soprano) and Cain (bass), singing against each other for all they are worth: three quarrelsome principles of human nature rocking the future of mankind.

The tuning-forks, which the Guardians of Part IV carry and occasionally use, represent a new dimension in the drama: a dispersed accompaniment of sounds which have symbolic function. A pistol-shot and blasts from a police-whistle mark the scene between Napoleon and the Oracle; the entry of the Envoy's party into the temple is preluded by orchestral music through which a gong resounds; the progress of the scene inside the temple is pointed by a series of musical motifs, beginning with the chimes of a carillon and continuing in bursts of "sacred" organ music, rolling and crashing of thunder, until finally: *"trombones utter three solemn blasts in the manner of Die Zauberflöte."* This is all part of the mummery with which the Guardians perfunctorily indulge the Shortlivers and that, ironically, is likely to impress an audience in the theatre, too; for the various qualities of sound are calculated to attune the mood of the auditorium to the dramatic movement through which Shaw conducts his characters. He uses the drum in *Major Barbara* with like symbolic force to increase the intensity of excitement at

[15] K. H. Gatch, loc. cit., refers to "those quick transitions to genuine feeling which everyone versed in Shavian comedy will recognize."

critical moments. In the third Act of *Man and Superman*, the Statue music from *Don Giovanni* was a setting for the dream convention and emphasized the extent to which the dialogue moved beyond "mere talk" towards pure rhetorical melody. So here Shaw is employing a device to remove his play still further from naturalism. It is not only in the perspective of time that *Back to Methuselah* is receding away from the present of the Brothers Barnabas; the later sections are distanced in the way that a self-contained work of art is remote from the "slice of life." The music of flutes, to which the Grecian figures dance farandole and sarabande at the beginning of Part V, is a frame to reveal the play as pure image, a moving icon of the dance of life.

A remarkable speeding-up begins with "The Tragedy of an Elderly Gentleman." The whole significant content of *Arms and the Man* is summed up in the scene between Napoleon and the Oracle. The debate between them is a commentary on the pantomime in which tragedy fizzles out and the epic hero dwindles, as later the clown will grow great. The sight of the Priestess compels Napoleon to sink to his knees; her threat to remove her veil forces him to yield his pistol to her. The development is repeated in yet more condensed form, as the melodramatic climax, in which she shoots him, is promptly followed by burlesque deflation:

The Oracle. . . . die before the tide of glory turns. Allow me [*she shoots him*].
    He falls with a shriek. She throws the pistol away and goes haughtily into the temple.
Napoleon [*scrambling to his feet*]. Murderess! Monster! She-devil! . . . No sense of
    the sacredness of human life! No thought for my wife and children! Bitch! Sow!
    Wanton! [*He picks up the pistol*]. And missed me at five yards! That's a woman all
    over.

As his abuse of her descends in bathos, he shrinks into a bad-tempered small boy who, pocketing his pistol, runs out blowing furious blasts on a whistle and glaring at Zoo as he brushes past her. So the dream of martial glory is abandoned for the rule of law; and the Nietzschean superman collapses gibbering at the base of a statue of Falstaff. This is the concentrated, allusive type of action that Shaw first perfected in *Misalliance* and that distinguishes *Heartbreak House* also. It may be described as symbolical farce.

In Part V, the speeding-up of time in the presentation of the Youths is even more evidently an aspect of the view of human life seen through the wrong end of a telescope. Chloe ages line by line in her dialogue with Strephon; at four, she is ready to put away childish things: "listening to flutes ringing changes on a few tunes and a few notes . . . making jingles with words." "Oh, this dreadful shortness of our lives!" laments the Newly Born, an hour out of the egg. "Nothing is great or little otherwise than by Comparison," Swift observed, and it is in relation to the virtual immortality of the Ancients, untouched by time in their eternity of contemplation, that the childhood of the Youths is scaled down to less than a butterfly's existence. This development was anticipated in Act I of "In the Beginning":

The Serpent. Love. Love. Love.
Adam. That is too short a word for so long a thing.
The Serpent [laughs]. . . . Love may be too long a word for so short a thing soon. But when it is short it will be very sweet.

Such is the experience of Strephon, the fool of love, in whom Granville Barker, had he produced the play, would have found the answer to his doubts about pure satire in the theatre. For Strephon is the token of Shaw's compassion, in whom the pain of becoming is concentrated. With him is identified the process of "heartbreak" that transports men against their will from folly to wisdom, as it tears them from all attainable desires. But, seen from so great a distance, the tragedy of the natural man is softened to a pathos that evokes a smile:

What is the use of being born if we have to decay into unnatural, heartless, loveless, joyless monsters in four short years? What use are the artists if they cannot bring their beautiful creations to life? I have a great mind to die and have done with it all.

The image recedes once again, now to minimal scale, as the Youths gather round, in their theatre on the stage of a theatre, to watch a play within a play. Pygmalion's automata, Ozymandias and Cleopatra-Semiramis, recapitulate in miniature the whole argument of *Back to Methuselah*, shifting from one style of dialogue to another, as they rapidly change from the satirized puppets of modern society, through the epic pose and the glorification of deterministic science, to creatures of evil and destruction. This is the last appearance of the theme of Cain,[16] the theme of usurping passion. At this point, when the female figure has given Pygmalion a mortal bite, the Ancients transfuse into them a measure of true life, a power of altruism, which takes them back to the truth of the relation between them, as Adam and Eve recognized it in Part I:

The Male Figure. . . . Spare her; and kill me. . . .
The Female Figure. Kill us both. How could either of us live without the other?

This is the moment of conversion, the climax of their play which is analogous to the climax of the whole play: the conversion of the Elderly Gentleman. It is Discouragement that strikes them to the ground; and out of the sense of life as "too heavy a burden," the immediate consequence of looking reality in the face, emerges the triumph of tragic death, such a resurrection in the spirit as Strephon shrinks from:

[16] Except in the musical recapitulation of the epilogue.

The Musicians play.

The Female Figure. Ozymandias: do you hear that? [*She rises on her knees and looks raptly into space*] Queen of queens! [*She dies*].

The Male Figure [*crawling feebly towards her until he reaches her hand*]. I knew I was really a king of kings. [*To the others*] Illusions, farewell: we are going to our thrones. [*He dies*].

The music stops.[17]

The Ancients' smile of compassion is apt comment on that.

This is the culmination of the theme of the Image, which Shaw has been developing to this fully dramatized form from the moment when the Serpent teaches the word "poem" to Eve and explains the meaning of "conception": "both the beginning in imagination and the end in creation." It has been sustained in the scattered imagery of dolls and disguises, in the Guardians' rejection of metaphors and in the static symbol of the television screen. It is rendered theatrically potent in the setting, and dramatically potent in the action, of Part IV, Act III. For the temple of the Oracle is the Platonic cave, where men are prisoners watching a shadow-show that they mistake for reality.

Major features of Plato's description are easily recognizable: the gloom and vapour of the abyss, and the violet light that flares up at intervals like the reflection of a fire; the raised gallery, brightly lit, along which move figures, some talking, including "*two men . . . holding their hats with the brims near their noses*"; the noises as of thunder that come from the void in answer to the tourists' questions. Shaw has not provided an exact reproduction of Plato's cave, but the whole scene is certainly closer to its original than the other great variant in modern drama: the cave-scene which is the climax of Strindberg's *Dream Play* and where are found the figure-heads of *Justice*, *Friendship*, and the rest, which have sunk in the sea of becoming.[18] Zoo sits with her back to the abyss and comments on the whole business of the Oracle as the conjuring trick that she knows it to be; yet the Shortlivers remain as much impressed by the illusion as the men chained in the cave, who disbelieve the explanations of their wiser fellows. The Elderly Gentleman, however, turns to face the Oracle in daylight, as the philosopher turns to the sun:

The Oracle [*with grave pity*]. Come: look at me. I am my natural size now: what you saw there was only a foolish picture of me thrown on a cloud by a lantern.

Edmund Wilson has read the last part of *Back to Methuselah* as evidence of Shaw's abandonment of politics for despair. It would be truer to say that here he turns away from politics in the same sense as Socrates turns away from his theory of the perfect state to the true concern of philosophy: con-

---

[17] Note the likeness to the masque in a Jacobean play.
[18] Shaw, of course, was among the first and most fervent of Strindberg's English admirers.

templation of the heavenly pattern of Ideas. *Major Barbara* stopped before
this, at the hypothesis: "If philosophers were kings in their cities. . . ." Now
the dramatist proceeds to demonstrate the relevance of the satirical art of
Back to Methuselah to the actual political business of men—to justify it as
political satire, indeed—by showing the distance between image and actuality which the political idealist ignores.

The mechanistic, deterministic creed recited by the unredeemed automata
takes its form and cadence from the First Epistle to the Corinthians:

> *The Male Figure.* . . . the king of kings and queen of queens are not accidents of
> the egg: they are thought-out and hand-made to receive the sacred Life Force.
> There is one person of the king and one of the queen; but the Life Force of the
> king and queen is all one: the glory equal, the majesty co-eternal. . . .

Parody such as this can work both ways, and Shaw quite often employs it
to an end which is the reverse of burlesque.[19] So now the tone of the passage
prepares for the heightening of seriousness in the Ancients' lengthy exposition
of the doctrine of Ideas. The furthest reach of consciousness to which Shaw
conducts us is visionary; for the Ancients are moving beyond philosophical
speculation to mysticism. Shaw has gone for its terms to the Pauline lines
which bear the closest relation to the turning away of Socrates. They provide
a viewpoint from which to look back on the entire design and intention of
the Shavian fable:

> There are also celestial bodies, and bodies terrestrial: but the glory of the celestial
> is one, and the glory of the terrestrial is another. . . .
> And so it is written, The first man Adam was made a living soul; the last
> Adam was made a quickening spirit . . . flesh and blood cannot inherit the
> kingdom of God; . . . we shall all be changed. . . .

There is undoubtedly an element of what Edmund Wilson calls "lunar
horror" in Part V. The power over life and death, as represented in the
delivery of the Newly Born from the egg, the making of man and woman
in a laboratory, and the calcining of unfit children, corresponds to the
eugenics and euthanasia of Plato's *Republic*, as well as to the potentialities
of modern science; these are such things as reason would always impose upon
the natural man. But the most significant figure in Part V is Pygmalion,
who takes us back to Laputa, the land of the machines, where the Watch-
maker is God. The scientist among the artists, he is identified with the false
relation between the ideal and the actuality which the philosopher-statesman
may labour to produce. For Pygmalion is so foolish as to do what Strephon

---

[19] A notable example is B.B.'s reaction to the death of Dubedat, where the power of
the Shakespearian words and rhythms into which he falls works against the effect of the
nonsense to which he reduces them.

is so foolish as to desire: bring images to life. The epilogue presents his true opposite in Lilith, who is the creative imagination.

The Ancients are no less relative and partial components of the total image of man than are the Guardians of Part IV, who do not understand imagination. In maintaining the opposition between rational soul and appetitive to the very end, Shaw acknowledges that the one cannot get on without the other. The tragedy of the Elderly Gentleman lies in the fact that the philosopher cannot escape from his humanity, though he may despise it. It is counterbalanced by the comedy of Pygmalion, with its theme of the destructiveness of pure intellect in the context of human life. The artist holds the scales, as Lubin—by one of those touches of truth with which Shaw keeps his caricatures alive—was allowed to observe:

> The poets and story tellers, especially the classical poets and story tellers, have been, in the main, right.

The Saint as Tragic Hero

by Louis L. Martz

Saints and martyrs have frequently been regarded as impossible subjects for true tragedy. The reasons have been forcibly summed up by Butcher in his standard commentary on Aristotle's *Poetics*. One trouble is, he says, that Goodness "is apt to be immobile and uncombative. In refusing to strike back it brings the action to a standstill." This is exactly the objection sometimes made to Eliot's presentation of Becket, who is certainly immobile and, in a sense, uncombative:

> We are not here to triumph by fighting, by stratagem, or by resistance,
> Not to fight with beasts as men. We have fought the beast
> And have conquered. We have only to conquer
> Now, by suffering.

But even in the case of more combative saints, such as Joan of Arc, Butcher would see a serious difficulty: "Impersonal ardour in the cause of right," he says, does not have "the same dramatic fascination as the spectacle of human weakness or passion doing battle with the fate it has brought upon itself." And in short, the chief difficulty is that "the death of the martyr presents to us not the defeat, but the victory of the individual; the issue of a conflict in which the individual is ranged on the same side as the higher powers, and the sense of suffering consequently lost in that of moral triumph." [1] This, I suppose, is what I. A. Richards also means when he declares that "The least touch of any theology which has a compensating

"The Saint as Tragic Hero" (original title: "The Saint as Tragic Hero: *Saint Joan and Murder in the Cathedral*") by Louis Martz. From *Tragic Themes in Western Literature*, ed. Cleanth Brooks (New Haven: Yale University Press, 1955). Copyright © 1955 by the Yale University Press. Reprinted by permission of the author. In the course of this study quotations are made by permission of the publisher from T. S. Eliot's *Murder in the Cathedral* (2nd. ed., New York: Harcourt, Brace & World, Inc., 1936; London, Faber & Faber, Ltd.) and *Four Quartets* (New York: Harcourt, Brace & World, Inc., 1943; London, Faber & Faber, Ltd.).

[1] S. H. Butcher, *Aristotle's Theory of Poetry and Fine Art, with a Critical Text and Translation of the Poetics* (4th ed., London, Macmillan & Co., Ltd., 1932), pp. 310–12.

Heaven to offer the tragic hero is fatal" [2]—fatal, that is, to the tragic effect. But we remember:

> Good night, sweet prince,
> And flights of angels sing thee to thy rest.

And we remember the transfiguration of Oedipus at Colonus. Hamlet and Oedipus, we might argue, are in the end on the side of the higher powers. I do not know what we should call Oedipus at Colonus, if he is not a kind of saint, and there is something almost saintly in Hamlet's acute sensitivity to evil. Butcher concedes that Aristotle does not take account of this exceptional type of tragedy "which exhibits the antagonism between a pure will and a disjointed world." [3] We are drawn, then, into some discussion of the nature of tragedy, into some discussion of the plight of tragedy today, and into some discussion, also, of another excellent kind of writing, sometimes called tragic, in which the modern world has achieved a peculiar eminence.

Let us begin with this other kind, for it lacks the touch of any theology. I am thinking of the kind represented by Hemingway's *A Farewell to Arms*. I am thinking particularly of the attitude represented by the dying words of Hemingway's heroine: " 'I'm going to die,' she said; then waited and said, 'I hate it' . . . Then a little later, 'I'm not afraid. I just hate it.' . . . 'Don't worry, darling, . . . I'm not a bit afraid. It's just a dirty trick.' " This scene is painful and pitiful as all that earlier misery in the same novel, during the rainy retreat from Caporetto, at the beginning of which Hemingway's hero sums up the central impact of the book, in words that are often quoted: "I was always embarrassed by the words sacred, glorious, and sacrifice and the expression in vain." And he proceeds to emphasize his embarrassment in words that echo a biblical cadence, faintly, and ironically: "We had heard them, sometimes standing in the rain almost out of earshot, so that only the shouted words came through, and had read them, on proclamations that were slapped up by billposters over other proclamations, now for a long time, and I had seen nothing sacred, and the things that were glorious had no glory and the sacrifices were like the stockyards at Chicago if nothing was done with the meat except to bury it." [4]

The tragedies of Oedipus, Phèdre, Samson, or Hamlet certainly include something like this sense of shattered illusions, this painful recognition of man's fragility, and this pitiful recognition of the inadequacy of human love—but along with, in the same moment with, equally powerful affirmations of the validity of these terms sacred, glorious, sacrifice, and the expres-

---

[2] I. A. Richards, *Principles of Literary Criticism* (New York, Harcourt, Brace & World, Inc., 1948), p. 246.

[3] Butcher, p. 325.

[4] Ernest Hemingway, *A Farewell to Arms*. (New York: Charles Scribner's Sons, 1929), pp. 353–54, 196.

sion in vain. Tragedy seems simultaneously to doubt and to believe in such expressions: tragedy seems never to know what Wallace Stevens calls "an affirmation free from doubt"—and yet it always seems to contain at least the Ghost of an affirmation. Oedipus the King and Samson Agonistes, blind and erring, still sacrifice themselves "gloriously," as Milton puts it. Racine's drama of Phèdre affirms the validity of the Law of Reason, even as the heroine dissolves herself in passion. And Hamlet sees mankind, simultaneously, as the most angelical and the most vicious of earthly creatures; like the Chorus of *Murder in the Cathedral*, Hamlet "knows and does not know."

This sense of a double vision at work in tragedy is somewhat akin to I. A. Richards' famous variation on Aristotle, where Richards finds the essence of tragedy to reside in a "balanced poise." In the "full tragic experience," Richards declares, "there is no suppression. The mind does not shy away from anything." But Richards himself, like Hemingway's hero, then proceeds to shy away from transcendental matters, when he declares that the mind, in tragedy, "stands uncomforted, unintimidated, alone and self-reliant." This, it seems, will not quite square with Richards' ultimate account of tragedy as "perhaps the most general, all-accepting, all-ordering experience known." [5]

A clearer account, at least a more dogmatic account, of this double vision of tragedy has been set forth by Joyce in his *Portrait of the Artist*. "Aristotle has not defined pity and terror," says Stephen Dedalus, "I have." "Pity is the feeling which arrests the mind in the presence of whatsoever is grave and constant in human sufferings and unites it with the human sufferer. Terror is the feeling which arrests the mind in the presence of whatsoever is grave and constant in human sufferings and unites it with the secret cause." [6] Tragedy, then, seems to demand both the human sufferer and the secret cause: that is to say, the doubt, the pain, the pity of the human sufferer; and the affirmation, the awe, the terror of the secret cause. It is an affirmation even though the cause is destructive in its immediate effects: for this cause seems to affirm the existence of some universal order of things.

From this standpoint we can estimate the enormous problem that faces the modern writer in his quest for tragedy. With Ibsen, for example, this power of double vision is in some difficulty. In *Ghosts* or in *Rosmersholm* the element of affirmation is almost overwhelmed by the horror and the suffering that come from the operation of the secret cause—here represented by the family heritage—the dead husband, the dead wife. The affirmation is present, however, in the salvation of an individual's integrity. Ibsen's *Ghosts*, which has the rain pouring down outside for most of the play, nevertheless ends with a view of bright sunshine on the glaciers: symbolizing, perhaps, the

---

[5] Richards, pp. 246–8.

[6] James Joyce, *A Portrait of the Artist as a Young Man* (New York: B. W. Huebsch, 1916), p. 239.

clear self-realization which the heroine has achieved. But it is not a very long step before we exit—left—from these shattered drawing rooms into the rain of Ernest Hemingway, where we have the human sufferers, "alone and self-reliant," without a touch of any secret cause. We are in the world of pity which Santayana has beautifully described in a passage of his *Realms of Being*, where he speaks of the "unreasoning sentiment" he might feel in seeing a "blind old beggar" in a Spanish town: "pity simply, the pity of existence, suffusing, arresting, rendering visionary the spectacle of the moment and spreading blindly outwards, like a light in the dark, towards objects which it does not avail to render distinguishable."

It seems a perfect account of the central and powerful effect achieved in many of the best efforts of the modern stage, or movie, or novel, works of pity, where pity dissolves the scene, resolves it into the dew that Hamlet considers but transcends. Thus *A Farewell to Arms* is enveloped in symbolic rain; in *The Naked and the Dead* humanity is lost in the dim Pacific jungle; and the haze of madness gradually dissolves the realistic setting of *A Streetcar Named Desire* or *Death of a Salesman*. In the end, Willy Loman has to plant his garden in the dark. "The pity of existence . . . spreading blindly outwards . . . towards objects which it does not avail to render distinguishable."

The problem of the tragic writer in our day appears to be: how to control this threatened dissolution, how to combine this "unreasoning sentiment" with something like the different vision that Santayana goes on to suggest: "Suppose now that I turn through the town gates and suddenly see a broad valley spread out before me with the purple sierra in the distance beyond. This expanse, this vastness, fills my intuition; also, perhaps, some sense of the deeper breath which I draw as if my breast expanded in sympathy with the rounded heavens." [7] Thus we often find that the modern writer who seeks a tragic effect will attempt, by some device, such as Ibsen's family heritage or his view of the glacier, to give us the experience of a secret cause underlying his work of pity—to give it broader dimensions, sharper form, to render the ultimate objects distinguishable, to prevent it from spreading blindly outwards. We can see this plainly in O'Neill's *Mourning Becomes Electra*, where O'Neill, by borrowing from Aeschylus the ancient idea of a family curse, is able to give his drama a firm, stark outline, and to endow his heroine with something like a tragic dignity. The only trouble is that this Freudian version of a family curse is not secret enough: it tends to announce itself hysterically, all over the place: "I'm the last Mannon. I've got to punish myself!" In the end we feel that this family curse has been shipped in from Greece and has never quite settled down in New England.

Eliot has described much the same difficulty which appears in his play

<hr />

[7] George Santayana, *Realms of Being* (New York: Charles Scribner's Sons, 1942), pp. 147–49.

The Family Reunion, where he too, even more boldly than O'Neill, has tried to borrow the Furies from Aeschylus. Eliot deploys his Furies, quite impolitely, in the middle of Ibsen's drawing room. As we might expect, they were not welcome: "We tried every possible manner of presenting them," says Eliot. "We put them on the stage, and they looked like uninvited guests who had strayed in from a fancy-dress ball. We concealed them behind gauze, and they suggested a still out of a Walt Disney film. We made them dimmer, and they looked like shrubbery just outside the window. I have seen other expedients tried": Eliot adds, "I have seen them signalling from across the garden, or swarming onto the stage like a football team, and they are never right. They never succeed in being either Greek goddesses or modern spooks. But their failure," he concludes, "is merely a symptom of the failure to adjust the ancient with the modern." [8] Or, we might say, a failure to adjust the ancient Aeschylean symbol of a secret cause with the modern human sufferer.

How, then, can it be done? It is in their approach to this problem that *Saint Joan* and *Murder in the Cathedral* reveal their peculiar power, in an approach that seems to have been made possible by this fact: that both Shaw and Eliot feel they cannot depend upon their audience to accept their saintly heroes as divinely inspired. The dramaturgy of both plays is based upon a deliberate manipulation of the elements of religious skepticism or uncertainty in the audience.

As Eliot's play moves toward the somber conclusion of its first half, the Four Tempters cry out in the temptation of self-pity ("It's just a dirty trick"):

> Man's life is a cheat and a disappointment . . .
> All things become less real, man passes
> From unreality to unreality.
> This man [Becket] is obstinate, blind, intent
> On self-destruction,
> Passing from deception to deception,
> From grandeur to grandeur to final illusion . . .

And a page later the Chorus too cries out from the world of Ernest Hemingway, with also, perhaps, a slight reminiscence of the millrace in *Rosmersholm:*

> We have seen the young man mutilated,
> The torn girl trembling by the mill-stream.
> And meanwhile we have gone on living,
> Living and partly living,
> Picking together the pieces,

[8] T. S. Eliot, *Poetry and Drama* (Cambridge, Mass.: Harvard University Press, 1951), p. 37.

> Gathering faggots at nightfall,
> Building a partial shelter,
> For sleeping, and eating and drinking and laughter.

And then, at the very close of Part I, Becket sums up the whole attitude when he turns sharply to address the audience:

> I know
> What yet remains to show you of my history
> Will seem to most of you at best futility,
> Senseless self-slaughter of a lunatic,
> Arrogant passion of a fanatic.
> I know that history at all times draws
> The strangest consequence from remotest cause.

It is exactly the challenge that Shaw has thrown at his readers in the Preface to *Saint Joan:* "For us to set up our condition as a standard of sanity, and declare Joan mad because she never condescended to it, is to prove that we are not only lost but irredeemable."

Eliot and Shaw, then, seem to be assuming that the least touch of theology in their plays will serve—to raise a question. And so the saint may become a figure well adapted to arouse something very close to a tragic experience: for here the words sacred, glorious, sacrifice, and the expression in vain may become once again easily appropriate; while at the same time the uncertainty of the audience's attitude—and to some extent the dramatist's own—may enable him to deal also with the painful and pitiful aspects of experience that form the other side of the tragic tension.

But this conflict, this double vision, is not, in these plays, primarily contained within the figure of the saint as tragic hero: Joan and Becket do not here represent humanity in the way of Hamlet, or King Oedipus—by focusing within themselves the full tragic tension. They are much more like Oedipus at Colonus, who, although a pitiful beggar in appearance, speaks now through the power of a superhuman insight. Most of his mind lies beyond suffering: he feels that he has found the secret cause, and under the impulse of that cause he moves onward magnificently to his death and transfiguration. The sense of human suffering in *Oedipus at Colonus* is conveyed chiefly in retrospect, or in the sympathetic outcries of the Chorus, the weeping of the rejected Polynices, and the anguish of the two daughters whom Oedipus must leave behind.

To see these plays as in any sense tragic it seems that we must abandon the concept of a play built upon an ideal Aristotelian hero, and look instead for a tragic experience that arises from the interaction between a hero who represents the secret cause, and the other characters, who represent the human sufferers. The point is brought out, ironically, by the Archbishop, near the end of Shaw's play, when he warns Joan against the sin of pride, saying, "The old Greek tragedy is rising among us. It is the chastisement of hubris." Joan replies with her usual bluntness, asking, "How can you say that I am disobedient when I always obey my voices, because they come from God." But when the Archbishop insists that "all the voices that come to you are the echoes of your own wilfulness," when he declares angrily, "You stand alone: absolutely alone, trusting to your own conceit, your own ignorance, your own headstrong presumption, your own impiety," we are reminded of Creon berating Oedipus at Colonus, and we are reminded too of Oedipus' long declaration of innocence when Joan turns away, "her eyes skyward," saying, "I have better friends and better counsel than yours."

There is nothing complex about the character of Shaw's Joan; it is the whole fabric of the play that creates something like a tragic tension. For whatever he may say in his preface, Shaw the dramatist, through his huge cast of varied human types, probes the whole range of belief and disbelief in Joan's voices. "They come from your imagination," says the feeble de Baudricourt in the opening scene. "Of course," says Joan, "That is how the messages of God come to us." Cauchon believes the girl to be "inspired, but diabolically inspired." "Many saints have said as much as Joan," Ladvenu suggests. Dunois, her only friend, senses some aura of divinity about her, but becomes extremely uneasy when she talks about her voices. "I should think," he says, "you were a bit cracked if I hadn't noticed that you give me very sensible reasons for what you do, though I hear you telling others you are only obeying Madame Saint Catherine." "Well," she replies, "I have to find reasons for you, because you do not believe in my voices. But the voices come first; and I find the reasons after: whatever you may choose to believe." *Whatever you may choose to believe:* there is the point, and as the figure of Joan flashes onward through the play, with only one lapse in confidence—her brief recantation—Shaw keeps his play hovering among choices in a highly modern state of uncertainty: we know and do not know: until at the close Shaw seems to send us over on the side of affirmation. We agree, at least, with the words of the French captain in the opening scene: "There is something about her. . . . Something. . . . I think the girl herself is a bit of a miracle."

She is, as Eliot would say, "a white light still and moving," the simple *cause* of every other word and action in the play; and her absolute simplicity of vision cuts raspingly through all the malign or well-intentioned errors of the world, until in its wrath the world rises up in the form of all its assembled institutions and declares by the voice of all its assembled doctors that this girl is—as Shaw says—*insufferable.*[9]

Thus Joan's apparent resemblance to the Aristotelian hero: her extreme

[9] See the amusing anecdote recorded by Archibald Henderson, *Bernard Shaw, Playboy and Prophet* (New York: Appleton-Century-Crofts, 1932), pp. 693–95.

self-confidence, her brashness, her appearance of rash impetuosity—all this becomes in the end a piece of Shavian irony, for her only real error in the play is the one point where her superb self-confidence breaks down in the panic of recantation. And so the hubris is not Joan's but Everyman's. The characters who accuse Joan of pride and error are in those accusations convicting themselves of the pride of self-righteousness and the errors of human certitude. It is true that the suffering that results from this pride and error remains in Shaw's play rather theoretical and remote: and yet we feel it in some degree: in the pallor and anguish of Joan as she resists the temptation to doubt her voices, in the rather unconvincing screams of Stogumber at the close, and, much more effectively, in the quiet, controlled sympathy of Ladvenu. It would seem, then, that some degree of tragedy resides in this failure of Everyman to recognize absolute Reality, the secret cause, when it appears in the flesh. Must then, cries Cauchon in the Epilogue, "Must then a Christ perish in torment in every age to save those that have no imagination?" It is the same symbolism that Eliot has evoked in the beginning of his play, where the Chorus asks: "Shall the Son of Man be born again in the litter of scorn?"

We need not be too greatly concerned with Shaw's bland assertions that he is letting us in on the truth about the Middle Ages, telling us in the play all we need to know about Joan. Books and articles have appeared—a whole cloudburst of them—devoted to proving that Shaw's methods of historical research in his play and in his preface are open to serious question. But Shaw gave that game away long ago when he announced: "I deal with all periods; but I never study any period but the present, which I have not yet mastered and never shall";[10] or when he said, with regard to Cleopatra's cure for Caesar's baldness, that his methods of scholarship, as compared with Gilbert Murray's, consisted in "pure divination." [11] The Preface to *Saint Joan* lays down a long barrage of historicity, which in the end is revealed as a remarkable piece of Shavio-Swiftian hoaxing: for in the last few pages of that long preface he adds, incidentally, that his use of the "available documentation" has been accompanied by "such powers of divination as I possess"; he concedes that for some figures in his play he has invented "appropriate characters" "in Shakespear's manner"; and that, fundamentally, his play is built upon what he calls "the inevitable flatteries of tragedy." That is, there is no historical basis for his highly favorable characterizations of Cauchon and the Inquisitor, upon which the power and point of the trial scene are founded.

I do not mean to say, however, that our sense of history is irrelevant to an appreciation of Shaw's play. There is a point to be made by considering such a book as J. M. Robertson's *Mr. Shaw and "The Maid,"* which complains

[10] Shaw, Preface to *The Sanity of Art* (New York: B. R. Tucker, 1908), p. 5.
[11] See Shaw's notes appended to *Caesar and Cleopatra: Nine Plays*, p. 471.

bitterly, upon historical grounds, against Shaw's "instinct to put things both ways." [12] This is a book, incidentally, which Eliot has praised very highly because it points out that in this kind of subject "Facts matter," and that "to Mr. Shaw, truth and falsehood . . . do not seem to have the same meaning as to ordinary people." [13] But the point lies rather in the tribute that such remarks pay to the effectiveness of Shaw's realistic dramaturgy.

Shaw is writing, as he and Ibsen had to write, within the conventions of the modern realistic theater—conventions which Eliot escaped in *Murder in the Cathedral* because he was writing this play for performance at the Canterbury Festival. But in his later plays, composed for the theater proper, Eliot has also been forced to, at least he has chosen to, write within these stern conventions.

Now in the realistic theater, as Francis Fergusson has suggested, the artist seems to be under the obligation to pretend that he is not an artist at all, but is simply interested in pursuing the truth "in some pseudo-scientific sense." [14] Thus we find the relation of art to life so often driven home on the modern stage by such deep symbolic actions as removing the cubes from ice trays or cooking an omelette for dinner. Shaw knows that on this stage facts matter—or at least the appearance of facts—and in this need for a dramatic realism lies the basic justification for Shaw's elaborately argued presentation of Joan as a Protestant and Nationalist martyr killed by the combined institutional forces of feudalism and the Church. Through these historical theories, developed within the body of the play, Joan is presented as the agent of a transformation in the actual world; the theories have enough plausibility for dramatic purposes, and perhaps a bit more; this, together with Shaw's adaptation of the records of Joan's trial, gives him all the "facts" that he needs to make his point in the modern theater.

Some of Joan's most Shavian remarks are in fact her own words as set down in the long records of her trial: as, for example, where her questioner asks whether Michael does not appear to her as a naked man. "Do you think God cannot afford clothes for him?" answers Joan, in the play and in the records. Shaw has made a skillful selection of these answers, using, apparently, the English translation of the documents edited by Douglas Murray;[15] and he has set these answers together with speeches of his own

[12] J. M. Robertson, *Mr. Shaw and "The Maid"* (London: Cobden-Sanderson, 1926), p. 85.

[13] T. S. Eliot, *Criterion, 4* (April 1926), 390.

[14] Francis Fergusson, *The Idea of a Theater* (Princeton: Princeton University Press, 1949), p. 147.

[15] *Jeanne D'Arc, Maid of Orleans, Deliverer of France; Being the Story of her Life, her Achievements, and her Death, as attested on Oath and Set forth in the Original Documents*, ed. by T. Douglas Murray (New York: McClure, Phillips, 1902; published in England the same year). See p. 42: "Do you think God has not wherewithal to clothe him?" This contains a translation of the official Latin documents published by Jules Quicherat in 1841–49.

modeled upon their tone and manner. In this way he has been able to bring within the limits of the realistic theater the very voice that rings throughout these trial records, the voice of the lone girl fencing with, stabbing at, baffling, and defeating the crowd of some sixty learned men: a voice that is not speaking within the range of the other voices that assail her. Thus we hear her in the following speech adapted from half-a-dozen places in the records:

> "I have said again and again that I will tell you all that concerns this trial. But I cannot tell you the whole truth: God does not allow the whole truth to be told. . . . It is an old saying that he who tells too much truth is sure to be hanged. . . . I have sworn as much as I will swear; and I will swear no more."[16]

Or, following the documents much more closely, her answers thus resound when the questioners attempt to force her to submit her case to the Church on earth: "I will obey The Church," says Joan, "provided it does not command anything impossible."

> If you command me to declare that all that I have done and said, and all the visions and revelations I have had, were not from God, then that is impossible: I will not declare it for anything in the world. What God made me do I will never go back on; and what He has commanded or shall command I will not fail to do in spite of any man alive. That is what I mean by impossible. And in case The Church should bid me do anything contrary to the command I have from God, I will not consent to it, no matter what it may be.

In thus maintaining the tone of that—extraordinary—voice, Shaw has, I think, achieved an effect that is in some ways very close to the effect of the "intersection of the timeless with time" which Eliot has achieved in his play, and which he has described in "The Dry Salvages":

> Men's curiosity searches past and future
> And clings to that dimension. But to apprehend
> The point of intersection of the timeless
> With time, is an occupation for the saint—
> No occupation either, but something given
> And taken, in a lifetime's death in love,
> Ardour and selflessness and self-surrender.

An obvious similarity between the two plays may be seen in the tone of satirical wit that runs through both—notably in the ludicrous prose speeches that Eliot's murdering Knights deliver to the audience in self-defense. These have an essentially Shavian purpose: "to shock the audience out of their

---

[16] Cf. Murray, pp. 5–6, 8–9, 14–15, 18, 22, 33.

complacency," as Eliot has recently said, going on to admit, "I may, for aught I know, have been slightly under the influence of *St. Joan.*" [17] The atmosphere of wit is evident also in the first part of Eliot's play, in the cynical attitude of the Herald who announces Becket's return:

> The streets of the city will be packed to suffocation,
> And I think that his horse will be deprived of its tail,
> A single hair of which becomes a precious relic.

Or, more important, in the speeches of the Four Tempters, who match the Four Knights of Part II, and who tend to speak, as the Knights also do in places, in a carefully calculated doggerel that betrays their fundamental shallowness:

> I leave you to the pleasures of your higher vices,
> Which will have to be paid for at higher prices.
> Farewell, my Lord, I do not wait upon ceremony,
> I leave as I came, forgetting all acrimony,
> Hoping that your present gravity
> Will find excuse for my humble levity.
> If you will remember me, my Lord, at your prayers,
> I'll remember you at kissing-time below the stairs.

In all these ways Eliot, like Shaw, maintains his action in the "real" world: and by other means as well. By keeping before us the central question of our own time: "Is it war or peace?" asks Eliot's priest. "Peace," replies the Herald, "but not the kiss of peace./ A patched up affair, if you ask my opinion." By the frequently realistic imagery of the Chorus, made up of "the scrubbers and sweepers of Canterbury." By the frequent use in Part II of the recorded words that passed between Becket and the Knights in the year 1170.[18] By throwing our minds back to the literary forms of the Middle Ages: to *Everyman*, from which Eliot has taken a good many hints for the tone and manner of Becket's encounter with the Tempters, and which, as he says, he has kept in mind as a model for the versification of his dialogue.[19] To this last we should also add a special device of heavy alliteration (particularly notable in the Second Temptation), which seems to work in two ways: it reminds us of the English alliterative verse of the Middle Ages, and thus gives the play a further historical focus, and it also suggests here a rhetoric of worldly ambition in keeping with the temptation that Becket is undergoing:

[17] Eliot, *Poetry and Drama*, p. 30.
[18] See William Holden Hutton, *S. Thomas of Canterbury. An account of his Life and Fame from the Contemporary Biographers and other Chroniclers* (London, 1889), esp. pp. 234–245.
[19] Eliot, *Poetry and Drama*, pp. 27–28.

Think, my Lord,
Power obtained grows to glory,
Life lasting, a permanent possession,
A templed tomb, monument of marble.
Rule over men reckon no madness.

Both Eliot and Shaw, then, have in their own ways taken pains to place
their action simultaneously in the "real" past and the "real" present: an
action firmly fixed in time must underlie the shock of intersection.

But of course, in Eliot's play the cause of intersection, the agent of transformation, the saint, is utterly different from Shaw's, and thus the plays
become, so obviously, different. Shaw's Joan is the active saint, operating
in the world; Eliot's Becket is a contemplative figure, ascetic, "withdrawn
to contemplation," holding within his mind, and reconciling there alone,
the stresses of the world. His immobility is his strength, he is the still point,
the center of the world that moves about him, as his sermon is the center
of the play.

One is struck here by the similarity between the total conception of Eliot's
play and of *Oedipus at Colonus*. Both heroes, after a long period of wandering,
have found, at their entrance, their place of rest and their place of death,
in a sacred spot: Becket in his Cathedral, Oedipus in the sacred wood of
the Furies or Eumenides. Both heroes maintain the attitude that Oedipus
states at the outset: "nevermore will I depart from my rest in this land."
Both reveal in their opening speeches the view that, as Oedipus says, "patience is the lesson of suffering." [20] Both are then subjected to various kinds
of temptations to leave the spot; both are forced to recapitulate their past
while enduring these trials; both remain immobile, unmovable; both win
a glorious death and by that death benefit the land in which they die. Both
are surrounded by a large cast of varied human sufferers, who do not understand the saint, who try to deflect him from his ways, and who in some
cases mourn his loss bitterly: the cry of Eliot's priest at the end is like the
cries of Antigone and Ismene:

> O father, father, gone from us, lost to us,
> How shall we find you, from what far place
> Do you look down on us?

I suspect that *Oedipus at Colonus* has in fact had a deep and early influence
upon Eliot's whole career: "Sweeney among the Nightingales" alludes to
this very wood, which Sophocles' Chorus describes as a place where

> The sweet, sojourning nightingale
> Murmurs all day long. . . .

[20] *The Tragedies of Sophocles*, trans. Sir Richard C. Jebb (Cambridge: Cambridge University Press, 1904), pp. 63, 61.

> And here the choiring Muses come,
> And the divinity of love
> With the gold reins in her hand.[21]

The fact that the Muses haunt this wood may throw some light too upon the title of Eliot's first book of essays, *The Sacred Wood*, the book in which he revealed his early interest in the possibility of a poetic drama.

But our main point here is the way in which this deeply religious tragedy of Sophocles, which had already provided a strong formative precedent for Milton's *Samson Agonistes*, now provides us with a precedent for regarding Eliot's saint's play as a tragedy. The precedent may also explain why a strong coloring of Greek-like fatalism runs throughout Eliot's Christian play: a coloring which some of Eliot's critics have found disturbing. But these classical reminiscences of Destiny and Fate and Fortune's wheel remind us only of the base upon which Eliot is building: they do not delimit his total meaning. We can see this amalgamation of Greek and Christian at work in Becket's opening speech—the most important speech of the play, which all the rest of the play explores and illustrates. It is the speech which Becket's Fourth Tempter, his inmost self, repeats in mockery, word for word, twenty pages later, and thus suggests that these Temptations—of pleasure, worldly power, and spiritual pride—are to be regarded as fundamentally a recapitulation of the stages by which Becket has reached the state of mind he displays at his entrance. He believes that he has found a secret cause, and he enters prepared to die in that belief: "Peace," he says to the worried priest, and then, referring to the Chorus of anxious women, continues:

> They speak better than they know, and beyond your understanding.
> They know and do not know, what it is to act or suffer.
> They know and do not know, that acting is suffering
> And suffering is action. Neither does the actor suffer
> Nor the patient act. But both are fixed
> In an eternal action, an eternal patience
> To which all must consent that it may be willed
> And which all must suffer that they may will it,
> That the pattern may subsist, for the pattern is the action
> And the suffering, that the wheel may turn and still
> Be forever still.

We can worry the ambiguities of those words "suffering" and "patient" as long as we wish: in the end Becket keeps his secret almost as stubbornly as Joan or Oedipus:

---

[21] Sophocles, *Oedipus at Colonus*, trans. Robert Fitzgerald (New York: Harcourt, Brace & World, Inc., 1941), pp. 55–56.

I have had a tremor of bliss, a wink of heaven, a whisper,
And I would no longer be denied; all things
Proceed to a joyful consummation.

But halfway between these two passages lies Becket's Christmas sermon,
presented as a four-page interlude between the play's two parts. It is one
of the most surprisingly successful moments in the modern theater, for who
would expect to find a sermon, and an interesting sermon, here? It owes its
success to an atmosphere of restrained and controlled mystery, and to the
fact that it is not really an interlude at all, but a deep expression of the
play's central theme, binding the play's two parts into one. Becket is speaking
of this word *Peace*, the word that dominates the play, for all the actors and
sufferers in the play are seeking peace, on their own terms. But the meaning
of the word for Becket is conveyed only obliquely, by Becket's tone, his poise,
his humility, his acceptance, "Thus devoted, concentrated in purpose." He
can display only by his own action and suffering what this word Peace
means to him, for he is trying to explain the meaning of the unspoken Word
that lies locked in the visible and verbal paradoxes of acting and suffering.

And only in this way, too, can Becket display that submission of the will
by which he avoids the final temptation of spiritual pride. The Temptations
make it clear that Becket has been a proud man—even an arrogant man:
the first priest, the Tempters, and the Knights all accuse him, with some
reason, of pride. And we hear him speaking at times, throughout the play,
and even at the very end, in a harsh, acid tone, which here and there is
uncomfortably close to condescension. Eliot's control of the character is not
perhaps as firm as we could wish; though there is nothing that a skillful
actor cannot handle, for the central conception is clear: like Oedipus,
Becket is still a man, and retains the marks of his natural character: but
in the sermon we grasp his saintliness.

At the same time Becket conveys to us the essence of the view of Tragedy
that we are here considering. Becket's sermon ponders the fact that in the
services of Christmas the Church celebrates birth and death simultaneously.
Now, "as the World sees," Becket says, "this is to behave in a strange
fashion. For who in the World will both mourn and rejoice at once and
for the same reason?" And this is true on other occasions, he adds: "so also,
in a smaller figure, we both rejoice and mourn in the death of martyrs. We
mourn, for the sins of the world that has martyred them; we rejoice, that
another soul is numbered among the Saints. . . ."

It is this tension, this double vision, that Eliot presents in his great choral
odes. What Eliot has done is to allow everyone in his play except the Chorus
and Becket to remain the simplest possible types—simpler even than Shaw's:
ciphers who serve their functions: to provide an outline of the action and
a setting for the problem. Into the cries of the Chorus he has poured the

tragic experience of suffering humanity, caught in the grip of a secret cause: "We are forced to bear witness."

The Chorus opens the play with fear and reluctance and hopelessness, asking who it is who shall

> Stretch out his hand to the fire, and deny his master? who shall be warm
> By the fire, and deny his master?

They know and do not know who it is—themselves—bending to the earth like animals seeking their protective coloring:

> Now I fear disturbance of the quiet seasons:
> Winter shall come bringing death from the sea,
> Ruinous spring shall beat at our doors,
> Root and shoot shall eat our eyes and our ears,
> Disastrous summer burn up the beds of our streams
> And the poor shall wait for another decaying October.

These dead do not desire resurrection; and when their Lord Archbishop reappears to them, they can only cry out, "O Thomas, return, Archbishop; return, return to France. . . . Leave us to perish in quiet." They would like to go on "living and partly living," like Shaw's Dauphin, who irritably shies away from Joan, saying, "I want to sleep in a comfortable bed." Eliot's Chorus starts from this point—by the fireside and the bed—a point which Shaw's chorus of varied actors hardly goes beyond. But Eliot's Chorus moves far beyond this point, undergoing what Kenneth Burke or Francis Fergusson might call a ritual of transformation. They are not at all the "foolish, immodest and babbling women" which Eliot's priest calls them, but the heart of humanity moving under the impulse of a half-realized cause. Under this impulse they have moved, by the end of Part I, into the range of a "stifling scent of despair," which nevertheless is not spreading blindly outwards: for the Chorus

> The forms take shape in the dark air:
> Puss-purr of leopard, footfall of padding bear,
> Palm-pat of nodding ape, square hyaena waiting
> For laughter, laughter, laughter. The Lords of Hell are here.

But after Becket's sermon the Chorus has taken some heart: they no longer seem to fear the spring:

> When the leaf is out on the tree, when the elder and may
> Burst over the stream, and the air is clear and high,
> And voices trill at windows, and children tumble in front of the door,
> What work shall have been done, what wrong

> Shall the bird's song cover, the green tree cover, what wrong
> Shall the fresh earth cover?

From this oscillation between despair and a half-hope arises the play's greatest poetry, as the Chorus moves on far out of the range of ordinary fears and hopes into a nightmare vision that renews and extends the animal imagery, and the dense imagery of taste and smell and the other senses, by which the Chorus had expressed its horror at the close of Part I; but now there is more than horror: the Chorus is moving on here to a vision of humanity's living relation with all being, to a sense that all of creation from the worm to the Prince is involved in this sacrifice:

> I have smelt them, the death-bringers, senses are quickened
> By subtile forebodings . . .
>   I have tasted
> The savour of putrid flesh in the spoon. I have felt
> The heaving of earth at nightfall, restless, absurd. I have heard
> Laughter in the noises of beasts that make strange noises . . .
>   I have eaten
> Smooth creatures still living, with the strong salt taste of living things
>   under sea . . .
>   In the air
> Flirted with the passage of the kite, I have plunged with the kite and
>   cowered with the wren. . . .
>   I have seen
> Rings of light coiling downwards, leading
> To the horror of the ape. . . .
> I have consented, Lord Archbishop, have consented.

Beyond this recognition of responsibility for the action and the suffering, there lies a step into the vision of ultimate horror which they face just before the murder: a vision of utter spiritual death: the Dark Night of the Soul:

> Emptiness, absence, separation from God;
> The horror of the effortless journey, to the empty land
> Which is no land, only emptiness, absence, the Void. . . .

This, paradoxically, is their moment of deepest vision, of greatest courage; the point at which they fully comprehend their need for the sacrifice about to be permitted, suffered, and which provides the answer to their cries during the very act of the murder:

> Clear the air! clean the sky! wash the wind! take the stone from
>   the stone, take the skin from the arm, take the muscle from the
>   bone, and wash them. Wash the stone, wash the bone, wash the
>   brain, wash the soul, wash them wash them!

Like King Oedipus they are, without quite realizing it, being washed in this "rain of blood" that is blinding their eyes.

As these cries from the conscience of humanity fade away, the lights fade out—and then come on again in the foreground with a glaring brightness—as the four Murderers step forward, make their bows, and present their ridiculous speeches of defense—in the manner of an after-dinner speaker: "I knew Becket well, in various official relations; and I may say that I have never known a man so well qualified for the highest rank of the Civil Service." Or in the manner of the parliamentary orator: "I must repeat one point that the last speaker has made. While the late Archbishop was Chancellor, he wholeheartedly supported the King's designs: this is an important point, which, if necessary, I can substantiate." Or in the manner of the brisk attorney: "I think, with these facts before you, you will unhesitatingly render a verdict of Suicide while of Unsound Mind."

The lights fade out again, the Knights disappear, and then gradually the lights come on once more, to reveal the priests and the Chorus in their old positions. It is as if the Knights had never spoken: the conscience of humanity has been working deep within while the Knights were speaking on the surface, and now the Chorus sums up its discoveries, its transformation, in a psalm of praise, in which once again it affirms a union with the whole creation, but this time in a tone of joy and peace:

> We praise Thee, O God, for Thy glory displayed in all the creatures
> of the earth,
> In the snow, in the rain, in the wind, in the storm; in all of Thy
> creatures, both the hunters and the hunted. . . .
> They affirm Thee in living; all things affirm Thee in living; the bird
> in the air, both the hawk and the finch; the beast on the earth, both
> the wolf and the lamb; the worm in the soil and the worm in the
> belly. . . .
> Even in us the voices of seasons, the snuffle of winter, the song of spring,
> the drone of summer, the voices of beasts and of birds, praise Thee.

Those words from the final chorus may remind us again of the long tentacles of correlated imagery that reach throughout these choral odes: imagery of beasts and birds and worms; of seasons, of violent death, of the daily hardships of the partly living life: with the result that these choral odes grow together into a long poem, interwoven with verse and prose pitched at a lower intensity; and by this interweaving of the odes, even more than by Becket, the play is drawn into unity.

We can see now the effect that these different manifestations of a secret cause have had upon the total construction of our two saint's plays. Eliot's play, focused on a contemplative saint, displays what we might call a semi-circular structure: with Becket as the still center, and the Chorus sweeping

out around him in a broad dramatic action, a poetical ballet of transformation. Shaw's play, based on an active saint, develops instead a linear structure, as of a spear driving straight for the mark. It is marred, here and there,
by irrelevant or maladjusted witticisms, and the whole character of
Stogumber is a misfortune. Yet Joan and her voices seem to work like key
symbols in a poem: appearing in a carefully designed sequence of different
contexts: six scenes, with six differing moods, moving from farce to high
comedy, to a romantic glimpse of the warrior Joan in shining armor, and
from here into an area of deepening somberness, until, by the fifth scene,
the world of Shaw's play, too, has been transformed—from the foolish to the
tragic. Now we have in his play, too, the dim silence of the Cathedral, with
Joan praying symbolically before the stations of the Cross: her white raiment
revealing the saint whose mission is now nearly complete. The king is
crowned; she has shown France how to win; and now, as her allies, one by
one, and even Dunois, fail to answer the unbearable demands of the superhuman, Joan goes forth to meet the cheering crowd who will kiss her gar-
ments and line her roadway with palms. The way is now prepared for the
massive trial scene, the tragic agon, which presents what Eliot calls "a
symbol perfected in death."

And then, the Epilogue. Many have found this a disconcerting, inartistic
mixture of farce, satire, and didactic explanation. I agree. But I do not see
why the Epilogue should spoil the play. An epilogue is no part of the dramatic
action: it is the author's chance to step forward, relaxed and garrulous, and
to talk the play over with the audience. Traditionally, it is true, the epilogue
is recited by only one performer—by Prospero, for instance. There is a slight
difference here: Shaw has had his entire cast recite the Epilogue. But it is
still appended commentary on the action, not a part of the action. Moreover,
this kind of thing is not without precedent in performances of tragedy. The
ancient Greeks appear to have liked exactly this kind of release in their
festivals of tragedy, since they demanded that each dramatist, after presenting his three tragedies, should provide them with their satyr-play, usually
of an uproarious and ribald variety, sometimes burlesquing elements of the
very story that had just been seen in tragic dignity. The Epilogue is Shaw's
satyr-play: a bursting forth of that strong sense of the ridiculous which Shaw
has, during the play proper, subjected to a remarkable control—remarkable,
that is, for Shaw.

It seems possible, then, to find some place, within the spacious area of
tragedy, for our two saint's plays. It seems possible, if we will not demand
an Aristotelian hero, and if we may view the area of tragedy as a sort of
scale or spectrum ranging between the two poles of doubt and affirmation:
or, to put it more precisely, between the pole of fruitless suffering and the
pole of universal cause. Not a scale of value, but a spectrum of various
qualities, with *A Farewell to Arms* marking one extreme, outside the area of

tragedy, and Shakespeare's *Tempest*, perhaps, marking the other extreme. In between, within the area of tragedy, would lie an enormous variety of works that would defy any rigorous attempt at definition, except that all would show in some degree a mingled atmosphere of doubt and affirmation, of human suffering and secret cause. Far over toward the side of fruitless suffering we might find the plays of Ibsen, or *Othello;* somewhere in the middle, *Hamlet,* or *Oedipus Rex;* and far over toward the other side we might find a triad of strongly affirmative tragedies: *Oedipus at Colonus, Samson Agonistes*, and *Murder in the Cathedral;* and still farther over, perhaps hanging on by his hands to the very rim of tragedy—we might even find a place for Bernard Shaw.

The Shavian Machine

by T. R. Henn

He understands everything in life except its paradoxes, especially that ultimate paradox that the very things we cannot comprehend are the things we have to take for granted.[1]

G. K. CHESTERTON

I

It is related that Yeats perceived, in a dream or vision, Shaw as a sewing-machine "that clicked and clicked continually." There is a pleasantly surrealist quality about such a vision, and we must discount many of Yeats's statements about his friends and enemies; but there is, as often, a germ of the truth here. The two Irishmen, opposed in almost every conceivable aspect of background, upbringing and personality, offer some interesting material for a consideration of twentieth-century Tragedy. Shaw professed an immense admiration for his own interpretation of the Ibsen tradition; Yeats and Synge, in different ways, rebelled against the "pallid and joyless realism" that they saw there, although Yeats had a far more sensitive understanding of Ibsen than had Synge. For Ibsen was a poet; Shaw, taking over from those elements of Ibsen's art which best fitted his own optimistic scepticism, could only produce poetry from the teeth outwards; in spite of three notable attempts.[2]

The social and intellectual climate of England in the period 1880 to 1920 was perhaps less fitted to provide favourable conditions for a tragic Anschauung than either the Norway of Ibsen or the Ireland of Yeats and O'Casey. The slowly-broadening freedom, the inanities and inconsistencies of a world that was still sorting out its own "complexities of mire and blood" offered magnificent material for the socialist satirist, but little or nothing towards a constructive vision based upon conflicting antinomies. The pres-

---

"The Shavian Machine" by T. R. Henn. From *The Harvest of Tragedy* by T. R. Henn (London: Methuen & Co. Ltd., 1956). Copyright © 1956 by Methuen & Co. Ltd. Reprinted by permission of Methuen & Co. Ltd.

[1] *George Bernard Shaw*, p. 192.
[2] In *The Doctor's Dilemma, John Bull's Other Island*, and *Saint Joan*.

sures, religious, philosophical or national, were either insufficient to provide a sense of urgency, or obscured in the indefiniteness of objectives suggested by twentieth-century warfare. The vast problems of centralization raised by new methods of communication, the bewildering impact of "news" upon the public mind, were beginning to exercise those peculiar powers of induration and confusion which persist today. But to Shaw it must have seemed that the only refuge lay in a creative scepticism extended impartially over militarism, feminism, journalism, economics, medicine, big business and political philosophy, and in the Nietzschean romanticism of the Superman.

II

Three only of Shaw's plays deserve consideration as tragedies: *The Doctor's Dilemma, Mrs. Warren's Profession*, and *Saint Joan*.

At first sight *The Doctor's Dilemma* affords a striking example of the Hegelian theory of tragedy, the conflict of two balanced and irreconcilable claims, which by their conflict raise important questions of value but which point to a division in the substance of The Good. If circumstances allow the salvation of only one life, which is to be preferred; that of the morally worthless artist or that of the worthy general practitioner? By what scale is the choice to be justified? The stage is set, the victim dies; the famous Epilogue is spoken by Ridgeon:

> Then I have committed a purely disinterested murder!

The play is well constructed, theoretically effective, with excellent characterization; and yet the tragic failure is complete.

There are, I think, several reasons. *The Doctor's Dilemma* is the supreme example of the multiple-aspect-and-object play whose artistic statement is wholly vitiated by the impurity of its intention and the failure (in spite of signs that Shaw attempted this late in the play) to achieve a true balance within that statement. As usual we must first consider the Preface with its ninety-four pages, in which Shaw tells us specifically what he is attacking: the shortcomings of doctors; the evils of poverty (generally, and specifically as regards doctors); inoculation; vivisection; cruelty; national health; medical training and organization. We must supplement these "topics," in the Ibsen manner, by ancillary discussions of the shortcomings of journalists, and the place of the artist in the State. The long and unrelieved first act is cumbered with endless medical debate, allowing just enough character to emerge to serve the developing mechanics of the plot, but adding appreciably to the subjects proposed in the Preface: criminal law, cremation, Jewish *vs.* Gentile commercial morality, bourgeois views on marriage, and Christian Science. Behind these is the oscillating attack of the Puritan-Moralist on the artist and his function in society. And because of the very multiplicity of these topics, the play fails utterly to accumulate momentum; the whole of the first act is "discussion." The third is concerned with the *anagnorisis* of Dubedat's character as a scoundrel with artistic gifts, and provides further material for the Shavian polemic; for a moment we have some hint of human relationship in the opening between Dubedat and Jennifer, which is not picked up again till the death-scene. In this there are two speeches, admirably designed to illustrate Shaw's idea of the power of the *false word*—his conception of rhetoric—to persuade to *that which is not*. But such an analysis is too simple; Shaw would, I think, like us to be carried away by Dubedat's eloquence, is aware that it is *pastiche*, and by sheer brilliance introduces,, as it were, a double falsification. The following piece of dialogue is illuminating, from Dubedat's death-scene:

Louis. I want you to be beautiful. I want people to see in your eyes that you were married to me. The people in Italy used to point at Dante and say "There goes the man who has been in hell." I want them to point at you and say "There goes a woman who has been in heaven." It has been heaven, darling, hasn't it—sometimes?

Mrs. Dubedat. Oh yes, yes. Always, always.

Louis. If you wear black and cry, people will say "Look at that miserable woman: her husband made her miserable."

Mrs. Dubedat. No, never. You are the light and blessing of my life. I never lived until I knew you.

Louis (his eyes glistening). Then you must always wear beautiful dresses and splendid magic jewels. Think of all the wonderful pictures I shall never paint. (*She wins a terrible victory over a sob.*) Well, you must be transfigured with all the beauty of those pictures. Men must get such dreams from seeing you as they could never get from any daubing with paints and brushes. Painters must paint you as they never painted any mortal woman before. There must be a great tradition of beauty, a great atmosphere of wonder and romance. That is what men must always think of when they think of me. That is the sort of immortality I want. You can make that for me, Jennifer. There are lots of things you don't understand that every woman in the street understands; but you can understand that and do it as nobody else can. Promise me that immortality. Promise me you will not make a little hell of crape and crying and undertaker's horrors and withering flowers and all that vulgar rubbish.   (Act IV)

Beneath the surface the weakness and sentimentality is apparent; partly because Shaw has failed to build up sufficient stature for either of the characters in the earlier part of the play, partly because the emotional pressure is insufficient to carry conviction. And two redundancies—the allusions to "the woman in the street" and to funeral customs—are admirable illustrations of Shaw's failure to achieve unity of tone.

III

By contrast, *Mrs. Warren's Profession* comes very close to a true tragedy in the Ibsen manner. It is not hard to see why. The theme and its characters are integral, the psychological insight more subtle than usual; and because the speech of the characters is wholly in tone with the playwright's conception of them, it does not jar by any attempt at the self-consciously poetic. The ending is modulated sufficiently into the unspoken to leave room for the imagination to work upon the whole; Shaw's fondness for abruptness and finality has for the moment been abandoned. And while the component themes are drawn from Shaw's stock-in-trade (poverty, morality, clerical hypocrisy, parent-child relationships) they are sufficiently absorbed into the idea of the play not to appear discordant.

In some strange manner, too, the play has links with the great classical themes; the nature of "nature" between mother and daughter, father and son; hypocrisy, and the power of the individual and of society to rationalize or mask it; perhaps, too, the shadow of incest in the discovery of the relationship between Vivien and Frank. Through them the "society" which Shaw attacks so constantly achieves a kind of monstrous objectivity of its own. The sentimental artist, Praed, produces the ironic criticism of conventional values, though he is a little distorted. There is indeed much truth in Shaw's statement in the Preface:

> Thus it comes about that the more completely the dramatist is emancipated from the illusion that men and women are primarily reasonable beings, and the more powerfully he insists on the ruthless indifference of their great dramatic antagonist, the external world, to their whims and emotions, the surer he is to be denounced as blind to the distinction on which his whole work is built. Far from ignoring idiosyncrasy, will, passion, impulse, whim, as factors in human action, I have placed them so nakedly on the stage that the elderly citizen, accustomed to see them clothed with the veil of manufactured logic about duty, and to disguise even his own impulses from himself in this way, finds the picture as unnatural as Carlyle's suggested painting of parliament sitting without its clothes.

We can remember with profit *Timon*, *Lear* and Swift. When this social criticism is successfully merged with the dramatic structure the ironies of speech and situation support the whole, and when Shaw's sense of the theatre allows him to trust his audience to complete the pattern of the unspoken, we have an approach to the only kind of tragedy his genius allowed him to compass, the tragedy of woman.

IV

Saint Joan is for our purposes the single most interesting play: not merely because controversy has raged for so long about its value as a tragedy, but because Shaw has in the Preface given us some account of what he conceives to be the essential tragic principles:

> There are no villains in the piece. Crime, like disease, is not interesting: it is something to be done away with by general consent, and that is all about it. It is what men and women do at their best, with good intentions, and what normal men and women find that they must do and will do in spite of their intentions, that really concern us. The rascally bishop and the cruel inquisitor of Mark Twain and Andrew Lang are dull as pickpockets; and they reduce Joan to the level of the even less interesting person whose pocket is picked. I have represented both of them as capable and eloquent exponents of the Church Militant and the Church Litigant, *because only by doing so can I maintain my drama on the level of high tragedy and save it from becoming a mere police court sensation.* A villain in a play can never be anything more than a *diabolus ex machina*, possibly a more exciting expedient than a *deus ex machina*, but both equally mechanical, and therefore interesting only as mechanism.

We are led by this statement to look for a Hegelian balance, like that proposed in *The Doctor's Dilemma;* a balance to "maintain the play on the level of high tragedy." This careful manipulation of the scales is predominantly intellectual; and it appears to involve the exclusion of any philosophy of evil[3] in favour of stupidity, ignorance, self-will; and a general blindness to the ultimate outcome of a given action in time. The conflict is, in the most generalized terms, between Genius and Discipline, as Shaw points out in the Preface.

But this intellectual framework, this immense care to present both sides of the conflict and to provide a rational basis for the supranatural,[4] has some interesting effects. Both sets of protagonists are deflated, impartially, by the darts of Shaw's wit; and have scarcely any breath left to sustain the moments of high tragedy in the trial scene. We have thus an interesting reflection on the whole question of comic relief in modern tragedy; it seems that the humour must be carefully adjusted to the characters without depriving them

---

[3] This is made clear by the irony of Ladvenu's reading of the confession she is required to sign.

[4] Cf. Shaw's care to stress the commonplace aspect of Joan's "voices"; as well as the commonplace character—from several aspects—of Joan herself.

of the potentiality for rising, momentarily at least, above the memory of their demonstrated weakness. And we are led to the suspicion that Shaw is obsessed with the idea of the "ordinary," as opposed to the theatrical, representations of his characters, an "ordinariness" which is itself treated theatrically in order to emphasize it even at the expense of a certain cheapness of wit. In the trial scene the Inquisitor alone retains his full dignity; the Chaplain is over-caricatured, the anti-imperialism handled with far too heavy a touch. It becomes very clear that the central problem of the modern writer of tragedy is to achieve this delicate balance between the ordinary and the theatrical, so that the ordinary is not robbed of its power of exaltation, nor the theatrical degraded to the sentimental. And the wit must, in some manner, be merged into humour, if we are to believe in the capacity of the main protagonists to rise, in the later stages of the play, to the high emotion that will be demanded of them. But most interesting of all is Shaw's attempt to solve the problem of lyric speech at the moment of greatest tension:

> Yes: they told me you were fools (*the word gives great offence*), and that I was not to listen to your fine words nor trust to your charity. You promised me my life, but you lied (*indignant exclamations*). You think that life is nothing but not being stone dead. It is not the bread and water I fear: I can live on bread: when have I asked for more? It is no hardship for me to drink water if the water be clean. Bread has no sorrow for me, and water no affliction. But to shut me from the light of the sky and the sight of the fields and flowers; to chain my feet so that I can never again ride with the soldiers nor climb the hills; to make me breathe foul damp darkness, and keep me from everything that brings me back to the love of God when your wickedness and foolishness tempt me to hate Him: all this is worse than the furnace in the Bible that was heated seven times. I could do without my war horse; I could drag about in a skirt; I could let the banners and the trumpets and the knights and soldiers pass me and leave me behind as they leave the other women, if only I could still hear the wind in the trees, the larks in the sunshine, the young lambs crying through the healthy frost, and the blessed church bells that send my angel voices floating to me on the wind. But without these things I cannot live; and by your wanting to take them away from me I know that your counsel is of the devil, and that mine is of God. (Scene VI)

The rhythms here are an interesting index to the quality of the emotion; having in mind the previous delineation of Joan's character; and the two stage directions in the first two lines show that Shaw could never leave the obvious to the good sense and tact of his readers. We suspect the playwright's integrity because of the lack of rhythmic unity in the passage as a whole, as well as for the occasional clumsiness. ("You think that life is nothing but not being *stone* dead.") The passage that starts "if only I could hear the wind in the trees" [5] is consciously "poetic," quite out of keeping both with Joan's character and with the sentences that precede and follow it.

The Epilogues to Shaw's plays, both in The Doctor's Dilemma and in Saint Joan, have been the source of endless controversy. They serve several purposes. They stand in part for a negation of the traditional ending, that of the death of the hero. The play and life continue; the extension is, perhaps, designed to tempt us to view them sub specie aeternitatis. Any intention of the kind is denied by the irresistible opportunities they offer for a deflation of traditional attitudes, and to hammer home some of the propositions already set in the play. Shaw takes a final critical and ironical look at what has gone before. Death is neither eloquent, nor just, nor mighty, nor yet "a queer untidy thing." It is a chemical change through cremation. Ideas live on, modify themselves; illusion and stupidity continue in different forms; and, standing aside, Shaw's world is seen to have some measure of intellectual pity, but not of fear.

But why? Does this mean that Shaw, or Shaw's audience, demand a Weltanschauung sufficiently distanced that, like Troilus, they can laugh "from the holwe of the seventh sphere," at human stupidity? There are grounds for believing that this is so. "The tragedy of such murders is that they are not committed by murderers" (cf. The Doctor's Dilemma). "They are judicial murders, pious murders; and this contradiction at once brings an element of comedy into the tragedy: the angels may weep at the murder, but the gods laugh at the murderers." [6]

But to extend the tragedy in time and space in order to perceive the comedy is to remove at a stroke the possibility of a full tragic response. Any tragedy, thus produced in time, is seen, from an altitude, to provide its own resolution; as in medieval religious drama. It removes from the audience the need for any individual response or responsibility in the present. There are none of the old misgivings, the crooked questions that lie at the roots of individual experience; and Joan's cry "How long . . . ?" fades into the commonplaces of history.

V

Such considerations, themselves negative as regards Shaw's position as a tragic artist, may yet suggest certain thoughts on the nature of tragedy. The

---

[5] I do not think it is fantastic to perceive curiously Synge-like rhythms as well as substance in this passage: "but you'll be hearing the herons crying out over the black lakes, and you'll be hearing the grouse and the owls with them, and the larks and the big thrushes when the days are warm . . . but its fine songs you'll be hearing when the sun goes up, and there'll be no old fellow wheezing, the like of a sick sheep, close to your ear." (The Shadow of the Glen.)

[6] Preface to Saint Joan, p. lvi.

tragic artist must present the problems which he handles as intrinsic with the plot, character, and imagery, the whole a colloidal mixture rather than a series of separate globules existing in a kind of surface-tension relationship. There would appear also to be a limit to the number of propositions that form the raw material; it is, for example, apparent that Shaw's "subjects" are far more numerous, and less relevant to the central theme, than say, those of Ibsen or of Brieux. The sense of a tragic pattern is all-important; if this does not emerge from the interaction of character, the pattern must be brought out by imagery or symbol in the broad poetic statement. That poetic statement cannot be *appliqué*'d, at those points of the play where the dramatist thinks that they are demanded by the theatrical context; it must be, as it were, latent from the very beginning of the play, as much in its Image[7] as in its language. Comic relief, in general, must illuminate, contrast with, or round off this total idea; it must not be designed merely to puncture, deflate or wound *for its own sake*. And finally, the dramatist must achieve a certain measure of identification with his characters and situations; if he stands (even for a moment) outside them to criticize them with his own lips, he has withdrawn from them in just that measure their whole poetic life. Arland Ussher's words are worth quoting in this context:

> The tension we miss in him consists of those wholly un-Shavian ideas—sin, temptation and remorse; or in an older language than the Christian, in fear and pity—those emotions which the adolescent superman-worshipper will always despise—pity for the unalterability of the human lot, fear of the forces which lurk under the most polished social surface.[8]

[7] I use the word in Abercrombie's sense. Cf. *Principles of English Prosody*.
[8] Arland Ussher, *Three Great Irishmen*, p. 58.

Bernard Shaw and William Blake

by Irving Fiske

Bernard Shaw, in the Preface to the volume of his plays containing *The Devil's Disciple*, acknowledges his indebtedness to William Blake for the philosophical basis of that play in these words: "Let those who have praised my originality in conceiving Dick Dudgeon's strange religion read Blake's Marriage of Heaven and Hell; and I shall be fortunate if they do not rail at me for a plagiarist."

In his Preface to *Man and Superman*, Shaw names Blake, together with Bunyan, Hogarth and Turner—"(these four apart and above all the English classics)" he adds—as pre-eminent among those "whose peculiar sense of the world I recognize as more or less akin to my own"; and he reproaches the "polite critics of the 19th century" for "ignoring William Blake as superficially as the 18th had ignored Hogarth or the 17th Bunyan." In regard to the people of his *Heartbreak House*, he speaks of their futility and purposelessness even though "you would find Blake among the poets" on their guestroom tables, and "Blake and the other major poets" on their library shelves. Blake, elsewhere, is to Shaw "the most religious of our great poets." The clue to the nature of the kinship that he feels with Blake is provided, it is true, by the fact that Shaw appraises both Blake and himself as dealing with man and the world from a point of view essentially religious.

"Art has never been great," says Shaw, "when it is not providing an iconography for a live religion." To Shaw, to be an "iconographer of the religion of my time, and thus fulfil my natural function as an artist," is his central task; and, he says, "the thought is the life." William Blake speaks of his own purpose as

. . . My great task!
To open the Eternal Worlds, to open the immortal Eyes
Of Man inwards into the Worlds of Thought, into Eternity. . . .

"Bernard Shaw and William Blake" (original title: "Bernard Shaw's Debt to William Blake") by Irving Fiske. From *The Shavian*, Tract No. 2 (The Shaw Society, 1951). Copyright 1951 by The Shaw Society, London, England. Reprinted by permission of The Shaw Society.

But for Blake, as for Shaw, it is a task in which any touch of false reserve or self-effacement would be meaningless and distasteful; and one to be pursued with no concern for that surface "originality" which Emerson stated was never the preoccupation of the first-rate artist.

"I, a playwright of Shakespearean eminence," Shaw describes himself. "I, William Blake, a Mental Prince," and "in heaven a Prince among Princes," says Blake. "I really cannot respond to this demand for mock-modesty," Shaw declares. "If a man is master of his profession, he cannot be ignorant that he is so," Blake puts it, and:

> . . . In melodious accents I
> Will sit me down and cry I, I.

"The cart and trumpet for me," cries Shaw.

"I should make formal acknowledgment to the authors whom I have pillaged," says Shaw of *Man and Superman*, "if I could recollect them all." "The Bad Artist Seems to copy a Great deal," says Blake. "The Good one Really does Copy a Great deal." Nevertheless, for both men, it is the magnitude or newness of an idea that produces true originality of substance and of form. "New Ideas make their technique as water makes its channel," says Shaw; and Blake: "The Great Style is always Novel or New in all its Operations."

But Shaw's indebtedness to Blake is in reality much broader than this, and extends quite unmistakeably through the entire range of speculation by both men in regard to art, science, literature, religion, and virtually every question of human nature and human destiny. "A genius," says Shaw, "is a person who, seeing farther and probing deeper than other people, has a different set of ethical valuations from theirs," with energy enough to express these valuations, he continues, "in whatever manner best suits his or her specific talents."

With all allowance for the fact that Blake's specific talent is lyrical, and Shaw's dramatic, there is still in the pronouncements of both men a similarity explicable only on the basis of their closely related creative positions—a similarity, however, which is the natural and inevitable result of that relationship. The prose and expository writings of both men are, moreover, very similar in their unadorned directness of statement, unflagging didacticism, and insistence on tightness and definiteness of idea. "Obscurity," says Blake (despite his supposed taste for it) "is Neither the Source of the Sublime nor of any Thing Else," and: "Grandeur of Ideas is founded on Precision of Ideas" . . . a statement paralleled by Shaw's "Lucidity is one of the most precious of gifts: the gift of the teacher: the gift of explanation." On comparison, Blake is, if anything, more inflexibly assertive, and more of a thoroughgoing extremist in his evaluations and conclusions.

Asks Blake:

. . . What is a Church & What Is a Theatre? Are they Two & not One?
can they exist Separate?

and "a theatre," Shaw says, "as a place where two or three are gathered
together, takes from that presence an inalienable sanctity." "Excess of sorrow
laughs. Excess of joy weeps," says Blake, and: "Fun I love, but too much
Fun is of all things the most loathsome." "Tears in adult life are the natural
expression of happiness," says Shaw, "as laughter is at all ages the natural
recognition of destruction, confusion, and ruin"; and of his own plays: "Any
fool can make an audience laugh. I want to see how many of them, laughing
or grave, have tears in their eyes"—an idea summed up by Blake's

> Joy & Woe are woven fine
> A Clothing for the Soul divine;
> Under every grief & pine
> Runs a joy with silken twine.

And yet, though Blake is still widely referred to, rather surprisingly, as a
romantic, he has as little use as Shaw for those three prominent romantic
emotions: nostalgia, romantic sorrow, and romantic love.

Nostalgia, to Blake, comes into being only under the pressure of stifled
and imprisoned lives:

> They view their former life: they number
>   moments over and over,
> Stringing them on their remembrance as
>   on a thread of sorrow . . .;

and "Sorrow," he says, "is not fit for Immortals & is utterly useless to any
one." Of romantic love, says Shaw's John Tanner in *Man and Superman:*
"But a lifetime of happiness! No man alive could bear it: it would be hell
on earth." Blake has it

> Grown old in Love from Seven till Seven times Seven.
> I oft have wish'd for Hell for Ease from Heaven.

Both men reject the notion of progress in art and human affairs—"this
goose-cackle about Progress," Shaw calls it. "Mankind," says Blake, "are
in a less distinguished Situation with regard to mind than they were in the
time of Homer." "My reason then," says Shaw, with exaggerated patience,
"for ignoring the popular conception of Progress in Caesar and Cleopatra
is that there is no reason to suppose that any Progress has taken place since
their time."

"To suppose that Art can go beyond the finest specimens of Art that are
now in the world," Blake declares, "is not knowing what Art is"; and he
places Shakespeare among those who artistically "are the extent of the

human mind." "No man will ever write a better tragedy than Lear," says Shaw, and: "Molière and Mozart, upon whose art no human hand can improve." But Shakespeare, for both, is intellectually incomplete. To Shaw, Shakespeare is "irreligious," "anarchical," without "constructive ideas," and ignorant "as to what philosophy means." Shakespeare, says Blake, was "curb'd by the general malady & infection from the silly Greek & Latin slaves of the Sword"—meaning the Greek and Latin classics, towards which Shaw, on the whole, is not hostile, but which Blake detests.

"Are not Religion & Politics the Same Thing?" asks Blake. "A vocation for politics," to Shaw, is "essentially a religious vocation." "If Men were Wise," Blake asserts, "The Most arbitrary Princes could not hurt them. If they are not wise, the Freest Government is compell'd to be a Tyranny." "Fools must be governed according to their folly," states Shaw, "and not to a wisdom they do not possess."

To both, the prophet is allied to the artist, and prophecy a direct expression of artistic insight into worldly affairs, with nothing supernatural about it. "A prophet in the true sense" is defined by Shaw as "a man of exceptional sanity who is in the right when we are in the wrong." "Prophets, in the modern sense of the word, have never existed," says Blake, and the true prophet, he elaborates, "utters his opinion both of private & public matters. Thus: If you go on So, the result is So. He never says, such a thing shall happen let you do what you will. A Prophet is a Seer, not an Arbitrary Dictator." Shaw alludes to Christ as "an artist and a Bohemian in his manner of life"; and "Jesus & his Apostles & Disciples were all Artists," says Blake.

All men, for both Blake and Shaw, are indissolubly bound together— "members one of another," Shaw states it, and Blake:

> Can I see another's woe,
> And not be in sorrow too?

"I feel his pain in my own heart," cries the poet of his rival in Shaw's *Candida*. But hardness, not softness of response, is for Blake as for Shaw the meaning of real compassion.

> . . . Pity divides the soul
> And man unmans,

writes Blake. Shaw speaks of a tale of brutality "with an edge that will cut the soft cruel hearts and strike fire from the hard kind ones." Pity is labelled "the scavenger of misery" by Shaw's Undershaft in *Major Barbara*. Pity, to Blake, is "Miseries' increase."

Shaw proclaims himself always inspired when he writes; and "Inspiration," says Blake, is "my Eternal Dwelling place." For both, however, inspiration is a thing of complete awareness, not unconscious rapture. "Plato has made Socrates say that Poets & Prophets do not know or Understand

what they write or Utter; this is a most Pernicious Falsehood," Blake asserts.
"Produce me your best critic, and I will criticize his head off," says Shaw.
Science, as it is practised, is to Blake "Thy self-destroying, beast form'd
Science"; and to Shaw a "revival of tribal soothsaying" responsible for the
modern idea of scientific predestination,[1] which he calls "so imbecile and
dangerous a creed." Predestination to Blake is "Cursed Folly."

Both are particularly incensed by the corruption of the substance of
religion into its forms and shadows. "Christ's Crucifix shall be made an
excuse for Executing Criminals," says Blake; and Shaw: "Christianity means
nothing to the masses but a sensational public execution which is made an
excuse for other executions." Abstruse theological mysticism is to Shaw
merely "artificial intellectual mystification"; but to Blake "the dismal shade
Of Mystery," "the Ashes of Mystery," and "Mystery Accursed."

The key to the creative point of view shared by Shaw and Blake is to be
found in their insistence on the fundamental unity and validity of all human
drives and human appetites. From this point of view, the profoundest and
most significant of man's appetites is his appetite for religion—and the central
one lying behind all of his activities. "There is only one religion, though
there are a hundred versions of it," Shaw writes. "All religions are one,"
says Blake, and "have one source," which he calls "the Poetic Genius."
"Art, science, and religion," says Shaw, "are really identical and inseparable
in their foundations." "The Thing I have most at Heart," Blake affirms,
"Is the Interest of True Religion & Science." But while all religions are true
enough in origin and inspiration, all established religions, to both, are otherwise greatly in error.

"Our religion," Shaw says, is "gravely wrong"; and: "At present there
is not a single credible established religion in the world." Formal religion
is to Blake "a pretence of Religion to destroy Religion," and "the Wheel
of Religion," of which he says

> Jesus died because he strove
> Against the current of this Wheel; its Name
> Is Caiaphas. . . .

The most formidable obstructions of man's religious impulse, to Blake and
Shaw, are the self-negating concepts invented by man himself as substitutes
for a genuinely satisfying religion. Among such substitutes are nature-
worship, morality, humility, and the idea of man's insignificance in the
universe. "Where man is not, nature is barren," Blake maintains. "The
mountains are corpses," says Shaw's Ancient in *Back to Methuselah*. "If

---

[1] [*Note by G.B.S.*] Science, as it is practised, is to Blake "Thy self-destroying, beast
form'd Science"; and to Shaw a "revival of tribal soothsaying" responsible for the modern
idea of scientific predestination, etc.—*altered by Shaw to read* responsible for the modern
idea of scientific *determinism*, etc.

Morality was Christianity," Blake caustically observes, "Socrates was the Saviour"; and:

> The Moral Christian is the Cause
> Of the Unbeliever & his Laws.

Shaw speaks of the "confusion of virtue with the mere morality that steals its name." "Our Fundamentalists," to Shaw, "are the worst enemies of religion to-day." "Jesus was all virtue, and acted from impulse, not from rules," Blake concludes. "Opinion is a dead thing and impulse a live thing," Shaw's Jesus says in the Preface to *On the Rocks*.

Humility Shaw calls "the wicked doctrine of docility in poverty and humility under oppression," conceived by the coward as "a religion of his cowardice." Humility is for Blake not of God, but of Satan:

> God wants not Man to Humble himself:
> This is the trick of the ancient Elf,

for

> Humility is only doubt,
> And does the Sun & Moon blot out.

To Blake it is the accepted scientists and philosophers—lumped together by him as "Bacon & Newton & Locke"—whose guilt it is that they "teach Humility to Man."

An excessive devotion to the gratification of physical desires, or an ascetic renunciation of them, are for Blake and Shaw equally irrelevant and unwholesome. "The substitution of sensuous ecstasy for intellectual activity and honesty is the very devil," Shaw expresses it. "Hell, in short," says his *Man and Superman*, "is a place where you have nothing to do but amuse yourself." "Hell," says Blake, "is the being shut up in the possession of corporeal desires which shortly weary the man"; and a state where "Intellect is no more. There is no time for any thing but the torments of love & desire."

But "I am the last man in the world to be cited as ascetic," Shaw says. He insists upon "the satisfaction of physical cravings before they become mental anxieties." "Sooner murder an infant in its cradle than nurse unacted desires," Blake asserts, much more emphatically. Of man's ultimate spiritual illumination he says: "This will come to pass by an improvement of sensual enjoyment."

Only by embracing all of his desires can man eliminate the destructive inversions arising from their repression, and so release his underlying religious impulse to manifest itself freely. What will then emerge, according to Shaw, is man's "evolutionary appetite"—the drive of the Life Force in him towards the creation of "higher and higher individuals." This is Shaw's

Creative Evolution—basically a substitution of the idea of biologic progress
for the customary concept of progress which he attacks.[2] The goal of Shaw's
Life Force is ever "greater power of contemplating itself" and "self-understanding." "If God is anything he is Understanding," says Blake.

To Blake, however, man's perfect state is always potentially present, and
need not wait upon any act of outer creation. "The outward Creation,"
says Blake, "is as the dirt upon my feet"—a denial not of its being, but of
its supposedly crushing magnitude to man.

Shaw's Don Juan in *Man and Superman* sings "the philosophic man," and
philosophy is for Shaw a valid instrument of search. But philosophy to Blake
is "Abstract Philosophy warring in enmity against Imagination"; and abstraction itself a "fleeing from Identity In abstract false Expanses." The
scientist-philosopher, in particular, he accuses of misleading men by "Calling
the Rocks Atomic Origins of Existence, denying Eternity." For Blake, all
the works of accepted science and philosophy are as nothing compared with
that awareness of man's inner magnificence and resources which Israel
brought into the western world:

> The Atoms of Democritus
> And Newton's Particles of light
> Are sands upon the Red sea shore,
> Where Israel's tents do shine so bright.

Caesar, in Shaw's *Caesar and Cleopatra*, shocks and bewilders his associates
by insisting on treating his personal enemies with magnanimous forgiveness—
not out of benevolence, but on the grounds that it is most profitable for him
to do so. "In order to produce an impression of complete disinterestedness,"
is Shaw's explanation, "he has only to act with entire selfishness." Profitable-
ness as a test of human behaviour is for Blake the practical essence of genuine
Christianity. "The Christian Religion teaches that No Man is Indifferent
to you, but that every one is Either your friend or your enemy," says Blake,
"And that he will be equally profitable both ways if you treat him as he
deserves."

One of man's most crucial errors, as seen by Blake and Shaw, is his habit
of appraising human conduct in measures of good and evil, of moral right
and wrong, instead of in terms of human profit and loss. Mere good intentions, to both, are not enough.

> . . . Caiaphas was in his own Mind
> A benefactor to Mankind,

[2] [*Note by G.B.S.*] This is Shaw's Creative Evolution—basically a substitution of the idea
of biologic progress for the customary concept of progress which he attacks.—*altered by
Shaw to read* basically a substitution of the idea of biologic *development* for the *utilitarian*
concept of progress which he attacks.

Blake says of the accuser of Jesus; and "the Mischief is just the same whether a Man does it Ignorantly or Knowingly." "Hell is paved with good intentions," says Shaw, "not with bad ones."

In place of moralistic self-righteousness, both preach the need of accuracy and thoroughness of intellectual judgment. "Severity of judgment is a great virtue," Blake contends. "The secret of forgiving everything is to understand nothing," Shaw says. In their view, every falsehood, evasion or confusion of the issue, deliberate or not, in man's weighing of human affairs must pay its price in misery and blood. If clarity of judgment, without preconception or illusion, is not displayed by individuals, it will be exercised by events. Illusion "is productive of the most dreadful Consequences," writes Blake, "even of Torments, Despair, Eternal Death" to those possessed by it. He attributes to incorrect habits of thought "A World in which Man is by his Nature the Enemy of Man." Shaw says of the devastations of the first World War that "They were all as preventible as the great Plague of London, and came solely because they had not been prevented."

This reprisal of events, to both, is the everyday actuality behind man's religious expectation of a Last Judgment. "In sober fact, every day is a day of judgment," Shaw asserts; and "Judgment is valuation." "Civilizations live by their valuations," he writes. "If the valuations are false, the civilization perishes as all the ancient ones we know of did."

Says Blake, savagely, "A Last Judgment is Necessary because Fools flourish"—which is exactly the theme of Shaw's *The Simpleton of the Unexpected Isles.* "We must stop making fools," that play declares, and "There just shouldn't be any fools." On the Day of Judgment with which the play deals, not only do man's illusory ideals "cease to exist," Shaw explains, "it becomes apparent that they never did exist." "Error," Blake says of the Judgment Day, "will be Burned up." "It is Burnt up," he adds, "the Moment Men cease to behold it."

Man's only real original sin, to Blake and Shaw, is his subjection to the concept of sin itself, which fills his mind and diverts it from the genuine issues. Man forgets that there was in the Garden of Eden not only the tree of the knowledge of good and evil, to eat of which was death; but also the tree of life, of which he was not forbidden to eat, but did not taste. "The original sin," Shaw says, "was not the eating of the forbidden fruit, but the consciousness of sin which the fruit produced." The concept of sin Blake describes as one of Satan's own delusions. "Satan thinks that Sin is displeasing to God," says Blake, "he ought to know that Nothing is displeasing to God but Unbelief & Eating of the Tree of Knowledge of Good & Evil."

A free exchange of ideas is therefore, to Shaw and Blake alike, a prime requirement of man's welfare, no matter how dangerous or appalling those ideas may at first appear. "The counsel men agree with is vain: it is only the echo of their own voices," Shaw's Jesus replies to Pilate. "But he who does not fear you and shews you the other side is a pearl of the greatest price." Freedom of expression Blake regards not merely as a human right, but a divine necessity. "As the breath of the Almighty such are the words of man to man," he writes.

Man's redeemed and illuminated state, for Blake, is a state in which man has emerged from "Satan's Labyrinth" of moral evaluations of good and evil, with his intelligence and imagination freed to operate creatively, unhampered by moralistic modes of thought. "Here they are no longer talking of what is Good & Evil," Blake says, "or of what is Right or Wrong, & puzzling themselves in Satan's Labyrinth, But are Conversing with Eternal Realities as they Exist in the Human Imagination." The same conviction, in essence, is summed up by the hero of Shaw's *The Shewing-Up of Blanco Posnet*. "There's no good and bad," declares Posnet, "but by Jiminy, gents, there's a rotten game, and there's a great game. I played the rotten game; but the great game was played on me; and now I'm for the great game every time."

Chronology of Important Dates

1856	George Bernard Shaw born in Dublin, Ireland, July 26th.
1876	Arrived in London to make his way.
1879–83	Wrote five unsuccessful novels in laborious succession: *Immaturity*, 1879; *Irrational Knot*, 1880; *Love Among the Artists*, 1881; *Cashel Byron's Profession*, 1882; and *An Unsocial Socialist*, 1883.
1882	Heard Henry George, American author of *Progress and Poverty*, address a London meeting. It "changed the whole current of my life." Read Marx's *Das Kapital* at the British Museum. It "made a man of me."
1884	Fabian Society formed; Shaw elected a member.
1890	Wrote *Quintessence of Ibsenism*.
1888–94	Brilliant success as music critic.
1892	First play, *Widowers' Houses*, produced.
1893	*Mrs. Warren's Profession* banned. First produced in 1902.
1894	*Arms and the Man* and *Candida*. Shaw's first stage successes.
1895–98	London's leading drama critic in Frank Harris' *Saturday Review*.
1895	*The Sanity of Art*.
1896	*You Never Can Tell*, perhaps Shaw's most underrated comedy.
1898	Married Charlotte Payne-Townshend, an heiress and fellow Socialist.
1899	Wrote *Captain Brassbound's Conversion* for Ellen Terry, and *Caesar and Cleopatra*.
1901–03	*Man and Superman* (produced in 1905) began Shaw's great period. First play to have full-scale Shavian preface.
1904–07	Vedrenne and Granville Barker Court Theatre productions of Shaw, Shakespeare, and Euripides established Shaw's permanent theatrical reputation with 701 performances of eleven Shaw plays.
1904	*John Bull's Other Island*, least known of Shaw's major plays.
1905	*Major Barbara*.
1906	*The Doctor's Dilemma*. Bought "Shaw's Corner" at Ayot St. Lawrence.
1908	*Getting Married*.
1911	*Androcles and the Lion*.
1912	*Pygmalion*. Shaw sculpted by Rodin.
1914	Courageous and much reviled attack on super-patriotism and the insanity of war, *Commonsense About the War*.
1913–16	*Heartbreak House* (produced in 1920).
1921	*Back to Methuselah*, Shaw's "Metabiological Pentateuch."
1923	*Saint Joan*.

1925	Awarded Nobel Prize for Literature.
1928	*The Intelligent Woman's Guide to Socialism and Capitalism.*
1929	*The Apple Cart* (his last play of arguable major stature).
1943	Mrs. Shaw died.
1947	Wrote last complete play at the age of 91: *Buoyant Billions.* His career as a publishing writer exceeded seventy years.
1950	Shaw died at his home in Ayot St. Lawrence, November 2nd.

Notes on the Editor and Authors

R. J. KAUFMANN, editor of the anthology, is Professor of History and English at the University of Rochester. He has written frequently about Shakespearian drama and aspects of modern literature and criticism.

ERIC BENTLEY is Brander Matthews Professor of Dramatic Literature at Columbia University. He has done much to raise the standards of contemporary theater in America through his work as a critic, reviewer, producer, anthologist, and translator. His numerous books include *A Century of Hero Worship*, *The Playwright as Thinker*, *Shaw*, *The Dramatic Event*, and *The Life of the Drama*.

BERTOLT BRECHT has been one of the revolutionary forces in the modern theater through his plays, through his fertile theorizings about acting, and through his genius as director of his own and other plays. His *Mother Courage*, *Threepenny Opera*, *Good Woman of Setzuan*, and *The Caucasian Chalk Circle* belong to the classic canon of modern drama.

ROBERT BRUSTEIN is Professor of Dramatic Literature at Columbia University and theater critic for the *New Republic*. In 1962 he won the George Jean Nathan award as the outstanding drama critic in the United States. *The Theater of Revolt* is his first book.

LOUIS CROMPTON, a Canadian who teaches at the University of Nebraska, is completing a book on Shaw. He has published on Ibsen, Dickens, Hardy, and other nineteenth-century figures.

ERIK H. ERIKSON is one of America's most distinguished psychiatrists. Professor of Human Development at Harvard University, his books include *Childhood and Society*, *Young Man Luther*, and *Insight and Responsibility*.

IRVING FISKE is an English Shavian.

T. R. HENN is Senior Lecturer at St. Catherine's College, Cambridge. He has written books on Longinus and on Yeats and is the author of *The Apple and the Spectroscope*, a book on the interplay of science and poetry.

G. WILSON KNIGHT, who retired in 1963 as Professor of English at Leeds, is one of the most influential modern interpreters of Shakespeare. Among his many books are: *The Wheel of Fire*, *The Imperial Theme*, *The Christian Renaissance*, *The Crown of Life*, and *The Golden Labyrinth*.

LOUIS L. MARTZ is Douglas Tracy Smith Professor of English and American Literature at Yale University. He is the author of the well-known *Poetry of Meditation* and, most recently, *The Paradise Within*.

MARGERY M. MORGAN is Senior Lecturer in English at Monash University, Australia. She is author of *A Drama of Political Man: A Study in the Plays of Harley Granville Barker*.

NORBERT F. O'DONNELL teaches at Bowling Green State in Ohio. He is the author of numerous essays on Shaw.

RICHARD M. OHMANN is Associate Professor of English at Wesleyan University. Besides *Shaw: The Style and the Man*, he has published *The Making of Myth*.

BRUCE R. PARK teaches at Brooklyn College. He is co-author of *The State of the Jazz Lyric* and is completing a book called *The Protocols of Comedy*.

Selected Bibliography

Shaw's own work in very extensive. All his fifty-two plays and playlets are reprinted in the thirty-six-volume Constable Standard Edition of the *Works of Bernard Shaw* (London, 1930–50). The Standard Edition also includes Shaw's important drama criticism (*Our Theatre in the Nineties*, 3 vols.), most of his music criticism, his major political and social criticism (of which *The Intelligent Woman's Guide to Socialism and Capitalism*, 1928, provides the most complete summary of Shaw's position), and *Major Critical Essays* (which contains Shaw's *Quintessence of Ibsenism, The Perfect Wagnerite*, and *The Sanity of Art*). Read together, these three latter works from the 'nineties shed as much light on the formation of Shaw's aesthetics as anything available.

Shaw was a busy letter writer and a good one. An edition of his complete correspondence is in progress by Dan H. Laurence, who has also issued three carefully edited volumes of material not in the collected edition. Respectively, they gather Shaw's fugitive music criticism, speeches (mainly on religious topics), and commentaries on Irish questions. Volumes of Shaw's correspondence with the great actresses Mrs. Patrick Campbell and Ellen Terry, and with his favorite co-worker in the theater, the actor and dramatist Granville Barker, have been published. Hardly anything better reveals the inner workings of Shaw's personality than these intimate exchanges.

The standard biography of Shaw is Archibald Henderson's *Bernard Shaw: Playboy and Prophet*, 1932. It is massive and critically heavy-handed but packed with information. Of the very numerous approximations to a definitive critical biography, William Irvine's *The Universe of G. B. S.*, 1949, is perhaps the best.

Being a contentious man, Shaw has provoked an immense literature of spirited critical comment. Much of it is marred by prejudice and journalistic improvisation. The early study by G. K. Chesterton, *George Bernard Shaw*, 1909, and Eric Bentley's *Bernard Shaw*, 1947, are recommended as keenly intelligent points of entry to Shaw's multifarious intellectual and artistic activities.

Aside from Richard Ohmann's *Shaw: The Style and the Man*, Martin Meisel's *Shaw and the Nineteenth Century Theater* (Princeton, 1963), perhaps contributes most originally to the scholarly reassessment of Shaw now in progress.

The periodical literature on Shaw is so copious that specific recommendations in so brief a listing are largely arbitrary and possibly unfair. However, Stanley Weintraub, Frederick McDowell, John Gassner, and Eric Bentley are devoted and accomplished Shavian critics. Their frequent essays and articles provide informed insights into the Shavian topics they discuss.

A two-part bibliography of books and articles on Shaw from 1945 to 1955 compiled by Earl Farley and Marvin Carlson appeared in *Modern Drama*, September and December 1959. More recent studies are chronicled annually in the *PMLA* bibliography.

Finally, Shaw's *Prefaces* compete with his plays for admiration. The most substantial and revealing ones are sometimes attached to relatively minor plays, as are those for *Getting Married, Misalliance*, and *Androcles and the Lion*. These prefaces are really little books in themselves and can be read independently as Shaw's systematic explorations of such topics as parenthood, marriage, education, Christianity, and poverty.